ON PATROL

True Adventures of an Alaska Game Warden

RAY TREMBLAY

FOREWORD BY
JIM REARDEN

"Whose book is this?"

FRANK PAULI
ANCHORAGE FEB 2006

Alaska Northwest Books®
Anchorage   *   Portland

In memory of my son, Ron

Text © 2004 Ray Tremblay

Photos © 2004 Ray Tremblay, unless otherwise credited

Excerpts on pages 89–91 appeared in "Land of the North Wind," from *Wildlife in America,* by Peter Matthiessen, line drawing by Bob Hines, copyright © 1959, revised and renewed © 1987 by Peter Matthiessen. Used by Permission of Viking Penguin, a division of Penguin Group (USA) Inc.

Portions of *On Patrol* were previously published by Alaska Northwest Publishing Co. in *Trails of an Alaska Game Warden,* © 1985 by Ray Tremblay.

Library of Congress Cataloging-in-Publication Data
Tremblay, Ray, 1926-
  On patrol : true adventures of an Alaska game warden / Ray Tremblay ; foreword by Jim Rearden.
    p. cm.
  Includes bibliographical references.
  ISBN 0-88240-573-X (softbound)
  1. Tremblay, Ray, 1926- 2. Game wardens—Alaska—Biography.
I. Title.
  SK354.T74A3 2004
  363.28—dc22   2004003060

Alaska Northwest Books®

An imprint of Graphic Arts Center Publishing Company

P.O. Box 10306, Portland, Oregon 97296-0306

503-226-2402 / www.gacpc.com

President: Charles M. Hopkins

Associate Publisher: Douglas A. Pfeiffer

Editorial Staff: Timothy W. Frew, Jean Andrews, Kathy Howard, Jean Bond-Slaughter

Production Staff: Richard L. Owsiany, Susan Dupere

Editor: Tricia Brown

Cover Design: Elizabeth Watson

Interior Design: Barbara Ziller-Caritey

Printed in the United States of America

CONTENTS

FOREWORD

We who worked beside Ray Tremblay in managing and protecting Alaska's fish and game in "the good old days" of the 1950s and 1960s, know the mark he made. Alaska's wildlife professionals have long been close-knit, the handful of men who in those years worked for territory, state, and federal governments knew one another intimately. Among these dedicated men, Ray Tremblay stood out. To his coworkers no higher praise could be given then to say, "He always put the resource first"—which is what Ray did.

We met in 1953 when I was at Minto Lakes, near Fairbanks, banding waterfowl for the U.S. Fish and Wildlife Service, a summer break from my job of teaching wildlife management at the University of Alaska. Ray Tremblay arrived to fly me home to Fairbanks in a Piper Pacer.

From that first meeting sprang a friendship that has lasted five decades. We are tied together by a mutual interest in Alaska's fish and game. We have crossed trails from the Arctic Brooks Range to the Alaska Peninsula. We have attended the same wildlife meetings. Some of my former wildlife students worked for and with Ray. Our mutual friends are mostly wildlife professionals or longtime Alaskans.

Ray Tremblay plunges at life with enthusiasm, which bubbles over on every page of this, his third book recounting his adventures in Alaska. He's interested in everything and everyone around him. He has always been genuinely concerned over the well-being of others.

In this book Ray briefly recounts the rescue of a prospector at Big River, near McGrath. His modest account needs expanding.

It was June 1959, and U.S. Game Management Agent Raymond H. Tremblay was on an aerial search for the lost prospector. After much flying he sighted the man waving from a sandbar of Big River. The river was winding and narrow, with bank erosion and sweepers—fallen trees hanging from the shores. The current was swift, the water muddy.

Ten times Ray flew low-and-slow over the stranded man, searching for a spot to land. He studied the roily water, memorized where the sweepers were, and tried to judge water depth.

He finally flew below overhanging trees, keeping the plane centered over the deeper fast water, and landed on a pinpoint he had located during his flyovers. He ran one float up on the river bar where the man stood, and held it there with power. The man plunged into the water, climbed up on a float, and crawled into the plane.

With the prospector aboard, Ray roared down the narrow river, dodging sweepers and shallow water, seeking a straight place where he could lift into the air without hitting bankside trees.

In this perilous manner he sped around three bends until he found a relatively straight stretch. Fire-walling the throttle, he lifted into the air and flew over the riverbank trees.

Fred A. Seaton, Secretary of the Interior, conferring the Valor Award of the Department of the Interior upon Ray for the feat, commented, "By foresight, follow-up, and skillful execution, without regard for his personal safety, Mr. Tremblay undoubtedly saved the life of a fellow citizen."

In December 1979, Secretary Cecil Andrus awarded him the Interior Department's Meritorious Service Award for a highly superior performance and devotion to duty—recognition for his years with the U.S. Fish and Wildlife Service.

Andrus commented on Ray's sincere concern for the well-being and wise use of the fish and wildlife in Alaska, and his efforts in adapting aircraft to accomplish U.S. Fish and Wildlife Service missions in Alaska.

Those of us who have known and worked with Ray also know the measure of the man: awards are nice, but Ray's real reward has always been his personal satisfaction for simply doing his job to the best of his ability.

As Ray has written in this modest volume describing some of his conservation work, the 1950s were truly "the good old days," when Alaska was wild and free, without today's acrimony and clutter of laws involving the use of fish and game. These lively tales recounting his adventures as an Alaska game warden (his titles were different, but that's what he was) are based on his diaries, and they will bring back fond memories for those of us who were there. They will entertain, inform, and excite those who weren't.

— Jim Rearden, Alaskan writer
Outdoors Editor of *Alaska* magazine, 1968–88
Field Editor for *Outdoor Life,* 1975–95

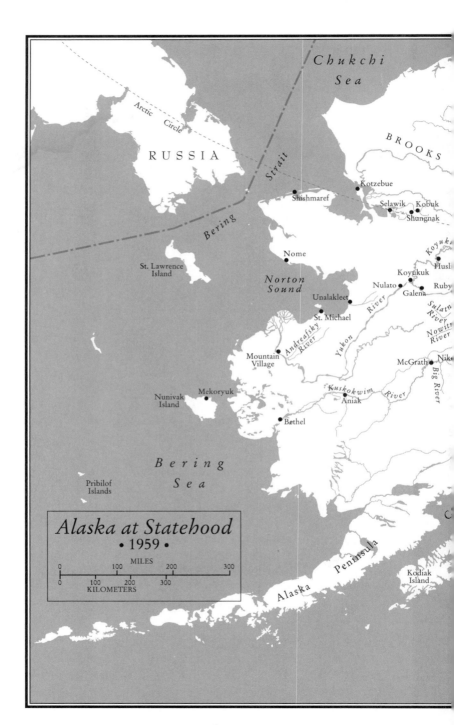

Chukchi
Sea

Arctic Circle

RUSSIA

B R O O K S

Strait

Kotzebue

Shishmaref

Selawik Kobuk
Shungnak

Bering

Koyuku

Nome

Husl

St. Lawrence
Island

Norton
Sound

Koyukuk

Nulato   Ruby
Galena

Unalakleet

Sulatn
River

River

Nowitr
River

St. Michael

Yukon

Mountain
Village

Andreafsky
River

McGrath   Nike

Big River

Mekoryuk

Kuskokwim   River

Nunivak
Island

Aniak

Bethel

Bering

Sea

Pribilof
Islands

Alaska at Statehood
• 1959 •

MILES

0   100   200   300
|————|————|————|————|————|————|
0   100   200   300
KILOMETERS

Peninsula

Kodiak
Island

Alaska

C

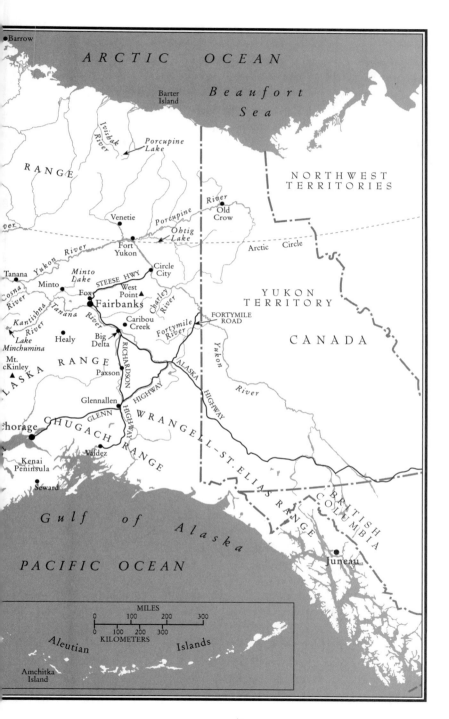

Barrow

ARCTIC OCEAN

Beaufort
Sea

Barter
Island

Ivishak
River

Porcupine
Lake

RANGE

NORTHWEST
TERRITORIES

River

Venetie   Porcupine   Old
Crow

Ohtig
Lake

Fort
Yukon   Arctic   Circle

Yukon River

Tanana   Minto   Circle
Lake   City

Minto   STEESE HWY

YUKON
TERRITORY

Cosna
River   Fox   West
Point

Fairbanks   Charley River

FORTYMILE
ROAD

CANADA

Kantishna
River   Tanana River   Caribou
Creek   Fortymile
River

Lake
Minchumina   Healy   Big
Delta   RICHARDSON   Yukon

Mt.
cKinley

ALASKA RANGE   Paxson   River

ALASKA HIGHWAY

Glennallen   HIGHWAY

horage   GLENN   HIGHWAY   WRANGELL-ST. ELIAS RANGE

CHUGACH   RANGE

Valdez

Kenai
Peninsula

BRITISH
COLUMBIA

Seward

Gulf   of   Alaska

PACIFIC OCEAN   Juneau

MILES

0   100   200   300

0   100   200   300
KILOMETERS

Aleutian   Islands

Amchitka
Island

7

INTRODUCTION

*M*y book, *Trails of an Alaska Game Warden*, published in 1985 by Alaska Northwest Publishing Company, went out of print some years ago. It was an unfinished saga. I had intended another volume to complete the story, which, in addition to revealing the trail I left, is a partial twenty-five-year history (1953–78) of the U.S. Fish and Wildlife Service in Alaska. *On Patrol* is built on the foundation of the previous book. Most of it outlines my experiences in territorial days. After statehood many changes dictated a new method of operation for the U.S. Fish and Wildlife Service. Thus, now, a continuation of my book, *Trails*...

In 1960, with Alaska's wildlife under management of the new State Department of Fish and Game, U.S. Fish and Wildlife (FWS) agents began functioning, as did agents in the other states. Our title had been changed in 1956 from "Alaska Enforcement Agent" to "U.S. Game Management Agent" to conform with our southern counterparts so no structural changes in the division were necessary.

Interestingly, about the time Alaska became a state, Congress was in the process of changing the 1925 Alaska Game Law and authorized hiring more enforcement agents. We had a force of twenty-five, and we were in the process of hiring twenty-five more. The Statehood Act changed all that, and the old game laws became moot. Instead of hiring, we started transferring agents away from Alaska, cutting the force down to twelve. I was transferred to Fairbanks from McGrath for two years and then to Anchorage, where I remained until my retirement.

Left: Fish and Wildlife Service Alaska Enforcement Agent 1953–1956

Right: Fish and Wildlife Service U.S. Game Management Agent 1956–1974

The Statehood Act required FWS to turn over to the Alaska Department of Fish and Game (ADF&G) all outlying stations, complete with housing, vehicles, patrol boats, and other equipment. A number of aircraft were also transferred, including several Grumman Goose. The federal property at Lake Hood, where the aircraft headquarters was located, was divided, giving the state a quarter parcel of the land including one of the hangars. We downgraded in a big way.

As the state organized, federal agents were deputized as Alaska Fish and Wildlife Protection Officers. In turn FWS deputized state officers as federal agents. This dual authorization created a force of fifty to sixty wildlife officers commissioned to enforce both state and federal laws. We worked in harmony, utilizing equipment from both agencies to protect Alaska's wildlife resources.

Eventually, with the help of a group of U.S. Attorneys General, Congress upgraded fines and penalties for violating some wildlife laws from misdemeanors to felonies. This put the needed teeth into the laws and regulations, which helped convince judges to impose heavier penalties for violations. It also included provisions for confiscating planes, boats, and other equipment used to take game illegally. Seizing an airplane in the middle of their paid hunting season made them sit up and take notice. When illegal wildlife was shipped out of Alaska, in violation of the Lacey Act, hunters, guides, shippers, and taxidermists all became liable, and with the added felony provisions, they were subjected to heavy fines and jail sentences. This slowed down some of

Left: Fish and Wildlife Service U.S. Special Agent #44 1974–1978

Right: Alaska State Dept. of Public Safety Aircraft Officer #1 1978–1983

the operators, but the hungry ones were still willing to take chances. They did, however, become more difficult to apprehend.

The big turn in the road was Congress setting aside money for undercover operations. The State Legislature followed suit with additional money, and we were both in business. Our agents were able to penetrate the operations of the worst offenders and collect evidence to make the big cases. Finally justice was being served and wildlife was being saved from the illegally operating big-time money hunters.

Much of my work involved flying, and my abilities had their ups and downs (pun intended), but improved with the hundreds of hours I flew each year. I can't say I'm proud of every landing I ever made. Some were controlled crashes. But somehow through it all, I became proficient enough to instruct other pilots in the finer techniques of landing on gravel bars, beaches, and mountainous terrain. As an old adage says, "Every takeoff is optional; every landing is mandatory."

When I started flying for the FWS, I was fortunate to become acquainted with some of Alaska's longtime Bush pilots. Many were still flying mail, passengers, and freight to villages, traplines, or mining camps on floats, wheels, and skis. These pilots had vast knowledge of bad-weather routes, how to evaluate landing areas from the air, and other skills necessary to land in out-of-the-way places. Not only were they skilled aviators, they were mechanics, woodsmen, businessmen, and jacks-of-all-trades. They were hardy and wilderness-wise, which was why they were still around. Friendly and willing to share knowledge, they became my mentors. I filed away every bit of valuable information I could collect, bringing it into play whenever needed, which was often with the type of flying I was doing.

I was one of the fortunate. However, it wasn't skill alone that brought me home. Many times it was the "powers that be" that interceded in my behalf and allowed me to fly another day. Read on and see if you don't agree . . .

— Ray Tremblay
February 2004
Anchorage, Alaska

PART I: THE 1950s

Enforcing Federal Game Laws in the Territory of Alaska

Packing out an illegal moose from Minto Flats, November 1955

Chapter 1

THE MAKING OF A FLYING
GAME WARDEN

I was a full-time professional trapper in interior Alaska, a life I had dreamed of as a boy. Trapping for a living was a demanding way of life, and it sometimes became very lonely. It was not exactly the romantic life I had envisioned; nevertheless, it suited me. I loved the wilderness and the independent life, as well as the challenge of wresting a living from the land. I felt I was in control of my life.

This way of life finally came to an end, however, because of forces over which I had no control. In the spring of 1952, a scant three years after I took to the trapline trails, fur prices dropped to an all-time low. As I took my winter's catch of marten, mink, otter, wolverine, and wolves to sell to fur-buyers in Fairbanks, I became downhearted with the prices I was offered for a hard winter's work.

I remember caressing the lovely dark pile of 122 marten skins as they lay on the counter of the highest bidder and being bitterly reluctant to part with them for the paltry average of twenty-seven dollars a pelt. The buyer was sympathetic, but his prices were based on the prevailing market demand.

"I'm giving you a break, Ray," he said, "even though I know you've pulled the matched sets from this bunch, and I'm not getting the benefit of your best skins."

This was true. I thought of the nine silky furs I had left in my room at the Nordale Hotel, wondering if they would bring enough to offset the low price I was receiving for the rest of the catch. Holding out matched skins was common practice among trappers, especially those in the Minchumina area where I trapped, and also in the upper Kuskokwim country, where marten vary from a light buff to chocolate brown. Some were even orange or light yellow and were humorously known as "Minchumina canaries."

I had sorted my catch in strong light and pulled out the matching skins, or "blenders," as they were called. Out of one hundred skins, I would usually get about four sets of perfectly matched furs. Most

*I was running a trapline in the Lake Minchumina area when
circumstances led me to a new career. (Photo by Val Blackburn)*

marten chokers were made in sets of three skins. These then brought a
premium price and I usually sold them by advertising in the *Fairbanks
Daily News-Miner* or by word of mouth around town. They brought
two hundred and twenty-five dollars to two hundred and fifty dollars
a set, depending on whether they were female or male pelts. The
males, being larger, were higher priced.

It took about six weeks before I got my price for the matched
sets. Meanwhile I had brought my outfit, including the sled dogs, to
Fairbanks for the summer. With fur prices so low, and grub and supply
prices rising, I figured I had to think about the future.

13

I started training for my commercial pilot's license, working at odd jobs to pay the cost. At midsummer all my sled dogs, which were boarded at a private kennel, contracted and died of distemper. This seemed to be the final blow.

I accumulated the required flight time and passed the test for a commercial pilot's license. With my background of living in the backcountry, I felt that I had the necessary talents to make my living as a pilot. A major obstacle was finding an air-taxi operator who was willing to take on an enthusiastic young aviator with a new, dripping-wet license and no practical experience. At that time a hardy breed of pilots operated from short, usually rough, landing strips hacked out by trappers, miners, and other backcountry dwellers. They were known as "Bush pilots." At least I was familiar with that part of the operation, having prepared a few strips myself at remote cabins. Preparing a marginal landing strip and landing on one, however, took training and practice.

As I explained my qualifications to one local air-taxi operator, he smiled and said, "After you've busted a few planes flying the boonies, come back and we'll talk about a job."

Catch-22. In other words, go practice with someone else's airplanes. The problem was how to find someone who had planes that were expendable, and how do you bust airplanes without hurting yourself or others?

No one at Fairbanks could help me. It became obvious I would have to look at other ways of achieving this goal. A thought occurred one day while I was talking with another trapper about the increased number of wolves around the country and the detrimental effect they were having on caribou and moose. Why not be a government trapper? I knew Frank Glaser, dean of wolf trappers for the U.S. Fish and Wildlife Service. He acquainted me with the wolf-control program. My trapping experience and flying knowledge seemed made to order for a career in this field. At the time, aerial hunting of wolves with a shotgun was becoming a common method of control used by the federal government. I submitted my application, but, unfortunately, no position was available.

The seed was sown, however, and I started to beat a trail to the Fish and Wildlife Service office in Fairbanks. I knew Jim King, one of the agents, and he acquainted me with the operations of the Enforcement

Division of the service. On one of my visits, the secretary casually suggested that I might consider working as a game warden. This caused a new set of mental gears to mesh, and I mulled it over for some weeks.

I had to answer several questions for myself. Would I be able to enforce conservation laws (which I fully endorsed) with sensitivity for the people as well as the wildlife? Would I be able to live the life of a civil servant under the regimentation required of a government employee after living the free life of a woodsman? These and other questions plagued me for the next few months until the day that fate struck again. A position opened for an enforcement agent pilot trainee. Would I accept it?

The pros and cons bedeviled me. Why not give it a try? Here was a chance to put my skills to work at something worthwhile. I knew the subsistence way of life, as well as recreational hunting and fishing; both are valid, and both have substantial impact on Alaska's wildlife. I had a good knowledge of poachers' tricks, not because I had used them, but because trappers and hunters often discussed them. My piloting skills were developing, although I hadn't busted any airplanes yet. I thought of the old saying, "If you can't whip 'em, join 'em." So join them I did. I spent the next quarter of a century protecting wildlife.

My first title was Alaska Wildlife Enforcement Agent. This title changed in 1956 to U.S. Game Management Agent, to conform to the title given federal agents in the Lower 48 states.

The early 1970s saw important new laws to protect diminishing wildlife. Taking wildlife illegally was big business the world over, and Congress enacted legislation to protect rare, threatened, and endangered wildlife. There are always those who are willing to take a species down to the last animal for the monetary reward, giving us an ever-growing list of extinct wildlife. Our agents tackled international smuggling rings that shipped endangered mammals, birds, and reptiles in and out of the United States.

Domestic wildlife was harvested in large numbers in violation of state and federal laws, and it became obvious that our investigative techniques needed to become more sophisticated. We then trained in the same academies as other federal enforcement agencies. My title changed again, this time to Special Agent (Wildlife), to more properly identify the work we were doing.

This progressive change of duties took me more and more out of the field and into the office. I was given more administrative responsibilities, more flying duties, and more advancement until I finally reached the position of Chief of the Enforcement Division in Alaska. My final title was Special Agent in Charge, or SAC.

I have never regretted my choice of career. After twenty-five years of federal service, which ended in 1978, I could look people in the eye and say I gave it my best. I tried to be fair in all decisions that affected many lives.

This book is the story of my life as a game warden pilot in Alaska. The first six years were the most rewarding and interesting, and are the basis for most of the chapters. Alaska was still a territory during those six years, and Alaska's Natives were still largely living from hunting and fishing, even though the transition to today's involved lifestyle had started.

Dog teams and snowshoes were the primary modes of travel for those living on traplines, since snowmobiles, or "snowmachines" as we Alaskans call them, had not yet made their debut. Liquor was a problem, but not an epidemic, as it is today. Drugs were unheard of in rural Alaska. Most people were honest, resourceful, and had a sense of pride in their way of life. Although Alaska's Wildlife Enforcement Agents never won any popularity contests, the people who lived by the old standards understood the need for conservation laws and respected our work.

Recreational hunters were just beginning to flex their muscles. All-terrain vehicles had not yet been developed (except in the form of the expensive military-surplus tracked Weasel), so these nimrods were confined to local areas accessible only by the few highways that existed. Small planes were taking hunters and fishermen into the backcountry, but they were not yet numerous enough to cause serious problems. Unscrupulous guides hadn't yet developed their devastating skills at flying Super Cub airplanes to drive bears and other wildlife toward a client stationed at a strategic location. Here the big-money killer waited with a high-powered rifle for the exhausted and bewildered quarry to show up and meet an undignified death.

Many of the old-timers were still around to tell stories of the "good old days," and they commonly started hunting tales by saying,

"Remember now, this happened before there were any game laws." Interestingly, the time frame they were talking about was thirty-five to forty years prior to my early years as a warden, which is about the same number of years that transpired between the end of that era and the first writing of this book.

A resident fishing license was one dollar; resident hunting and fishing, two dollars; and resident trapping, hunting and fishing license, three dollars. There were only six game and fur districts (today there are twenty-six major ones, with numerous subdistricts), and the hunting, fishing, and trapping regulations were simple and easy to understand.

How times have changed. I remember conducting the annual game hearings in Fairbanks at the Tanana Valley Sportsmen's Club on the bank of the Chena River. The meeting was open to the public as a forum for hunters and fishermen to request changes in the regulations—and/or to vent their frustrations at the U.S. Fish and Wildlife Service. The meeting lasted well past midnight, which I felt was much too long. Little did I realize how short a meeting it was by today's standards.

Nowadays the boards of fisheries and game meet annually for several weeks to consider changes recommended by the Alaska Department of Fish and Game, advisory committees, regional councils, sportsmen's groups, and the public. The boards commonly spend fourteen hours a day listening to testimony and making decisions based upon recommendations of wildlife experts, professional biologists, attorneys, environmentalists and, of course, the antihunting fraternities.

The state is cut up into so many districts and subdistricts that it is difficult to locate some of the boundaries. Some of the regulations are so complex that state Fish and Wildlife Protection Officers cannot agree among themselves on how to interpret the intent, causing confusion in enforcement. The same holds true for prosecuting attorneys and courts. Imagine the plight of the poor hunter confronted with the maze of regulations. I know several ex-hunters who have hung up their rifles rather than take a chance of being prosecuted for an unintentional mistake.

In retrospect, it seems that life was infinitely simpler in the 1950s, and now many Alaskans regard that period as the "good old days." Wolf hunter Frank Glaser, now hunting wolves in a happier land, and that dean of the old-time guides, the late M. W. "Slim" Moore, would have argued that the "good old days" were the 1920s and '30s.

Most of the real old-timers who are now gone would have called it the turn of the century—the last one, that is—a time when a trapper or hunter could make his livelihood off the land through his own merits without a myriad of laws and restrictions to hem him in. Whatever the time span claimed as the "best" had its bad and good features, but there is no denying that because of increasing human pressures, wildlife management becomes more complicated with each passing year.

It seems fitting to me that an account of the 1950s should be documented from at least the perspective of one flying game warden. This era, followed by the changes made during statehood, can perhaps be used in future years to measure the progress of civilization and conflicts with wildlife in Alaska.

Chapter 2

MODUS OPERANDI

*H*istorically, game law enforcement is the oldest tool of game management. The original goal was to preserve breeding stocks of wildlife and manage the harvests. We find the first written game law in the Old Testament, Deuteronomy 22:6, which forbade the taking of game in such quantities that would reduce basic breeding stocks. Marco Polo wrote of the Great Kublai Khan [1259–1294], who enforced the first system of open and closed seasons on many game animals and birds during breeding periods. The Magna Carta, signed in 1215, recognized the importance of wildlife to the people of England, and it became the legal foundation of the present system of game administration in the United States. In 1646 the Rhode Island town of Portsmouth closed the "deere" hunting season from May until November; any violator was to be fined five pounds. Half the fine went to the person who brought the culprit to court, and the other half to the town's treasury. By the time of the American Revolution, twelve of the thirteen colonies had closed seasons, and methods and means of taking game.

At the end of the Revolution, the Common Law of England was applied and determined that the State (in the same capacity as the King) owns all wildlife within its boundaries, and holds it in trust for the people. Game within the territory acquired by the national government after the adoption of the federal Constitution became the property of the United States in trust for the benefit of the people and of the states subsequently organized out of such territory. Until the organization of such states, the federal government can regulate the taking of game.

Federal laws, then, prevailed in Alaska until statehood was granted. Alaska, as a state, assumed responsibility for its fish and game on January 1, 1960. The federal laws were attempts to give protection to mammals, birds, and fish through a series of congressional acts beginning in 1868.

On January 13, 1925, Congress passed the Alaska Game Law, which superseded all previous federal laws and regulations for the protection of game animals, land fur animals, and birds in the Territory of Alaska. This did not include the Migratory Bird Treaty Act, the Lacey Act, and laws protecting animals and birds on federal reservations.

It authorized the secretary of agriculture to make suitable regulations to accomplish the purpose of the respective laws and the employment of personnel and equipment to enforce the acts and regulations. This function was transferred to the secretary of interior with the creation of the U.S. Fish and Wildlife Service in 1940.

Alaska Wardens, later known as Alaska Enforcement Agents, enforced provisions of the Alaska game laws and regulations, federal wildlife and commercial fisheries laws, as well as territorial acts in Alaska and on the high seas. The small staff of agents was supplemented with the use of deputies, temporary patrolmen, and stream guards during the busy seasons.

Before 1925, moose, sheep, and caribou were legally killed and sold on the market or to supply meat to road crews, roadhouses, and dog teams. Although "market hunting" had its place in the early days, it became illegal under the Alaska Game Law. It took years of firm enforcement to stop the slaughter of game animals for profit by market hunters. Strychnine poison was commonly used in the early days of trapping for the taking of fur animals and required an intense effort on the part of the "fur warden" to eliminate the practice. Strychnine was much easier to transport into new trapping areas than packing in heavy steel traps.

The first wardens patrolled their districts by boat, snowshoe, and dog team. Theirs was a lonesome and, at times, unrewarding life. They were enforcing game regulations that had little support from Bush residents, most of whom were dependent on wild meat, fish, or fur-bearers for subsistence. Hunters who once sold meat on the open market in Fairbanks and other towns became outlaws when they bartered or sold parts of game animals to others. Trappers who once carried cans of poison instead of a bunch of steel traps or snares were arrested and fined. Those dog-team drivers who hauled freight and mail, and depended on moose and caribou as dog feed, had to find another source of food for their teams. The sale of dried salmon became big business along the river towns. Logging and mining camps that used wild meat in the mess halls had to ship in domestic meats. Additionally, there were seasons and bag limits to be concerned with.

Old reports that I found in the files at McGrath gave a real insight into what early game wardens were up against. The reports of one of my predecessors, Wayne House, were full of his frustrations in trying to enforce the game laws. Catching Bush-savvy people with illegal goods was extremely difficult. Everyone knew what direction the game warden was headed when he left headquarters, and the word went out by "moccasin telegraph," which some said was faster than a speeding bullet. Knowing this, the warden often doubled back and headed in a different direction. His hope was to arrive at a particular poacher's place of business before the warning got out.

If and when the warden was able to catch a poacher with the goods, he faced another monumental task—prosecuting the person in court and obtaining a conviction. Word got out that the best way to beat the system was to demand a jury trial. This way the defendant went before a jury of other people living the same lifestyle, and as long as he wasn't an outcast, he would probably receive a not-guilty verdict. Each member of the jury probably thought, "There, but for the grace of God, go I—and next time it might be me!"

One old report in the file about the "Highpower Swede" was particularly interesting because the accused was still living in a cabin upriver from McGrath. He came to town regularly to sell loads of wood and to pick up supplies. His gas-powered scow flew an American flag over the stern, and his wife, a local Indian woman, stood in the bow ready to help beach and unload cordwood. I enjoyed their visits and the stories he told in a thick Swedish accent of the early days.

As our friendship developed I asked him about his nickname of the "Highpower Swede." Most of the monikers handed out back then were the result of an interesting occurrence or a particular trait, so I was sure there was an interesting story here. (One local was named "Bearpaw," because he had lost his fingers on both hands to frostbite.)

In his case it was attributed to a difference of opinion between him and his brother, both of whom had trekked from Sweden to Alaska during the early 1900s. Both were stubborn and each had a definite idea on what type of hunting rifle was best. The brother was an advocate of older rifles with low muzzle velocity. He claimed they wasted less meat. Highpower, on the other hand, was more interested in the newer calibers that were being developed, figuring that they anchored the larger game animals in their tracks when shot and what meat was wasted was more than compensated for by fewer animals being wounded or lost. The argument went on through the years, and those who got involved ended up naming the brothers "Lowpower" and "Highpower." It was probably a lot easier than trying to pronounce their Swedish names anyway.

Wayne House wrote the case report on Highpower after he'd been apprehended on the North Fork of the Kuskokwim River with a boat containing three moose. The regulations at the time stated that a resident could take a total of five moose and a nonresident, two; however, only one moose could be in possession at any one time. The season was September 1 through December 31. As an alien, Highpower was allowed to take only two moose, with one in possession. In this case he had more than the bag limit and more than the possession limit—caught but not convicted. He requested a jury trial in McGrath. Six men, tried and true, were chosen as jurors, and the trial took place in the local meeting hall (probably one of the bars).

Warden House presented his case, which was taken from his written report on the events of the day he apprehended Highpower. He gave an exact count of the number of pieces of meat in the boat and indicated that twelve legs added up to three freshly killed moose. Next, it was Highpower's turn to tell his story. No doubt he looked back and forth from the U.S. Commissioner to the jury before making a brief statement on where he went hunting, how he needed the meat to survive the winter, and could he help it if his moose had twelve legs? That was his total defense. The jury's verdict: not guilty.

Years later, when I asked him about the circumstances of the case, he just shrugged his shoulders and said, "Ya, shure, that was funny-looking moose—twelve legs."

There were still a few of the old wardens around when I first went to work for the FWS. Sam White, the world's first flying warden, was a great source of information, and we developed a long-lasting friendship during the years I was in Fairbanks. He came from Maine, where he had worked as a lumberjack. After a few years doing odd jobs around the Territory, he went to work as a game protector in 1927. With his background as a woodsman and believing in wildlife conservation, he felt he was qualified to take on Alaska's poachers. Looking back at his career, he said he had the satisfaction of putting out of business several of the hard-core poachers who indiscriminately used poison and slaughtered big game for profit. At the same time he was able to look the other way when those in need took an occasional animal out of season. Like so many of his colleagues, he found that the poachers were not the biggest problem—it was the administrators dictating unrealistic policies from Juneau and Washington, D.C.

Sam did his patrolling with a dog team, boat, snowshoe, and motorcycle. The motorcycle was used in Fairbanks and on the limited road system. When running errands around town, he tied his dogsled behind the two-wheel vehicle to haul groceries and freight.

His goal was to promote the use of an airplane to more effectively patrol his vast area of responsibility. All his pleas and memos fell on deaf ears, however, since his superiors failed to envision the aircraft as an enforcement and management tool. In desperation he finally bought his own plane, a Bone Golden Eagle monoplane, and started using it at no cost to the government in a last effort to promote its use.

Every spring one of his assignments was counting the moose in the Blair Lakes district south of Fairbanks using his dog team and snowshoes. This area, which encompassed approximately one hundred square miles, had a high density of animals and was used as a barometer to gauge the winter survival rate of the animals. The year he bought his aircraft he used it for the spring count and made the first aerial census of moose in Alaska. He proudly submitted his report of what he felt was the most reliable tally ever accomplished in the territory. For his efforts he received a terse and nasty memo from the regional administrator telling him they would not accept his report as accurate and to go back out and count the moose on foot as he was supposed to.

He continued using his plane to patrol his Northern District at no charge and proved its worth on many occasions. Grudgingly the bureaucrats acknowledged the merits of his efforts, but Sam felt little credibility in the position shift and finally resigned in disgust. Not long afterward the service bought a few aircraft and put them to use, finally realizing how effective they really were. A new era emerged. Years later Sam was finally credited for his efforts, but by then he felt little pleasure in the accolades.

Sam started his own flying business and became known as a safe and trustworthy pilot. He eventually went to work for Wien Airlines, and when he was in his seventies was still flying a Cessna 180 out of the villages of Huslia, Hughes, and Bettles. It was about that time that the airline decided to require company Bush pilots to get an instrument rating. That meant a considerable amount of studying and forty hours of flight training, so Sam decided to hang up his goggles and retire. When people asked him why he quit flying, he would chuckle and tell them it was due to the lack of a formal education.

With the advent of the airplane, the entire enforcement program changed direction. Wardens popped into the most remote areas of Alaska unannounced, making it difficult for hard-core poachers to continue their activities without the fear of arrest. This was especially true in the winter, when trails and tracks in the snow were like road maps of a person's activities. Wardens became proficient at tracking from the aircraft, and were able to determine how individuals were conducting their illegal activities. Once their mode of operation was established, deputy wardens could be dropped off at strategic locations and snowshoe into the area to gather evidence and arrest the offenders. It was a whole new way of doing business, and the results were rewarding.

Also, attitudes among the general public were changing. The majority condoned the taking of game by the Bush dwellers, regardless of seasons, as long as it was needed. They started supporting the law banning the sale of wildlife for personal gain and the use of poison. It was a slow process, but little by little conservation laws were being recognized as necessary, and the tide started to turn in favor of the enforcers.

Most wardens were not hard-nosed individuals, and they realized they needed the support of the people in their uphill fight to regulate the harvest. This became especially true as the population boom began. They turned their backs on minor infractions and avoided confrontations with the locals on traditional taking as long as it was within the bounds of a "needed food source."

Sam White told how he handled one of the traditional illegal practices in Fairbanks. Every spring it was customary to hunt a few of the incoming ducks and geese on the open sloughs and ponds around town. This was not a major problem in the 1930s, since the take by Alaskans was limited and made a minor dent into the population. Still, the Migratory Bird Treaty Act closed the hunting season between March 10 and September 1, so the taking was an infraction of the

Jim King checks out a violator's camp up on the Yukon River, 1955.

federal law. The warden had his duty to uphold the law and arrest anyone observed in the act of hunting. Sam took care of this by announcing
in the local newspaper when he was leaving town and how long he
would be gone. This was the signal that allowed a few days of harvest-
ing, and the ritual was observed without problem for several years.

Finally, as Fairbanks grew, the practice had to be stopped. It came
to a head for Sam when he returned to Fairbanks and found that a
few individuals were hunting on the edge of Weeks Air Field, the local
airport. Some of the pilots complained to Sam about the shooting,
especially as they were taking off. The noise of the plane departing
would scare the birds into flight and the shooting went on in earnest.
The last straw was when he went to his hangar and found that some of
his airplane parts had been used for constructing a blind.

The large influxes of people to the North during and after World War II prompted an increase in the number of wildlife enforcement agents and a crackdown on all infractions. Clarence Rhode became regional director in 1947 and made a big push for airplanes. As a pilot, he saw the need for an agent force equipped with aircraft to effectively patrol Alaska. He manipulated the transfer of surplus equipment and parts from the military, and finally the FWS had the mobility it needed to get around.

The U.S. Fish and Wildlife Service was growing out of its infancy into a larger, more complex conservation organization. Biologists were hired to learn the intricate patterns of animal, bird, and fish populations. The breeding potential of wildlife in the North was different than any population dynamics studied in the Lower 48 states, so new baselines had to be designed. The new biologists were a hardy breed and spent most of their time in the field. Reports were written by hand and in tents. Valuable information was documented that is still being used today.

Ron Skoog was a good example of those dedicated biologists. He spent a good part of one winter alone as he followed the Fortymile caribou herd. His only equipment was what he carried in his pack. Ron remembered the time that he lost complete track of day and night during the short days of December. He woke one morning, looked at his watch, thought it was evening and went back to sleep. When he woke up again he realized he had slept twenty-four hours. Trying to live like these nomadic caribou was definitely a problem. As I recall, it took him several days to catch up with the herd again.

Commercial fishing was a big business and required a large division of both biologists and enforcement agents to handle the complexities and politics of that industry. For many years the salmon-canning industry controlled many of the decisions made in Washington, D.C., regarding the management, or mismanagement, of commercial fish stocks. For Alaskan fishermen, one of the biggest complaints was about the large fish traps that caught millions of salmon headed for the spawning streams. They were mostly owned and operated by big fish companies outside Alaska. Shortly after statehood, Alaskan legislators finally outlawed them.

A separate Sport Fish Division was required to study the effects of the increasing numbers of fishermen and determine the consequences of sport fishing on the slow-growing game fish. A Predator Division was added when it was shown that a balance was needed between wolves, moose, and caribou if the hunting stocks were going to be increased.

When I went to work, there were approximately twenty-five enforcement agents in the Alaska Region. Four of us were at Fairbanks. We had two aircraft to patrol the northern half of the Territory, a Piper Pacer and a Gullwing Stinson. Each of us had a Suburban patrol vehicle except our chief, Ray Woolford, who drove a sedan. We also had a specially designed riverboat to patrol the river systems. There were no shortages of snowshoes, and we could replace worn pairs any time through army surplus. Usually they were broken in transportation or when we used them under an airplane ski to get turned around on slick snow or ice.

We traveled constantly and were effective because nobody knew where we were going to show up next. Jim King and I were bachelors in 1953 and 1954 and seldom took a day off, working in excess of eighty hours a week most of the time. We altered our patrols as the seasons dictated and tried to maintain a visible profile knowing our efforts were token, at best. We were pleasant and amiable with sportsmen who were in the pursuit of legal hunting and fishing activities, but hard-nosed and calloused with poachers.

One avid sport fisherman is probably still telling his friends that the game wardens in Alaska were everywhere and that there was just no way to violate the game laws. This individual was an army officer who was stationed in Fairbanks at Ladd Air Field (now Fort Wainwright) in the spring of 1954. He went on his first fishing trip in April at Fielding Lake with a small group of military friends. The ice on the lake was still solid, so fishermen could walk a mile or so across the lake to reach the inlet streams, which were open and filled with spawning grayling. When Jim and I walked in to check licenses and bag limits that Sunday, about ten fishermen were there. The officer was enjoying the fishing and engaged us in a conversation about fishing and hunting in Alaska, indicating he was going to be stationed in Fairbanks for two years and planned to get out every chance he had. We briefed him on the laws and regulations and wished him luck.

Three weeks later we launched the riverboat for the first trip up the Chena River. About ten miles upstream we checked a boat with several men enjoying a day of fishing and relaxation. One turned out to be the army captain we had checked at Fielding Lake. "Boy," he said, "you guys sure get around." We advised him we knew he had a license and not to bother getting it out. After acknowledging the fact that we tried to cover as much of the district as possible we said our good-byes. When we returned home we remarked that the contact with the captain was an interesting coincidence.

That summer Jim and I were involved in weekend aircraft patrols of the Yukon River from Kaltag to the Canada border. One Saturday we took a detour up to Old John Lake, about one hundred miles north of Fort Yukon. This large crystal-clear lake produced excellent lake trout and grayling fishing, and a few of the air-taxi operators were beginning to take sport fishermen up there from Fairbanks. We spotted a camp on the sandy beach by the inlet and landed. Three men were fishing by themselves in the middle of the wilderness. Much to our surprise, one of the fishermen turned out to be the army captain again. He threw up his hands, shook his head in disbelief and stated in a loud voice, "I give up, there's no way anyone could ever break the game laws in Alaska." While we were just as amazed at this meeting, we were very professional and agreed we had a very tight reign on all of Alaska and few violators were able to escape our efforts.

Back in the airplane we looked at one another and wondered how, with a population of more than forty thousand people in the Fairbanks area, we had checked one sportsman three times in an area of over hundreds of square miles in a period of three months. It had never happened before and it never happened to us again.

Chapter 3

THINK LIKE A BEAVER

*W*ith the buildup of beaver populations came the age-old problem of man and animal trying to live in harmony. In this case, the problem was the animal's need for deep water to build a house with an underwater entrance. Beaver accomplish this by building a dam across a stream, which then creates a pond. All well and good, but if people have built homes in these lowlands, the rising water level can cause havoc. The dams never seem big enough to these engineering marvels, and if a particular valley has enough feed they will keep adding to the dam size creating large lakes. This gives them a place to build homes free from predators and enough water to float tree branches for feed and, you guessed it, to build a bigger dam. The flood plains can inundate roads, cultivated lands and homes, and it means only one thing, "The beaver must go!" However, getting rid of the beaver isn't as easy as it sounds.

We had constant complaints from the Alaska Road Commission on plugged highway culverts in areas of good beaver habitat. Plugged is a good word because the culvert would be so jammed with sticks, stones, and mud that it would take one or two men hours with crowbars and axes to pull it apart. Then within one or two nights it would be plugged again—such is the tenacity of these animals.

How to control the problem without killing off the animals was the question. Killing them seldom worked if there was more than one colony anywhere else on the watershed. Younger beaver from upstream would just move in. Supervisors in charge of maintaining the highways would often lose patience. One even tried dumping diesel oil in the water to discourage the intruders. As you can imagine, this didn't set well with the local folks. Then one of the engineers came up with a simple but effective solution: heavy-duty screen panels fitted into slots on the sides of the culvert. The beaver would build against the screen, but one man patrolling the road system could pull the panel and free the debris in a matter of minutes. Eventually the animals became discouraged and vacated the stream.

Another sticky problem was dams that flooded roads and homes in the bottomlands. The owners wanted the dams lowered to control the water level, yet most did not want to hurt or lose the beavers.

They enjoyed them as neighbors until they became nuisances and caused damage.

Meetings were held, dams blown, beaver moved, but still the problem persisted. Finally someone came up with a simple solution by using a twenty-foot length of four-inch pipe. Using an ax and crowbar, a notch was cut into the middle of the dam down to the level of the desired water table. One end of the pipe was placed into the slot so it protruded out from the end of the dam. The upstream end was set into a cradle in the river bottom. This allowed the water to flow through the dam at the proper depth.

Upon confronting this situation, the beaver would pack the notch solid but were never able to figure out how to stop the water flow. They weren't able to find the source of the leak since the pipe opening was fifteen feet or so upstream. Most times they gave up and lived with the new water level. The pipe kept the water at a constant level, deep enough in most cases for their purposes and low enough to keep from flooding the neighborhood. Everyone was happy, and we were heroes.

In some areas the only solution was to trap the beaver and move them to another location. We soon found out that they had to be moved a considerable distance and into a different watershed or they would return. The Bailey Live Trap was made from a heavy-duty metal mesh and designed similar to a suitcase. To set the trap, I laid it open on the ground and baited it with fresh birch or willow branches.

The beaver walking over the mesh eventually set off the trigger and, thanks to a powerful spring assembly, the animal was immediately "suitcased" and ready for a ride or flight to a new location. Most times I flew them to a new lake or stream many miles away.

On one occasion I had a trap set on the bank of a slough in the vicinity of several homeowners who were losing their birch trees to a rogue beaver. The next morning, I found the trap sprung, but no beaver. This was the first time the trap failed and I was curious as to how it had missed. At first I suspected that someone tripped it until I talked with one of the local residents. The previous evening, he'd seen a large beaver approaching the trap so he sat back to watch. After sniffing the surrounding area, the giant animal stepped on the trigger. The trap sprung, but the beaver was so big that instead of snapping shut around him, it just catapulted him into the air, over the bank, and into the slough. When the witness last saw him, the beaver was moving downstream like a boat with its throttle wide open. We never did capture that rascal, and he continued to plague the neighborhood until some poor sport shot him. It was costly, though, as the man had to pay a healthy fine for his indiscretion.

Often beaver would dam important salmon streams completely, stopping a run of fish from reaching the spawning ground. When this occurred, it was, and still is, necessary to blow up the dam with dynamite, then keep it open until the run is complete. In spring, a follow-up is usually required to allow the smolt to swim downstream.

It was during my first dam-busting operation that I became acquainted with Slim Moore, one of Alaska's original and oldest registered hunting guides. He was licensed as a master guide, and for his dedication to guiding and devotion to fair chase in the taking of game, he was the first recipient of the prestigious Simon–Waugh Award given by the Alaska Professional Hunters Association. He spent some fifty years as a guide and trapper and was well known and respected by conservationists and wildlife managers for his commitment to wildlife.

In the early 1950s Slim was operating a lodge located on the shores of Summit Lake off the Richardson Highway. The outlet of Summit Lake flows into Paxson Lake and then into the Gulkana River, which in turns meanders into the Copper River. The Copper River winds its way through the Chugach Mountains and empties into the Gulf of Alaska near the town of Cordova. This entire watershed plays host to enormous runs of spawning salmon and is vital to the survival of several species, especially the sockeye, or red salmon. Finding their way to the headwater lakes after traveling hundreds of miles of glacier-silted waters is a miracle in itself for the fish. Being stopped by a beaver dam must be the ultimate frustration.

Such was the case with the outlet stream of Fish Lake, which feeds into the river connecting Paxson and Summit Lakes. In 1953 beaver built a large dam several hundred feet downstream from Fish Lake, causing it to rise several feet. The lake is about four miles long, so the two-foot rise was significant in the volume of water held back. Downstream from the dam were thousands of red salmon trying unsuccessfully to enter the lake to spawn along the shoreline. The dam had to go, and I was sent to Summit Lake with a Super Cub and a load of dynamite to do the job. As I gingerly loaded the ominous-looking cardboard box of explosives I wondered, "Why me?"

I was told to protect the caps carefully and not load them near the dynamite, for an inadvertent jar could cause the plane and me to disappear. I knew nothing about dynamite, so I believed what I was told. The explosives were in the back beside a movie camera. I put the caps, carefully wrapped in cloth, inside my shirt. I was told to find Slim Moore for advice since he had worked around mining camps and would have experience on the use of explosives.

I landed at Summit Lake with the float-equipped Cub, and Slim was right out to help me beach and tie down. I explained to him the problem of the beaver dam and asked if he would help with removing the dam. "When do we start?" he asked.

"After lunch please," was my reply. I wanted to relax away from the dynamite-laden plane. It had been rough flying through the pass, which is not unusual for that route through the Alaska Range. I'd sat on the edge of my seat all the way there, as if a few more inches between the caps and the box would have helped. When you know nothing about explosives, your mind can play cruel jokes.

Years later I had to haul over a ton of dynamite with a Grumman Goose from a lake in the Kenai Mountains to the town of Lawing for the Forest Service. Seems like one of the fellows working on the project blew himself up tapping the powder into a pipe. Even though I was more comfortable about this flight (the caps were flown out separately), I had to admit that my landings with the Goose were the smoothest ever and nary a pebble was disturbed. It's interesting how our senses get so finely tuned when we're apprehensive, even though we can act so nonchalantly on the outside.

Late in the afternoon I took off with Slim, who barely fit in the back seat. The box of dynamite was in his lap. He was in his usual jovial mood and kept joking about how we should make a pass over his competitor at Paxson Lodge so he could drop one of the sticks down the chimney, just for sport. On the approach to Fish Lake, I dragged the Cub in over the marshy end to touch down as close as possible to the lake edge. I got a tap on the shoulder and a, "Hey, boy, get my butt out of the grass if you don't mind!" Things always look different from the back end.

Once on the ground Slim eyeballed the dam like a log driver searching out the key log to blast. Finally satisfied with the right location, he took several sticks and taped them together onto a pole. As he made a slit into one stick and inserted a cap and fuse, I readied the camera. He waterproofed the opening with grease and poked the pole into the dam. Once the fuse was lit we made a beeline to a pre-picked spot where we could watch in safety.

I started the camera to capture the event on film for future PR work. Just before the big blast a female mallard swam into view, and I yelled to Slim, "Chase her away before she's hamburger." He yelled back, "Forget it, friend—better her than me. It's too late now." Thirty seconds later it blew, and although the mallard didn't suffer the fate of being minced, she made the most spectacular catapulting takeoff I ever did see. It would have made a dandy movie sequence except that I jumped when the blast went off and all I got was a picture of the sky.

The dam opened and the water poured through, filling the stream bank full. Many unfortunate salmon were washed downriver a good distance before recovering and some got carried all the way to the mouth. What an inglorious ending to a super migration effort. Fortunately, several days later the creek stabilized and we watched hundreds of salmon making their way into the lake. I camped on location for about a week, keeping the dam open until the major share of the run passed through.

I went back to Summit Lake and had a long talk with Slim about the fate of this family of beaver. I had counted seven, all told and felt they had to be removed. Slim indicated that it would be too difficult to do during the open trapping season because of the snow depth. He agreed to give it a try if we issued him a permit to trap in November and December when he would be able to get to the lake on snowshoes. It was agreed, and I told him the necessary paperwork would be issued in plenty of time. I reported back and told my supervisor that once we issued the permit we could forget about the beaver house because it was just like the Mafia negotiating a contract—Slim the hit man would do the job.

I thought no more about the problem until one day in December, when I got a call from Slim's wife saying he was in the hospital recuperating from an appendectomy. When I went up to visit I found him propped up in bed looking all tanned and ruddy against the white sheets with no indication that he had just been through an operation. He was his good-natured self as he gave me the details of the incident that put him in the hospital. Fortunately, his wife, Margaret, had been accompanying him on his jaunts up to Fish Lake to trap out the beaver. She was adept on snowshoes herself and often helped. That particular morning Slim hadn't felt up to snuff but not bad enough to stay home, so they put on the webs and plodded the four miles up the creek to the lake and checked the traps. They had one beaver and were proceeding back home when Slim was hit with a severe attack of abdominal pains. Somehow Margaret assisted him back to the road, although I don't know how because Slim was one big guy. She got him into the pickup and drove to Fairbanks. As Slim put it, if Margaret hadn't been there he would have cashed in his chips right then and there on the trail. Then he grinned and said he got a ribbing from his doctor who claimed Slim's appendix was chock full of ptarmigan feathers.

"He told me I should clean my birds before I ate them. Now ain't that a hell of a note to have to change my ways this late in life?"

Slim recovered and finished trapping out the family of beaver. The next year there was no dam for the fish to contend with and I had gained the lasting friendship of a great Alaskan. I was honored years later when he sponsored me for membership into the Pioneers of Alaska after I had fulfilled the thirty years' residency requirement. All of this as a result of my continuing encounters with beaver.

Chapter 4

FOR THE WANT OF SNOWSHOES

*W*e didn't need them last trip."

That's what we told each other, and so began the unforgettable trip of the forgotten snowshoes. It was to be a routine beaver-pelt sealing trip to the villages of Ruby, Galena, Koyukuk, Nulato, and Huslia, combined with a patrol of some of the heavily trapped areas in between. The date was March 9, 1954, a beautiful clear day with the temperature about –30°F, and my partner as usual was agent Jim King. We planned to use the ski-equipped Piper Pacer because of its ability to get in and out of the small ice- and snow-covered lakes or rivers where most of the trapping activity was taking place. Our gear for the trip was packed accordingly. First, there were 1,500 consecutively numbered locking seals with the necessary affidavit books carefully stacked in a canvas bag. Then came the travel necessities: a rifle, ax, tie-down ropes, emergency gear, sleeping bags, cameras, wing covers, engine cover, and a specially designed oil can for draining the engine oil at night. Also there was a plumber's firepot for preheating the engine in mornings, and our personal belongings. Enough to last for the five or seven days away from headquarters.

At the Fairbanks hangar, a Herman Nelson heater warmed the ski-equipped Pacer as we loaded our gear. About the time we were ready to depart, Jim noticed that we had forgotten to bring snowshoes. One never traveled without these rawhide-laced wooden frames since they were the only way of walking out traplines in the deep snow. Also if the plane should get bogged down they were the only means of packing down a runway for takeoff. To retrieve them would require a drive back to town and at least an hour's delay in our departure. We were already behind schedule, so the prospect of a further delay was not encouraging.

Then came the famous last words, *We didn't need them the last trip*, which was true as very little snow had fallen this year. The previous week we had walked over much of that same area in only ankle-deep snow, which was highly unusual for this time of the year. Because the Interior was still under the influence of a large high-pressure system with cold weather prevailing, we had every reason to believe that conditions would be the same this trip. We agreed—unwisely—that we would go without the snowshoes.

I took off at 11:55 A.M. and headed west into flawless flying conditions. It was severe clear without a bump in the air and visibility was unlimited. A pilot's dream. We flew alongside Ester Dome, continued over the Minto Flats and crossed the Tanana River at a cruising altitude of about two thousand feet. The monotonous droning of the engine and the bright sun soon lulled Jim to sleep while I struggled to stay awake. We had both been out late the night before taking part in bachelor activities.

As we crossed the Cosna River flats I remarked aloud that with visibility this clear, we would be able to spot an illegal moose kill five miles away. Jim cocked open his eyes, looked out the right window and remarked, "There's one right there." I banked the aircraft and sure enough there were two men butchering a freshly killed moose. By following their snowshoe tracks we found a tent camp about three miles from the kill, and by backtracking the main dog-team trail to the north, determined they were beaver trappers probably from the village of Tanana.

There was only one area suitable for landing, a snow-covered meadow about halfway between the moose kill and the tent camp. Our plan was simple. After landing, Jim would walk to the kill site, and I would go to the tent to intercept the individuals involved, in the event they tried to take off with the dog teams.

I evaluated the landing site and made a pattern over the spruce trees, easing the plane gently onto the snow patch. The aircraft settled, and settled, and settled, finally coming to rest in snow clear up to the windshield. It was impossible to taxi, for the Pacer was completely bogged down in loose, fluffy snow and when I shut the engine down, the shock set in—no snowshoes. We had landed in a valley that had received substantially more snow than the rest of the country. How would we get out? It was now imperative that we make contact with these men we were pursuing since they had the only snowshoes and a dog team. They were mobile and able to travel while we had no means of getting out of this valley of the deep snow. The time was 1:25 P.M.

We forced the aircraft door open and made our way into four feet of powdery snow. Jim floundered off toward the moose kill while I made like a land otter, floundering my way to the tent. At times I literally pulled myself through the alder bushes. After three hours of half-swimming or pulling myself through the brush, I finally found the tent. All the time I was fighting my way to the tent I was thinking of Jim who was going in the opposite direction. He would have to retrace his steps to get back to the plane, and then follow my trail to the tent site. It was obvious that we would be spending the night here due to impending darkness.

As I was inspecting the campsite, an Indian trapper arrived and asked why I was there. I introduced myself and explained the situation about the moose kill and our stuck plane. He said that the trappers we had observed must be his partners and he confirmed they were all from Tanana. They had arrived three days earlier after several days on the trail with two dog teams. The beaver-trapping venture had been planned with the idea that it would take about three weeks for the three of them to get their limit of beaver. I told him that unless they had another food cache somewhere, the outfit he showed me was insufficient to sustain three men and eleven dogs for that long. When I questioned him further he said they had planned to eat mostly beaver meat once the traps started producing. The high-protein beaver carcasses would also feed the dogs, providing the traps and snares were productive. So far prospects didn't look very good, he admitted, which was the reason his partners left this morning on snowshoes to try to find a moose.

After we got a fire going in the tent, I told him that Jim and I were stuck for the night and would have to somehow make arrangements with him for our night's lodging. He looked around and I guess we both had the same question. How can five men sleep in an eight-by-ten wall tent equipped with a stove and cooking equipment? It was crowded quarters for three, and it appeared that would be impossible to stuff two more bodies in there. Somehow we would have to manage, though, so I went out and started cutting and splitting a rack of wood to last the night. No doubt it would drop to at least −40°F before morning.

Later the other two Indian trappers snowshoed into camp. I asked about Jim, and they said he was on his way from the kill site and that they were going back to pick him up with one of the dog teams. About an hour later they were back in the darkness with an exhausted Jim, who agreed that the tent, as small as it was, looked mighty good.

After he rested we talked over our problems. The big concern of course was a place to spend the night and a runway for the aircraft the next day. Here we had in effect arrested two trappers for killing a cow moose out of season, and we were at their mercy for shelter in the bitter cold. We resolved the situation by offering to pay them to snowshoe out a runway in the morning and for allowing us to stay the night in the tent. The illegal moose incident would be handled separately at a later date in Tanana and would not be an issue at this time. Both of our sleeping bags were in the aircraft and we decided not to ask our hosts to make another trip with their teams to get them since there was not enough room for five people to stretch out. It would be a matter of keeping the fire going all night to make us as comfortable as possible.

We busied ourselves with woodcutting while the trappers cooked their evening meal. This additional exercise sharpened our already keen appetites, but unfortunately there was little prospect for a meal this night. The meager supplies and strained relationship with our new associates did not give much prospect for filling our empty stomachs. All of the emergency rations were also back in the plane, and as with the sleeping bags, we did not think it wise to ask them to hook up the dogs. We stacked all the split spruce near the entrance of the tent where we could easily reach out during the night and feed the small Yukon stove.

By nine o'clock we were finished and poked our heads through the tent flap to observe the three trappers finishing up a slim meal of rice and biscuits. We entered the crowded quarters after taking off our heavy outer clothing and tried to make ourselves as inconspicuous as possible. After they finished eating they gave us each a biscuit, some tea and what was left of the rice. This did little for the hunger pangs, but would have to take care of our needs until we got back to town.

The night proved to be exceptionally long and cold. While the three trappers slept nice and snug in their sleeping bags, we dozed in fits and starts while in the sitting position. The stove kept going from hot to cold as the wood burned. The tent cooled immediately, causing one of us to wake with a start and fill it with wood again. When daylight finally arrived we both looked like we had been dragged through a knothole.

The trappers' breakfast consisted of some dried fish. The fish was also fed to the dogs. We had to settle for growling stomachs. Finally the dogs were hooked up and the five of us went to the plane with the two teams. Jim and I rode while the drivers walked behind the sleds, helping them through the tangled alder and willow brush. One walked ahead on snowshoes breaking out a trail.

At the plane, they immediately went to work snowshoeing out a runway of about five hundred feet long while we preheated the aircraft engine. Since we had not been able to drain the oil the night before, it took twice as long to heat the engine. The plane's skis were dug out, propped up, and scraped clean of frost that had accumulated during the night. It was important to have these surfaces polished for fast acceleration since the runway was not going to be any too long. What we needed was enough packed-down snow for the plane to build up the speed necessary for the wings to develop lift. This would then allow the skis to run on top of the powdered snow until takeoff speed was attained.

After the men finished packing the runway, I started the engine and warmed it carefully until all gauges said it was a go. Then with Jim and the trappers pushing, I was able to get the aircraft positioned for a takeoff run. We said our good-byes and told the trappers we would fly back over the camp in two days with whatever supplies they requested in exchange for the lodging and work they had performed. The supplies would be air dropped, so anything breakable was not to be considered. They went into a huddle for about five minutes and gave us the group decision: two cartons of cigarettes.

Jim and I looked at each other in disbelief and asked if they were kidding. They said no, that they would be getting plenty of beaver, which would provide food, and with the season ending March 30, they would be home in Tanana in just over three weeks. We agreed and advised them we would be dropping the cigarettes they requested plus some grub. We also told them we would meet them in Tanana about April 15 to take care of the illegal moose situation and we would advise the U.S. Commissioner about all the cooperation they had given us.

It took three tries to get airborne. Jim and the trappers had to assist after each attempt by pushing the taxiing plane back through the deep powdered snow to the packed runway. Finally we were off, and with great relief we headed back to Fairbanks. The first thing we did was get a big meal. It was then that Jim told me that the moose they had killed was a sick one with big cysts in the lungs and wasn't fit to eat.

What a series of events: a sick moose met its demise because three trappers went on a beaver-hunting expedition without adequate food supplies, and a routine landing that turned into a nightmare because two experienced wardens forgot to take snowshoes.

We departed two days later to complete the trip we had started on the ninth. When we flew over the trapping camp, the three trappers waved. We dropped several packages with food, coffee and, of course, the most needed items, three cartons of cigarettes.

On April 15 we met the trappers in Tanana as prearranged and kept our part of the bargain. The commissioner listened to our story when we filed the complaints. He allowed them to pay a minimum fine with the understanding that in the future they would plan trapping expeditions with an adequate food supply that would last the duration of the trip. Even though the moose in question had been a sick animal and not fit for food, it was still an illegal kill and could not be ignored. Any action or inaction we took would travel around the area like wildfire and we could not allow the wrong message to get out. The Alaska Game Law allowed the killing of game for an actual "emergency," however, the law was very explicit, and going out without adequate provisions was not considered an emergency.

As for us, we never forgot snowshoes again. In fact, maybe I went overboard, for one of our aircraft mechanics at the Anchorage hangar was overheard asking another, "How come Ray keeps his snowshoes in his plane until it's time to go on floats?"

Chapter 5

THE GULLWING STINSON

*T*he Gullwing is my airplane, I shall not rest." So said Sig Olson, a good friend and biologist for the FWS, in a poem he'd written after our many adventures with Stinson N782.

When I checked out in that Stinson on September 1, 1953, I felt I had reached the peak of my flying career. The big five-place aircraft, boasting a round 300-horsepower Lycoming engine, constant-speed propeller, and graceful wings had for years proven a reliable Bush plane in Alaska. As the Gullwing had established its credibility, so I was eager to prove mine, and a great love affair was born that lasted until she was sold in 1961. We flew together over all of northern Alaska on enforcement patrol, game counts, freight hauls, and trips for VIPs.

On one of the first trips with the Gullwing, I was flying out of Point Barrow with Ray Woolford, my supervisor, and Walt Ahmaoyak, a local Eskimo. That day I learned a valuable lesson in radio navigation as well as the Eskimo method of travel without a compass. We had flown several hours north of Barrow to record the condition of the ice pack and document the number of polar bears observed. When we found a fresh track, we followed it until we found the bear, made notes of direction of travel, and recorded any seal kills in the vicinity. When we had used up about half of our fuel, we decided it was time to head back to Barrow. I tuned the plane's Aircraft Directional Finder (ADF) and after the needle settled down, headed in the direction it pointed.

After about an hour of droning along over the vast ice fields, Walt, who was sitting in the copilot's seat, asked where I was going. When I said Point Barrow, he pointed to the right about 90 degrees and said "Barrow that way." I explained to him how the ADF worked and how once the receiver was tuned, the needle would point to the station, and for all practical purposes you just had to follow it home. I did not go into correcting for wind drift since we were not encountering any noticeable drift. He listened patiently and shook his head saying he didn't know anything about the gadget I was following, but, "Barrow that way," pointing to the right again. Nothing was on the horizon but more ice and pressure ridges.

The good ol' Stinson and I had many adventures together, April 1955.

Ray, who was in the back seat, poked his head between us and looked at the ADF, listened to Walt, and then asked me for the radio headset. After a few minutes he smiled, gave me back the headset, and said, "You're not tuned to Barrow." Stunned, I listened carefully to the Morse code identifier and sure enough, I had tuned in Barter Island, 265 nautical miles east of Point Barrow. This meant we were paralleling the coast about 150 miles out and with our limited gas supply would never have reached land. A stupid mistake that could have been costly if it hadn't been for Walt. I properly tuned the radio and the needle swung to the right just where Walt was pointing, and when I turned in that direction, he smiled and we all relaxed again.

We landed at Barrow with little fuel remaining. After we secured the plane for the night, I asked Walt how he knew we were going in the wrong direction. He said the predominant winds in this part of the world are northeast–southwest, and the snow on the nonmoving ice always formed hard drifts that lined up in those directions. This was the way Eskimos navigated on the ice when hunting miles off shore. They cut the drifts at whatever angle was necessary to go in a straight line and then reversed the procedure on the way back.

I had learned two valuable lessons on that trip. The first was to positively identify the station being used for navigational purposes.

This is critical especially with instrument flying and was a good lesson to learn early in my career. In my later years when I flew larger aircraft by Instrument Flight Rules (IFR), I would always remember this incident and check and recheck my instrument identifiers. The second lesson taught me to be more aware of nature's compasses when flying Visual Flight Rules (VFR).

Although this was not the only time the old Gullwing humbled me, we always accomplished our missions with nary a scratch on her fuselage. There was the time I was asked to fly some Canadian dignitaries north of Fairbanks to observe the caribou calving grounds. It was June 3, 1955, during a science conference at the University of Alaska. Biologists from several countries were presenting wildlife research papers at the conference and the major topic was the Alaska–Canada caribou herds. It seemed that the Canadians had lost a major segment of that herd in the Yukon and Northwest Territories, while Alaska was enjoying a great abundance of the critters. Several teams from both countries were studying the migration patterns of these travelers. There was a great deal of speculation that they traveled great distances back and forth across the border, giving them dual citizenship. This, of course, has been confirmed and the movements of the different herds are now well established.

Dr. Francis Banfield, Canada's caribou expert, and two of his colleagues were my passengers. Sig Olson, big-game biologist working out of the Fairbanks office, would ride in the copilot's seat to act as guide and tour director. Our plan was to fly to the Preacher Creek area of the White Mountains, north of Fairbanks, and observe the large number of caribou and calves in that area.

The Gullwing was parked at the Fairbanks Airport, which had just been opened the previous year. The only building was the control tower, and we had permission to park on the apron just opposite and in full view of the operators. I had completed a preflight prior to the arrival of the biologists, so I invited them to climb aboard when they were ready. There is only one door on the aircraft, aft of the wing strut on the left side. If the rear passengers get in first, which was usually the case, the pilot and the person sitting in the right seat have to be careful as they squeeze their way into the front seats. The passengers didn't like to have their feet stepped on by clumsy pilots, so I made it a habit to make sure everything was a go before getting in last.

After everyone was settled I cranked up the engine and allowed it to warm up as I monitored the gauges. Since my passengers were not pilots I was naturally going to impress them with my flying skills, so I activated the switch making all the radio transmissions audible on the overhead speaker. I was sure they would be interested in hearing me talk to the tower operator and to the FWS secretary monitoring us on the radio. I would file a flight plan with her after takeoff and keep her advised periodically of our progress.

After everything was ready, I called the tower in my most professional voice, "Fairbanks tower this is Stinson N782 parked in front of the tower and ready to taxi to the active runway." There was a pause and finally the tower operator answered, "N782 you are cleared to taxi to runway 019, wind calm, suggest you untie your wings first!"

Bummer, boy, what a first impression. I think if I had been one of the biologists I would have said, "See you later." Obviously they were dedicated scientists because they stayed in the airplane. I had committed another cardinal sin. "Check and recheck what helpers do for you." I had relied on Sig to untie the wing on the right side of the aircraft, which he normally did on our flights. Since I had been there before he had arrived, he had assumed that I had taken care of it. Talk about eating humble pie! I had to shut down the engine and step on everyone's feet while climbing out to release the tie-down rope. After that I shut off the overhead speaker.

Experienced pilots have a saying about Stinsons: "They're built like a bridge and they fly like one." This was true. They were one of the strongest planes ever constructed, but they were ground-lovers. It was not a short-field aircraft, but once airborne they were a great comfort, especially while flying in turbulence. The stout gear was also appreciated when landing on rough rocky runways or when botching a touchdown. I did a good job of proving this point one night during the fall hunting season in 1954.

We had set up a check station at Paxson that year to keep track of the harvest of moose and caribou being taken along the newly opened Denali Highway. Several temporary employees were hired to man a trailer at the junction of the Denali and Richardson Highways. They were to inspect each vehicle passing through. I was assisting this effort by making daily flights in the Gullwing to make sure no hunters were hunting in the closed areas. The airstrip I was using paralleled the road and was about 1,500 feet long. At the north end there was a hill. This significant obstacle prompted all takeoffs to the south and landings to the north with the Stinson.

Two of the temporaries had to be flown to Healy one evening to assist with some problems that had developed in that area. This meant a late return flight, and I knew I would be arriving after dark. The only possible landing would be toward the hill and touchdown would have to be precise on the first part of the strip. To add zest to this adventure, the landing light on the plane wasn't working.

Before departing, I requested the other temporary worker, now by himself at the check station, to help me by placing a gas lantern on the left side of the runway at the exact end of the usable strip. This would act as my guide for my descent and landing.

As anticipated, it was dark when I returned and after several passes, the lantern appeared and finally became stationary at the end of the runway. I made a long approach with my eyes on the lantern and when I came up even with it, chopped the power and hauled back on the stick ready for touchdown. Suddenly, a sickening, sinking sensation surged through me as the bottom fell out. The airplane stalled and plunged for what felt like an eternity before hitting the ground. Needless to say, what was supposed to be a featherlight landing turned into a bone-jarring, soul-quaking crash, which would have destroyed the landing gear on any airplane but that of the big Stinson. After gingerly bringing the plane to a halt and finding how many teeth I had left, if any, I walked shakily back to find out what had happened.

Nothing much, except for the fact that my young friend had really wanted to help me out. To do so, he had attached the gas lantern, my handsome guiding light, to a twenty-foot pole, which he had then proudly held high into the air above his head. Another valuable lesson! Be careful when you ask for assistance and make sure that the helper, especially if he is a non-pilot, knows exactly what you want. It did prove one thing. She was a stout ship.

Another feature of this plane that sometimes caused problems was the non-steering tail wheel. Most modern planes have the tail wheel assembly connected to the rudder pedals; when the rudder is moved right or left while taxiing, the tail wheel follows. This simple tracking mechanism greatly assists with more positive steering on the ground, especially in crosswinds. The fully castored tail gear of the Gullwing was easily kept aligned with the use of brakes while the aircraft was on wheels; however, once skis were installed, the situation changed considerably. Now the only turning force available was the effect of the propeller blast on the rudder, and when fully loaded in deep snow or glare ice, a large turning area was required to complete the turn.

There were several ways to assist in getting the plane turned into the wind for takeoff. One was to wrap several turns of a rope on one of the skis to slow down the sliding action of that ski which in turn acted as a brake. The big trick was figuring out a knot that did not jam as the rope slid back on the bottom and became taut. Usually the line had to be cut, so good tie-down ropes were not used for this purpose.

Another big problem with this method was having to get out with the engine running, tie on the rope, get back in and complete the turn, get back out to take the rope off, and back in again to take off. Shutting down the engine would have been safer; however, cold-weather starts were hard on an aircraft battery, and it was unwise to take the chance of not having enough juice to get the engine going again.

A better method was having a "skookum" (strong) passenger who would get out and push the tail around while the pilot applied full power. Volunteers were hard to come by, however, because it was a nasty job, especially when the temperature was below zero. The wind and chill factor from the propeller required the hardy person to be adequately dressed in a heavy parka and big mitts. Because visibility was restricted due to swirling snow, the pusher could only follow the tail around, not really knowing when it was in the proper position for takeoff.

The pilot, on the other hand, would have to apply enough power to get the plane moving so that inertia could help move the tail ski in the direction required. Left turns were planned when possible to take advantage of the engine and prop torque. When the turn was completed it was sometimes necessary to keep the plane moving forward and get aligned in a set of ski tracks or hard-packed snow so the skis would break free for takeoff. The pusher working in the blowing snow oftentimes would not know when to quit and sometimes ended up getting knocked over by the horizontal stabilizer. Strained feelings could result if the person did not have a sense of humor, so pushers were chosen carefully, when possible, and pilots cherished the good ones.

Sig Olson had many a good story to tell about being on the tail end of the tail of the Stinson, and it was he who categorized the positions of the pilot and passenger as "blasters" and "pushers." When we were issued uniforms in 1957, the regional director considered designing a set of wings for pilots to wear. Sig suggested that pushers be considered for a badge of distinction also. His idea was a set of crossed snowshoes on the uniform sleeve with a hashmark below for each time the pusher had been run over by the tail! In his case, however, we determined that the sleeve of this coat was not long enough to support that many hashmarks. Sig was definitely our most devoted pusher.

In the spring of 1955, Lt. Bill Trafton called me for assistance. He said that territorial officials had determined it was time to acquaint people in the outlying areas with the new territorial laws and introduce them to the Troopers charged with enforcing them. He asked if it was possible to take one of his Troopers on a trip to some of the Interior villages. At the time I was flying to most of the villages sealing beaver skins, so taking a Trooper along posed no problem. Since he wanted to make the proper impression, he picked his biggest officer, Ray Hill. Ray was at least six-feet-six-inches and very impressive in full uniform. He was also a gentle and well-liked cop.

On April 11, I departed Fairbanks in the Gullwing on skis with Ray in his best uniform to make a tour of all the villages down the Yukon River from Tanana to Kaltag and up the Koyukuk River to Bettles. It was warm with the snow soft and melting. Most of the winter landing strips were on the river in front of the villages. We had no problems until we arrived in Nulato. The strip on the river ice was narrow and, except for the packed snow from other planes, there was a considerable amount of overflow (water on the ice) beneath the deep snow along the edges. After landing I told Ray I would need his help turning around. I advised him of the procedure and explained that if we didn't complete the turn and get back on the packed surface, we would be there indefinitely getting the plane out of the overflow. Ray dutifully got out and, with most of the villagers standing on the bank watching, I proceeded to make a turn with my Trooper pushing the tail around. As the turn progressed, I realized it was going to be nip-and-tuck, so I advanced the throttle all the way to get back into the ski tracks. I knew Ray was in big trouble back there, but felt I had no choice. Sure enough, Ray could not get away from the tail when the plane surged forward and he got wrapped over the horizontal stabilizer, the part of the tail assembly that supports the elevators.

When I finally got back on the packed surface of the runway, I looked back to see a most disheveled officer limping back in the ski tracks to retrieve his clip-on tie and whatever else had been blown off his uniform. I wish there were some way to describe the guffaws and knee-slapping that were going on up on the riverbank. I'm sure this is not what Lt. Trafton had in mind when he envisioned his handpicked officer walking into a village for the first time.

Ray rose to the occasion, however, like the real Trooper he was. He clipped his tie on, straightened out his uniform, put on his Trooper Stetson and introduced himself to all the folks. This was the first uniformed officer many had seen and they were dutifully impressed. He held a brief meeting to advise who the Territorial Police were and how they would be functioning in the outlying areas in the future. We traveled to all the other villages with no further troubles, gaining recognition for the future State Troopers.

Taxiing on glare ice was especially tricky, particularly going downwind. The plane wants to weathercock, or turn into the wind and go in circles, if the breeze is strong enough. The pusher must walk along the back of the aircraft keeping the tail heading in a straight direction.

On one occasion, Ray Woolford and I had landed on the lake behind the village of Kobuk. It was spring and the ice was free of snow, making it very slick. When we were ready for departure, Ray asked if I wanted him to walk behind to steer the plane in the twenty-knot wind. I had to taxi downwind the full length of the lake, which would be difficult, but I felt I could do it and suggested he climb aboard.

After warming the engine I started very slowly down the middle of the narrow lake. When we had advanced about a hundred yards, the plane started to veer to the left. There was a split decision to make—either stop and have Ray get out or blast the tail to straighten it out.

I chose the latter and gave the engine a good burst of power. Instead of straightening out, the Stinson swerved even more, gathered momentum and headed off the lake into the willows. I shut down, and Ray's only remark was, "I really didn't mind walking behind, you know." No I didn't know, and after all, he was my supervisor, and I didn't think it proper for him to be walking the plane in full view of all the villagers that were out to see the takeoff.

Fortunately, the onlookers were a happy bunch, because we were turned 90 degrees to the lake in the dense brush with no way to turn the plane around, and we desperately needed them. Only one solution was available—brute force pulling and pushing backwards. After several tries with little effect, some of the men went back to the village and brought back several dog teams and all the available manpower. The dogs were hooked up to a long towline and were assisted by several of the men who helped by pulling on the line. Others pushed on the gear, skis, and inboard wing struts. They were having a ball, thankfully. This was their kind of challenge. After much yelling and grunting, it moved, and once started, made its way backward to the center of the lake.

Without a word, Ray stayed outside as I cranked up and slowly taxied to the other end of the lake while he walked the tail keeping it from wandering again. His only comment as he climbed back into the airplane was, "Do you suppose, as a pilot, I would have been entitled to a hashmark if I had been on the back of the tail when you blasted it?" No answer was necessary and the incident wasn't mentioned again except to wonder what we would have done had we been alone when the Stinson decided to make a dive into the brush.

Another call came from Deputy Marshal Mike McRoberts. There was a deranged trapper at the village of Beaver who had to be transported to Fairbanks. He was presently tied up and held in a cabin by some of the men in the village. Could we assist? Another trip for N782. On the trip north, Mike and I discussed where we would put him especially if he was violent. We decided Mike would have to put him in restraints and put him on the floor in the back of the plane. The back seat was removable.

On our arrival we were met by some of the men, and Mike gathered all the information he needed to incarcerate the man. He was a white trapper who lived part of the time in the village when he wasn't out on the trapline. A few days before he had returned and was acting strangely. Apparently he threatened a few of the villagers and they had had to restrain him. We went to the cabin where they were holding him. He appeared okay when we questioned him, until he started talking about voices inside that were telling him to do certain things. Since he was now obviously calmed down, we just put handcuffs on him and walked him to the plane.

When we got to the airstrip he looked at the plane and shouted "A GULLWING STINSON, THE BEST PLANE EVER BUILT! Can I ride up front?" I looked at Mike and he nodded stating he could watch him closely from the back seat. On the trip to Fairbanks the man was a model passenger, taking an interest in every instrument and continuously asking questions on how they worked. When we landed, there was a patrol car to meet us. He thanked me over and over and said this had been the greatest trip of his life. Good old N782, she came through again. I later learned the trapper had to be sent to a mental institution in Oregon.

I became involved with a project being conducted by Wilbur "Burt" Libby, a graduate student at the University of Alaska Wildlife Research Unit. The unit had a contract with the Air Force to produce a survival manual for pilots. The idea was to catalog plant and animal life in different parts of Alaska. The manual would be a part of the pilot's kit, and if forced down he could look into the book and determine what was available for his survival at that location. Burt was in charge of the project under the direction of Dr. John Buckley, the unit leader.

In the spring of that year I had to fly transects, or predetermined lines that were laid out on a map, across the Interior. Some were several hundred miles long. While I held a compass course following the line on the map, Burt in the copilot's seat and another student sitting behind me watched the snow very carefully, making observations of tracks, animals, and vegetation. Each had a portable recorder. The flying had to be accurate according to Dr. Buckley: exactly one hundred feet over the terrain, covering the line drawn on the map from the specific starting point to the precise spot at the end.

One day we were running a rather long transect that ended in a narrow valley of the Minto Hills. As we entered the valley I planned my turn at the exact point where the transect ended, knowing it would be tight. At the right moment I banked sharply to the left, extending the flaps to shorten the steep turn. Just as we started around, the engine sputtered. I had neglected to switch gas tanks, and the left one had just run dry. (Remember the adage: "Flying is hours and hours of boredom broken up by moments of stark terror." This was the stark terror.)

In my confusion, I reached beside my left leg for the selector valve. This was natural reaction, because the day before I had been flying a Piper Pacer and that's where the valve is located. Lo and behold, no selector valve; it was on the console directly in front of me. My right hand reached up and turned the valve just as we were about to enter the trees. The engine caught and the turn was completed at a very low altitude. Hell, we weren't very high to begin with. Nothing much was said.

We continued on our way and finished the day's flying. When we were back at the office, we reviewed the tapes to make sure the recorders had been operating properly. I listened attentively for Burt's reaction as the recorded voice reached the point when we were in the canyon. It went something like this, "We're approaching the completion of this transect which ends in a narrow valley. As the terrain climbs, the vegetation is changing from willows and black spruce to birch and alder. Tracks of several moose are meandering up the side hill. One moose at the end of the transect. We are in a steep turn, the engine has just quit (pause), there, it started again and we're completing the turn rather close to the ground. Now we will continue on to transect number 33." No emotion, no change in voice pitch, just matter-of-fact reporting routine data. I shrugged and thought he's either fearless or has lots of confidence in my piloting. Naturally, I chose the latter; no sense both of us being scared.

We parted company, the Gullwing and I, when she was sold in 1961. Then N782 ended her career a few years later in McGrath when the new owner tried to use the aircraft as a mosquito sprayer. The plane crashed and burned after a steep turn at the end of the runway.

As a fitting tribute, and with permission from my good friend Sig Olson, here is the poem he wrote recounting the many trials and tribulations we had with N782, including a final note regarding Hutch, the mechanic who worked on the Stinson in Fairbanks.

ODE TO N782
(With apologies to King David)

The Gullwing is my aircraft,
    I shall not rest;
It flyeth me above the tundra
    And leadeth me amongst mighty mountains;
It maketh me to lie down after each flight
    To recover my strength.
    It scareth my soul.

Verily, thou taxieth like a lumber wagon,
    Thou lovest the ground
And no airstrip is too long.
    Thine airspeed riseth but slowly;
The end of the runway approacheth rapidly.

Yea, though I near the valley of the
    Shadow of Death,
Thou art airborne! My sweat runneth over
    But thy manifold pressure and tach needle
They comfort me. I shall fear no evil!

Thou flyeth for hours and my bladder overfloweth,
    For I dare not land short of a 3,000-foot
    airfield.

Alas! Thou preparest an emergency before me
    In the presence of mine passengers;
Thy prop seals giveth out
    And I getteth a mere 1400 RPM from thee.
Thine oil pressure droppeth
    And again my sweat runneth over.
I calleth on the radio and receiveth no sympathy;
    Smoke filleth thy cockpit and I cannot see—

Thy smelleth overpowereth.
    Surely goodness and mercy hath deserted me forever.

I fighteth to maintain altitude,
    I turneth thee back to Fairbanks International;
At least thy rods and mains, they comfort;
    Thou never stoppeth completely.
But I forgetteth thy gas tanks and lo!
    Thou hast stopped completely!
My heart leapeth, my throat suddenly parcheth,

My hand flyeth to my left knee to switch tanks,
    Alas, thou are no Pacer!
Ah, Thy switch before my eyes—
    38 gallons more for thy gulping cylinders,

Thy flaps commeth down, thy airspeed droppeth
    Anyway thy landing seemeth normal!
I taxieth thee and the pushers pusheth thee;
    I leaneth thee out and thy engine stoppeth.
Surely I shall consign thee to Hutch.
    Forever!

                   Amen

Chapter 6

CAPTURE OF THE BLUE PARKA BANDIT
& OTHER TRAPLINE PATROLS

*I*n the 1950s the trapping season for marten, mink, land otter, fox, lynx, and weasel extended from November 16 through January 31 in the Interior. These furbearers could be taken by any means except by the use of a set gun, a shotgun, artificial light, or traps with jaws having a spread exceeding nine inches. Nor were poisons, dogs, chemicals, fish traps, or smoke allowed. Traps could not be set within one hundred feet of a fox den, and homes, houses, or dens were not to be disturbed.

The reason for the season's beginning and ending dates was to ensure a prime pelt. The Alaska Game Commission, backed by years of experience and studies that had been conducted by FWS biologists, believed that fur animals should only be taken when they were the most valuable, and not before or after. Skins taken early are thin, having few guard hairs, and the hide is blue, indicating the hair roots are not fully set. After the end of January, the longer guard hairs tend to become singed and split, also making them less desirable.

Other regulations prohibited methods that would be detrimental to the resource, other wildlife, or to humans through the misuse of poison or the large bear traps that were capable of breaking a man's leg. Disrupting homes and dens is self-explanatory, and the use of smoke and chemicals was prohibited because many animals suffocated in the dens and could not be retrieved. It was also considered inhumane.

Trapping was an important means of maintaining an existence for many people and the only way for some, especially Natives, to provide a livelihood for their families. As with any other occupation, there were those who cheated. Some advanced the season because it was easier trapping during the warmer weather, even though the fur was not fully prime and brought lower prices. They felt quantity versus quality would put them ahead in money. Others who operated near villages trapped early to beat out competitors. Some broke the law just because they believed it was their right to take wildlife whenever and wherever they felt like it. Others were just inefficient or lazy.

It was our job to ensure that those who took furs did so in accordance with the regulations. Having been a trapper for several years and having developed a pride in the profession, I took a special interest in this part of the job.

Normally, the Interior's lakes froze over by November 1 and enabled us to use ski-equipped aircraft. This gave us two weeks to check for illegal trapping activities before the season opened. Because the fur-producing areas were so vast, we picked one section of the district and concentrated our efforts there. If extensive violations were found, we went back to the same area the following year to determine if our efforts had a deterring effect. If not, we worked the area again, oftentimes picking up the same violators a second time.

A typical patrol would have us operating out of a centrally located village that had a roadhouse and gas facility. Before dawn we would be out heating the aircraft with a plumber's firepot. After the firepot was primed and generating a good blue flame, it was put inside a canvas engine cover which covered the cowling and prop. The engine cover draped to the ground, which in effect formed a tent around the front of the plane. The firepot was set on the ground beneath the engine, and before long the inside of the engine cover was warmed and the thawing process began. When it was zero or below, the engine would turn white and slowly the frost would melt and drip. The warming was continued until the prop turned freely. (At −30°F or lower it couldn't be budged, and you could do chin-ups on it prior to heating the engine.) The oil that had been drained the night before and kept warm inside was poured back into the engine.

Depending on the temperature, it took from thirty minutes to an hour to prepare the engine. The wing covers were removed while the engine thawed. These were necessary to keep the frost from building up on the surfaces of the wings during the night. Frost is detrimental to lift and has caused many accidents in the North. If the wings are not covered, the frost has to be brushed with a rope or broom to allow a smooth airflow over the top surface. At last the engine was started and allowed to run until all the gauges indicated it was a go. At this point we put the engine cover on to keep the engine warm and went back to the roadhouse to eat breakfast.

We had Herman Nelson heaters at our headquarters at Fairbanks and McGrath. These were large gas-fired heaters with a blower and two hot-air ducts. One forced hot air into the engine and the other

Warming up three FWS planes from −35° on the Kuskokwim River at Aniak,
March 1959. In the foreground is the Herman Nelson heater; the two other
planes have firepots under the engine covers.

warmed up the cabin, a real luxury, and one that we enjoyed only on
our departure from headquarters.

One day in 1954, I was bemoaning the problems of this long,
drawn-out procedure to Hutch, an old-time mechanic who maintained our aircraft in Fairbanks. He listened patiently as I mentioned
what a time-consuming chore it was to put on wing covers, drain
the oil, and secure the aircraft at night. This required even more time
when we had to cut tie-downs out in the ice on lakes or rivers. These
were chopped out in the form of a bridge so the tie-down rope could be
secured through the opening and then fastened to the wing. Otherwise
we tied off to full fuel drums, logs, or whatever else available. I continued about how we agonized with the firepot, especially with the
Gullwing Stinson, which required two firepots because the nose was
so high in the air. One of us had to stand by the engine cover continuously to make sure the wind did not blow the canvas into the flame or
that the firepot did not go out, shooting raw gas into the air. (Many a
plane has been lost due to carelessness on the part of a pilot who
decided to get a cup of coffee during this operation.) One could not
get inside the engine cover to stay warm because of the fumes. It was a

long wait when the temperature hovered around the −40°F mark or lower, and it seemed to take forever for the engine to thaw. During the short winter days, we spent more time taking care of the airplane on the ground than we did flying.

When I was finished, Hutch grinned and said, "You young fellers sure have it easy. When I was doing this years ago, we had water-cooled engines and had to drain the water as well as the oil. Both had to be taken inside and kept warm." What a balloon buster. After that I chose my audiences more carefully.

Now I can throw my weight around with the modern pilots of today because most have fitted, insulated engine covers. Just wrap it around the engine and plug in an electric heater, or fit a Thermax heater inside the cowling, and everything is nice and toasty warm in the morning. Young guys today don't know what tough is.

When it was full daylight, we started patrolling dog-team trails. By flying low and reading tracks, we were able to determine what activities the traveler was up to and planned our work accordingly. Often the trapper was supplying his camps for the season or checking fur sign, and being satisfied that he was legally engaged, we moved to another line. If, on the other hand, the tracks indicated that traps were being set, we had to land and walk out parts of the line. At times this proved difficult, especially when the only place to land was a lake, slough, or river several miles from the trapline. Often I would land at one end of the line, drop off my partner, and then proceed to another part of the line where I would walk in to meet him.

There were occasions when we would take our packs, snowshoes, and sleeping bags and walk out different parts of a line, returning to the plane several days later. These excursions were undertaken only when we were after a particularly active poacher who was savvy enough to set his traps miles from any place a plane could land. These fellows were difficult to catch without a lot of planning and hard work. Many times I walked miles of line wondering if I was tracking an honest trapper, only to find an illegally killed moose or caribou used as bait, or a string of traps set in dense timber so as to remain undetected from the air. Yet there were times when the trapper was completely legal, which was rewarding, and many times we left him a note congratulating him on his legal operations.

One year early in my career, one of our deputy agents, Dave Lanni, and I operated out of my old trapping cabin at Lake Minchumina. We were trying to locate several trappers who had been reported operating illegally in the Nowitna River area. From the air we found one line that was more than sixty miles long. With no place to land within walking distance of the trail, we backtracked it to the main cabin. This trapper was smarter than most, and determining if he had any traps set out would require several days of traveling on foot checking out his activities. By this time darkness was fast approaching, and a threatening snowstorm was considerably reducing the visibility. It would be a night of "siwashing" (a term old-timers used, meaning to get caught out from camp and having to sleep with whatever was available). We had sleeping bags, an ax, and emergency rations, so we could make a shelter in the spruce timber. Plenty good for any predicament that forced us to spend the night out. A cabin would be a lot nicer, so we circled the trapper's cabin situated on the bank of the river and could not see any smoke or other signs of life.

I was leery of landing on the river ice because we had no idea if it would support the weight of the airplane. We looked over a small pothole lake about five hundred yards away and made several passes to check the length and ice conditions. Very soon, it began snowing hard, and the sky darkened by the minute. I lined up with the longest part of the lake and "floundered" in for a landing. I say floundered because when we came in over the trees I realized they were much taller then they had appeared in the restricted visibility, and I had to do some not-too-fancy maneuvers to get the plane down before running out of lake and crashing into the bank on the other end. It turned out to be a "controlled crash," complete with a slalom ski turn at the end.

Once we had shut down and looked around we realized that we would have a heck of a time getting back out of this hole. The trees were seventy-five to one hundred feet high with a ten-foot bank and in the now-complete darkness, they looked formidable, to say the least. We drained the oil, put on the wing covers, and blocked up the skis on spruce poles. This is always necessary to keep them from freezing down. With little talk we packed our gear to the cabin.

The cabin showed signs of use, with two sets of moose quarters hanging on a meat pole in the back and dirty dishes on the table. A white trapper and his Athabascan Indian wife from the village of Ruby had come up by boat before freeze-up. They were obviously using it with the intention of staying all winter. We cooked up a meal from our grub sack and played a few games of gin rummy before turning in. No mention was made about the size of the lake we had landed on or how we were going to get out in the morning. Finally, we threw our sleeping bags on the bunk, which had a mattress of layered grass, and called it a day.

I spent a fitful night of nightmares. Each was the same: I would try to fly the plane out of the small lake and end up crashing into the trees at the other end. To add to the zest of the nightmares, there were mice living in the straw, and they kept running around searching for food. One got into my hair, causing me to sit upright and start slapping the bedding with a stick to get rid of the pesky critters. All Dave could say was, "It's the pits, ain't it?" as he pulled down into his sleeping like a caterpillar in a cocoon. Nothing worked for me, though, and between the mice and the crashes of my dreams, I might just have well have stayed up all night.

I finally got up about 5:00 A.M. and made a pot of coffee. While I was waiting for it to boil, I looked around and behind the stove in a box I found a cow moose head. Athabascans enjoy eating the nose of a moose. This head had been skinned and the nose obviously had been consumed. I showed the head to Dave and indicated that obviously one of the moose on the rack had to be a cow. When it was daylight we went out and examined the meat pole that we had casually observed the night before in the dark. We were not too happy with what we found. The quarters were uncovered and a few appeared to have soured. The birds had been busy and had eaten big holes in the meat. They had also defecated over the moose, leaving a deplorable mess. We took pictures and decided to take the cow head back to town as evidence. We would discuss the taking of the cow and the waste of meat with the U.S. Attorney. Back in the cabin, we did the dishes, cleaned the cabin, and gathered our gear. I grabbed an ax and went out to the river to test the thickness of the ice. Several test holes showed that it was about five inches thick, which was plenty adequate to support the aircraft, so we marked off a runway on the smoothest portion of the ice. The plan was that I would take off empty from the lake and pick up Dave and the gear on the river.

On the walk back to the lake with the warm oil, I kept thinking of my nightmares and wondering if it was a bad omen or if I was letting my imagination get the best of me. Once at the lake, I realized that I had reason to be concerned because it was definitely small, and the banks and trees were obstacles to be reckoned with. As Dave firepotted, I walked it all out and made sure there was no overflow to slow down the skis. Then I paced it off and d etermined the direction that would give me the longest takeoff run. When all this was accomplished, I warmed up the engine and taxied to the far end of the lake, where Dave and I pulled the tail back as far as it would go against the bank.

Looking ahead was not encouraging, but it was time to bite the bullet, firewall the throttle, and coax the plane to its limits. I remembered the old axiom that said, "Use up all the available runway and pull it off, then if you don't make it, it's the airplane's fault."

I did just that. At the end, I popped the flaps and exchanged airspeed for altitude and, lo and behold, the plane jumped over the trees without any shuddering or threats of stalling. "Nothing to it!" I remember shouting, but my sweaty palms and the rivulets running down my forehead told a different story. The shout was just relieving a lot of inside tension.

The rest was academic. I picked up Dave and the gear on the river, and we were on our way. We would have to check out this trapper's line next year. The legal season would be open the next day.

We flew up the Nowitna and then up the Sulatna River, one of its tributaries. We cut a trail and followed it back to a cabin just as a dog team was arriving. I landed on the river and made contact with the young trapper as he was unhitching his dogs. The first thing I noticed was some skinned marten carcasses on the roof of the cabin, which the trapper hadn't fed to his dogs yet. After several minutes of questioning he admitted to trapping early and produced the illegal marten and mink skins. Because of the distance involved to his home village of Ruby, I requested he pull up all his traps. He was then advised to meet us there in ten days to answer the charges of trapping fur animals before the legal season.

One of the U.S. Commissioners was a resident of Ruby. I had used this method of apprehension successfully throughout the years for non-aggravated violations. The violator could take care of his dog team or have someone in a village care for them in the event he had to be taken to Fairbanks. He agreed and we took off to continue our patrol effort. We checked several more lines, picking up a few traps that had been set illegally, and we proceeded to Minchumina for the night. The following day we went back to Fairbanks.

The next two days were spent writing up reports on the patrol and preparing complaints to be filed with the different commissioners. Then two things occurred that changed my plans considerably in the next few days.

"Go to the Big Bend of Birch Creek and dig in the snow. There's something waiting for you."

The suspicious message came over the air on "Tundra Topics," a program broadcast by local radio station KFAR. Folks could mail or radio in messages for transmission to friends or relatives in the Bush. For some it was the only way of communication with family members on traplines. Most everyone in the Bush listened to the program. We listened because there were times when the person sending the message was not discreet and would talk about activities that we knew were not legal. In the past we had found illegal moose meat that had been cached with the location mentioned in a coded message.

"Go to the Big Bend of Birch Creek and dig in the snow. There's something waiting for you." Was this such a message?

Sometimes we were able to get to the spot first and seize the illegal meat. After that it was a matter of good detective work to determine who was involved. We made a big case one year involving sheep meat that was being sold from a message on "Tundra Topics."

Usually, however, it was someone advising when they were arriving for a visit or to expect a shipment by plane on a certain day. There were important messages about births, deaths, and people in the hospital, as well as the general-interest messages like this one that really caught my attention.

It was from a trapper and his wife on the Nowitna River to friends in Ruby. A local Bush pilot had landed at their camp to deliver provisions and check on their welfare. Through him they delivered their message to the radio station the next day. In effect it said that Billy and Mary had arrived at their trapping camp late in September by boat. All was well, and the only incident of concern had happened a few weeks before. A cow moose had charged Mary, and it had to be shot. They had salvaged the meat, but could not turn it over to the Fish and Wildlife Service due to their isolation. So they would utilize it as best they could.

I thought about the cow moose head in the evidence locker and realized I had been outwitted. It was obvious the story was a fabrication; however, it had enough merit and that was all that mattered.

The next day I took the head to the dump, thinking to myself that sometimes you win and sometimes you lose. I had just lost this one. I was learning.

Later that afternoon another occurrence took place that significantly added importance to the previous week's events. Mike McRoberts, Deputy U.S. Marshal, came to the office requesting information. He was trying to locate someone who was trapping out of the Ruby area and wanted for robberies in Fairbanks. The thief had been nicknamed the "Blue Parka Bandit," because he always wore a blue parka and a handkerchief mask.

I was surprised to learn that the suspect fit the description of the trapper we had apprehended on the Sulatna River. I told Mike he was due in Ruby in seven days, that is, if he followed my directions.

"Could you find him again on his trapline before he returned to Ruby?" Mike asked. I nodded and we decided to leave the next morning.

We departed before daylight and flew directly to Ruby. An inquiry in the village determined that the trapper had not returned, so we flew up the Sulatna River. A pass over the cabin showed it to be empty, so we followed his trails and located him about twenty miles out in the opposite direction from Ruby. Either he was still trapping or he was pulling traps. My guess was he was still trapping, but there was no place to land and determine this. Somehow we had to find a way to make contact without alerting him to the fact that he was to be arrested; otherwise he could play a cat-and-mouse game in these woods indefinitely. We decided the best plan was to drop off Mike at his cabin and I would go back to Ruby, returning in the morning. We circled the dog team once more, then took a direct heading for Ruby.

After five minutes we felt he would no longer be able to hear the aircraft engine, and we circled back just over treetop level and landed at the cabin. I dropped off Mike with his sleeping bag and grub and headed back to Ruby for the night.

The next morning I heated the aircraft and departed for the cabin. I circled, and after Mike gave the sign that he had made the arrest, I landed. The suspect was in handcuffs. I told him we would leave his dogs behind, and I would fly back with someone from the village to take care of them. He gave me the name of a friend whom he felt would do this for him. I went back to Ruby, and flew the man to the cabin with his gear. When everything was in order, I flew Mike and the trapper to Fairbanks. The next day he was taken before the U.S. Commissioner and sentenced to fifty days in jail for illegal trapping. Later, faced with the evidence against him, the trapper confessed to three armed robberies, which netted him four years in a jail.

Sometimes you win, and sometimes you lose. This time we won.

Chapter 7

WILDLIFE SURVEYS:
LOW FLYING, QUICK THINKING

*W*hen I started my career with the U.S. Fish and Wildlife Service, my primary duty was enforcing the wildlife laws and regulations in the Territory of Alaska; however, I was often assigned other jobs such as assisting biologists with wildlife surveys, hunter surveys, predator control, etc. All of these activities were compatible with enforcement duties since I was continuously traveling all over Alaska, and any violations observed took priority over whatever else was taking place. I became involved in counting moose, caribou, musk ox, Dall sheep, eagle nests, bison, polar bear, spring bear dens, and tracking and hunting wolves.

So it was that I was assigned to fly the first waterfowl counts in Alaska. Dr. John Buckley, head of the University of Alaska Wildlife Research Unit, was in charge of the project. The powers-that-be in our Washington office sent a series of aeronautical charts covering all of Alaska with what they said were the appropriate lines drawn on them. We would be required to fly these lines as they appeared on the map at exactly 100 feet altitude and at precisely 100 miles per hour. Two observers would be required to count all ducks and geese within one-fourth mile on each side of the plane.

I met with Dr. John to go over the maps with him prior to setting up the date for departure. Examining the charts I made the observation that this wasn't going to be an easy job of flying. Dr. Buckley explained the transects had been set up randomly and would later be modified to better fit the needs of the waterfowl scientists.

"They certainly are set up randomly," said I. "They must have put the charts on the wall and then thrown darts to mark out where the lines should begin and end." They were scattered from the Canada border to the west coast of Alaska. They were marked off east and west and others north and south with no regard for terrain. *Didn't these guys know what duck habitat looked like?* As an example, there were north and south transects over the Tanana River. Some started in the mountains and ended in another range of hills. I casually asked Dr. Buckley if we could eliminate those that were obviously not in waterfowl areas. Nope. Doc was a perfectionist and we would follow the lines wherever they went according to the chart. It was obvious I would be one busy airplane driver locating the lines and following them according to the instructions.

Dr. Buckley and Dr. Brina Kessel, an ornithologist from the University of Alaska, were to do the counting. We started at the Canada border and worked our way westward. Imagine circling up to five thousand feet to locate the starting point of a transect on a mountain top and then coming down the side of that mountain one hundred feet above the terrain at exactly one hundred miles an hour looking for ducks and geese. Eventually we would get to the river valley, where there was genuine waterfowl habitat.

Being true biologists, Dr. Buckley and Dr. Kessel counted all wildlife, so on these transects they documented sheep, moose, ravens, raptors, etc. Once across the valley I would have to circle to gain altitude so we could count the ducks on the mountainside at the end of the transect. Sometimes scientists have weird ways of doing things.

As we flew across Alaska it became obvious we wouldn't make the deadline. The object was to count the birds while they were in flocks and before they paired off in their nesting areas. So several other agents were delegated to fly some of the western transects. These were in the Kuskokwim River and Yukon River delta country, where they expected to find waterfowl. Lucky them!

On the last segment that encompassed the upper Kuskokwim River, we used a Piper Pacer aircraft because my favorite Stinson was needed to haul freight for some other projects. The Pacer was much smaller and more cramped than the Gullwing, but adequate for the job and required less fuel. We operated out of McGrath for a few days. After we finished the segments in that area we said our good-byes to Agent Reynoldson's wife, who had hosted us, and we gassed up for the trip back to Fairbanks.

One transect ended at Lake Minchumina, my old stomping grounds. We stayed that night at my old cabin. As I was checking the Pacer for flight the next morning I realized we had lost one of the gas caps. The person who fueled the aircraft in McGrath had obviously forgotten to replace the cap, and the pilot had obviously not checked the plane very thoroughly before departing. My responsibility, and I

I'm pointing out a moose snare here. Unfortunately, these snares remained in place for far too long, and many animals died needlessly.

had made a serious error. Interestingly, the tank with the missing cap was the one I had used fuel from the day before and the other was full, so there didn't appear to be a big problem except with my ego. We flew on to Fairbanks without any problems but that incident came close to causing an accident later on that summer.

In July, Agent King and I responded to a violation at the village of Venetie located one hundred and fifty miles north of Fairbanks. The teacher there met us at the small airstrip behind the village and briefed us on his concerns. While he had no problems with a moose being killed out of season by the Natives when there was a need for food, he was disturbed by the numerous hunting trips being made upriver since breakup. On each trip several moose were killed. The hunters then built boat frames from willow or spruce poles, stretched moose hide over it for a cover, and stacked the meat inside. The boats were then floated to the village.

His biggest concern, which had been the subject of his letter to us, was the brush barricade that extended several miles from the village to a large lake. The inhabitants had built the fence to force moose and caribou through narrow openings where snares were concealed. Before the use of firearms, Natives had probably built this type of barrier. From what we were able to learn these snares had been made from braided spruce roots and were very strong. It was an ingenious way of taking game and worked quite well in the natural game trails between the village and the lake.

While it may have been a necessary way of obtaining meat at one time, it was not needed in this day and age. However, according to the teacher, some of the villagers were still setting snares made of steel cable. He knew it was illegal to use snares so he had cut loose several moose he had found caught and thrashing around. We walked out the fence line and removed several snares and took pictures of two places where two moose had obviously been taken. The ground was torn up considerably indicating the animals had died a slow, agonizing death.

At the village we held a meeting with the few men who were in town. No one admitted knowledge of the snares. It must involve some of the men hunting upriver, they said. When questioned about the number of moose being taken, they were just as vague. The teacher would not involve himself for obvious reasons, so there wasn't much we could do. They agreed there was little need to continue hunting, and we emphasized our plans to make unannounced visits during the closed seasons. They said they understood and would advise the other hunters.

When we left we flew up the East Chandalar River, we located several boats that appeared to be the hunters we were told about. There was no gravel bar in the vicinity suitable for landing so we headed back toward Fort Yukon for fuel. Then, suddenly the engine sputtered. Looking around wasn't comforting because we were just coming out of the mountains and the terrain didn't appear promising for a forced landing. Not to worry, however, because the engine picked up again and didn't miss a beat the rest of the way to Fort Yukon. We shrugged it off and decided it must have been water in the fuel.

After fueling and draining the sumps thoroughly, we continued on to Fairbanks. It was a beautiful, clear day and the flight was smooth as we headed on a direct course that took us over the White Mountains toward the Tanana Valley. Then it happened again as we crossed Beaver Creek, a slight hesitation in the engine followed by purring all the way to Fairbanks. This time we suspected a little carburetor ice and shrugged it off again.

The next day was Friday, and we were in the office filing our reports and writing up an account of the patrol. Bob Scott, one of the game biologists, asked about the Pacer, indicating he was planning to use it the next day to make a caribou survey of the Fortymile Country. I told him about the way the engine had acted and suggested he might want to have it checked by one of the mechanics before taking it out. Unfortunately, he ignored the advice.

Saturday morning, the next day, Ray Woolford received a relay call from a ham radio operator stating that Bob Scott had aircraft problems in Piper 702 and had made a forced landing at Caribou Creek. This was a mining strip on the headwaters of the Salcha River, about sixty-five miles northeast of Fairbanks. Fortunately, we were able to locate a mechanic and departed about noon in the Gullwing Stinson to investigate the problem. On the way to Caribou Creek, I briefed the mechanic about the way the engine in the Pacer acted on our last trip. He strongly suspected dirt in the fuel system.

After landing, the mechanic questioned Bob about the engine. It had sputtered a few times after about an hour of flying and then lost power. Bob could not get more than about 1,400 RPM out of it no matter what he did so he chose to land at Caribou, which fortunately was near—a real piece of luck, since strips are few and far between in that part of the country.

First thing the mechanic did was pull the fuel strainer and, lo and behold, it was full of feathers. Each time he drained the sump more downy feathers flushed out. He kept draining until it appeared the system was clean. Bob started the engine and it ran without further problem so he flew back to Fairbanks while we followed in the Stinson in case another problem occurred. The return trip was uneventful, and the Pacer was tied down next to Fairbanks Aircraft Service for a complete going-over on Monday. Before going home we checked the fuel strainer again. More feathers.

Monday afternoon I went to the shop to see how work was progressing on the plane. The entire fuel system had to be flushed and mechanics were removing the empty fuel tank from the right wing. After it was lifted from its recess the tank was taken to a sink for cleaning. Something was rattling inside so the mechanic held it upside down and shook it until the object fell out. I picked up the culprit that had caused all the problems and sure enough, it was the remains of a small bird with most of its feathers missing. Now the head-scratcher— How did he get into the fuel tank?

I took the mummified bird back to the office and from the remaining feathers on the wing and tail we identified it as a swallow. Then we pondered the mystery of why a swallow would be in a gas tank. The first thought was sabotage. Somebody at Venetie could have stuck the bird in the gas tank while we were inspecting the fence, or it could have happened at Fort Yukon where we had stopped for fuel and lunch. We knew we weren't popular with some of the villagers because of the trapline patrols we had conducted the year before; however, we had doubts that the people were responsible. These folks had never been vindictive, but then, times were changing.

We pondered the mystery for quite awhile, coming up with many possibilities, and then it dawned on me. I remembered the overnight stay at Lake Minchumina and the missing fuel cap. There had been swallows flying around the aircraft when we had prepared for the flight back to Fairbanks. It was nesting time and I was well aware of the fact that swallows will build nests in any convenient hole or cavity so I had looked the plane over very carefully for any activity. Finding none we proceeded with the flight

After discussing this with the group at the office we all agreed that the swallow had probably been circling the open gas tank as a possible building site, became asphyxiated, and spiraled in. That had been a month earlier and it had taken this long for the feathers to dislodge themselves from the carcass and start traveling through the fuel system. When I thought about all the forlorn country we had flown I decided we were very fortunate. Like oil and water, birds and aircraft don't mix. I've heard of many accidents since, which were caused by fuel contamination but never again of one that was downed by a bird in the gas tank.

I would be remiss if I didn't end this chapter without mentioning the hazards a pilot faces when conducting wildlife surveys. Observers can and do get airsick! Think about flying several hours to a survey site and beginning the counts, only to have your assistant tell you he or she is suffering. Most were wildlife students who were training as biologists. You have a choice of going back to base or trying to continue with someone that's barfing and not able to concentrate on the ground. On one occasion, in order to complete a bison survey in the Big Delta area on a windy day, I provided the observer with a large plastic bag and advised him to put his head inside while counting. That way he could get sick but continue counting. He was a willing observer not wanting to be the reason for not finishing. We did manage to complete the tally; however, I have doubts to the accuracy. After several aborted counts on other missions, I refused to make the surveys unless I was provided with a person that had a record of not getting airsick.

One particular waterfowl survey was memorable. We were surveying the Minto Lakes area, where large concentrations of nesting birds arrived every May. The transects were set up in a checkerboard fashion over the area and required eight hours of flying to complete. They were flown early each morning and took three or four days to finish. On the morning in question, the floatplane we had been using had to go on another assignment, so we decided to proceed anyway using the wheel Pacer. It was turbulent so I had my hands full flying a compass course at the usual one hundred feet and at the required one hundred miles an hour. The two biologists were busy identifying and counting the ducks as we bounced up and down.

About an hour into the flying I could see out of the corner of my eye that the woman observer beside me was getting sick. You developed a special sense about this after years in the business. Then I noticed her get a manila envelope ready, and sure enough her breakfast came up. It's always embarrassing for the person and very unpleasant for the pilot and other passengers, especially because of the odor. I continued flying straight ahead and again in my peripheral vision I could see her opening the side window. Before I could shout, "Don't try to throw that out!" she attempted to get rid of the envelope. Yep, it all came back in and I was hit, big time, with lumps on my sunglasses, etc.

Naturally we immediately ended the count and headed for a runway. Nenana was the closest airport and required about thirty minutes of miserable flying to reach the strip. I looked in the back at the other passenger and it was obvious he had been hit also. I parked on the side of the runway and we did our best to clean up and flew back to Fairbanks. Not a nice day for all concerned and another item to add to future pre-flight instructions before going out on game counts.

No matter how seasoned the passenger, I would make sure that there were adequate sick sacks aboard. I would also give full instructions that if they had to be used they were to be sealed, and under No Circumstances would there be any attempt to throw them out of the aircraft!

Chapter 8

MARRIED TO THE
FISH & WILDLIFE SERVICE

*B*ehind every successful man stands a devoted woman, so the saying goes, and when applied to the FWS agents of fifty years ago, the word "devoted" took on a special meaning. We were expected to be on call twenty-four hours a day, and there was no such thing as an eight-hour day, forty-hour week, overtime pay, or compensatory days off. Extensive travel was required due to the vast size of the area we patrolled. Consequently, our home life suffered greatly.

It was during one of these patrols in the spring of 1954 that I met Elsie Sommer at her dad's store. I was sealing beaver in Nulato when we first met. For some reason, afterward I seemed to have a reason to go into that village more frequently than any agent had in the past. The people began to realize that it wasn't because there were more violations occurring in that area, but that there was another attraction for me. Since I had to overnight somewhere on that end of the district on long patrols, and because Mrs. Sommer occasionally put up travelers, and because she served excellent meals, and because she had an attractive daughter, common sense dictated that it was a good place to stay.

Then another change in operations occurred that year requiring my continued presence on the Yukon River. The Bureau of Commercial Fisheries finally realized they knew very little about the salmon runs on the river. The Yukon is over two thousand miles long with the headwaters in Canada. One of the biggest king salmon runs in the world occurs in that waterway and its tributaries. Some of these fish travel the entire distance of the river to spawn and fulfill nature's destiny.

The Alaska Natives had been taking kings and other species of salmon with fishwheels and nets for generations. Suddenly a group of biologists decided that maybe, just maybe, the fishermen were taking too many fish. Until they knew the number of fish entering the river and the number being taken, there was no way they could manage the runs. So until they had a handle on the problem, they decided to close down all fishing on weekends. Fishwheels had to shut down and nets were removed from the water. This way, according to the scientists, the salmon would have an unrestricted run upriver for two days. The regional director required my partner, Jim King, and me to tour the villages, hold meetings, and explain the regulations to the people. We were about as popular as a hernia at a weight-lifters convention. But again the law was the law, right?

All summer I patrolled the Yukon River on weekends. One week I would start at the Canada border and patrol downriver to Kaltag and stay overnight with Elsie's family in Nulato. The next weekend I would stay at Nulato with Elsie and patrol the river from Kaltag to the Canada border. It was the one time I didn't complain about having to enforce a very unpopular regulation. As a side note, we didn't file any complaints that summer. If we found a fishwheel running or a net in the water, we located the owner and suggested he stop fishing. The unpopular regulation was a failure and wasn't attempted again in subsequent years.

Elsie was in Nulato that year to help her dad run the store. She had been away to boarding school in Portland as a youngster, and in San Francisco during her nurse's training. It was not in her plans to remain in Alaska but to return to the States after a year to pursue a career in nursing. However, as one of the nuns at the Catholic mission in the village later stated, it became obvious as time passed that she wouldn't return. It was also obvious that my bachelor days were coming to an end. This was confirmed when I borrowed a friend's plane and flew more than three hundred miles to Nulato from Fairbanks to propose marriage.

I tried to be honest in telling her what our life would be like after we were married, but I look back now and wonder if I was completely truthful with her in explaining how much traveling I would be doing— but then, love has a way of jumping over hurdles and not bringing them into complete focus.

When Elsie and I married on October 2, 1954, the Fairbanks district where I worked encompassed the area from Big Delta in the east, west to Unalakleet on the coast of Norton Sound, and everything north to Point Barrow. There were four of us agents to patrol the district with only Ray Woolford, the enforcement chief, and myself doing the flying. Since Ray was required to do most of the administrative work, most of the flying was delegated to me. That kept me busy and away from home many nights.

During our first year of marriage in Fairbanks, Elsie kept busy with her nursing career until our first daughter was born, and after that she became a full-time mother. In addition to putting up with my absences, she got out of bed with me at all hours of the night when I had to go out on calls. Most were in response to moose that been crippled or killed on the highway. I had to go out and dispatch the animal if it was crippled and field dress the critter for distribution to the needy. You'd be surprised how fast you can butcher a thousand-pound animal when it's −50°F and −60°F. Other calls concerned violations in progress, which we responded to as quickly as possible. By the time I was up and ready to go, Elsie would always have a welcome cup of coffee and a thermos for me to take along.

In 1956 I was transferred to McGrath, a district encompassing the Kuskokwim and lower Yukon Rivers. I worked alone for more than two years before another agent was hired as an assistant. Most of my patrols required up to two weeks of travel; however, on occasion I was gone three weeks or more. I didn't realize how much I was away from home until my wife presented me with her tally of days on the road for one year, and it amounted to more than six months of traveling. All this time she was at home caring for our small children, the house, and the Fish and Wildlife Service office. Fortunately, she was strong and understanding or our marriage surely would never have survived.

Occasionally I brought home an orphaned animal for Elsie to care for until I could find it a home. Once it was a fox pup that had been smoked out of its den by some military men. They had been reported taking the animal to the NCO Club and feeding it beer to the amusement of patrons. They had their day in court, and we had a fox with a badly burned nose. Elsie named him Hoikle and we kept him in a spare bedroom where he slept all day and he kept us awake all night with his puppy antics. Later I released him at Minto Lake where Pete Shepherd, a young biologist, was building a cabin for the Wildlife Research Unit and doing a study on muskrats. The fox stayed around Pete's tent all summer long enjoying food handouts and acting more like a domestic dog than a wild animal. Before the project ended that fall I watched as Pete tried to teach him to hunt mice for his survival that winter. We often wondered what became of Hoikle, hoping that he had finally learned to catch his meals and live to a ripe old age.

*Like other women who married into the FWS, my wife Elsie was very
self-sufficient during the hours and sometimes days that I was on patrol.
She also served as a superb radio operator.*

Our move to McGrath occurred in August. After getting established in the government log house that had been built two years
earlier, I departed for my first tour of the district with a float-equipped
Cessna 170. I had instructed Elsie on the use of the radio in my new
office, which was located in the front of our home. She was reluctant
to become a part of the FWS communication system until I told her I
would be dependent on her to keep track of my position by monitoring
my radio calls. She finally agreed to "talk to you only." It wasn't long,
however, before she became adept at radio procedures and became an
important link in our system by keeping a log of the pilots' position
reports. Our radio system operated on the high-frequency channel of
5907.5 and atmospheric conditions at times caused radio calls to skip
over the intended receiver. A plane flying in the southeastern part of
Alaska might try to radio Juneau without success, but his transmission

would be loud and clear in McGrath. Consequently we kept the radio on day and night, and she assisted many pilots during off-hours when the main offices were closed.

On this, her first time to log my radio transmissions, I advised her I would call only when I was landing or departing. I had written out my itinerary so she knew my route of flight. I followed the Kuskokwim River, stopping at each village to introduce myself, ending up at the Aniak Roadhouse for the night. I beached and secured the plane along the riverfront. Sometime before morning a big wind came up, forcing me to spend the rest of the night in the Cessna checking and rechecking the tie-down lines. Eighty-mile-per-hour gusts threatened to flip the plane until I pumped water into the floats to partially submerge them. The extra weight probably saved the aircraft.

When the wind subsided the following day, I pumped out the floats and took off in the direction of Bethel. I contacted Elsie and told her of the problems I had encountered during the night and where I was headed. Her response was that maybe I had better consider returning home because the same wind hit McGrath and half our metal roofing had blown off. I did an immediate 180-degree turn and flew directly back to McGrath.

I was more than a little upset with my spunky wife. Here she was six months pregnant with our second child and she had chased around in the big wind trying to save the metal sheets as they flew off the roof. Disregarding her condition, she ran after each piece that blew toward the river only ninety feet away. Several times when she picked up a two-by-twelve-foot sheet, she nearly went into the river herself, and she was also in danger of being struck by other pieces of roofing. Luckily, a neighbor came along, grabbed a ladder, hammer, and nails and secured the remainder of the roof.

After all that, I couldn't tell her that her troubles were for naught since none of the sheets she saved could be used again. Thankfully she wasn't hurt and I pleaded with her not to jeopardize herself again while I was gone. She shrugged and said, "You do what you have to do at the time and worry about it afterwards." I appreciated her all the more, but I could see I would have reason to be concerned each time I traveled.

The humorous part of the wind-and-roof episode occurred while she was calling on the radio, hoping I was on the air so she could advise me of the problem. Our assistant aircraft supervisor in Anchorage, Tom Wardleigh, responded to one of her calls and after being appraised of the problem gave her some sage advise. "Just remember, Elsie, when you go out there in the wind, keep a cool head!" Pearls of wisdom in a time of crisis are always appreciated.

We spent Thanksgiving that year in Fairbanks waiting for the birth of our second daughter. It was extremely cold on December 10, the day we were to return to McGrath with our new baby daughter. Because of the temperature, Northern Consolidated Airways was having trouble getting the DC-3 aircraft heated and ready for the run to McGrath. We were supposed to depart at 8:00 A.M. but did not take off until after 1:00 P.M. Because there was no phone at the home where we were staying, I was kept busy driving back and forth to the neighbor's to get the actual time of departure, which changed hourly. On the last effort the car stalled and wouldn't start again. I frostbit my ears and nose running back to the house to advise Elsie that one of the agents was on his way to take us to the airport. We made it at the required time with Renee, our one-year-old, and Michelle, our newborn. Outside it was in the –40s, but the cabin of the plane was like a blast furnace from the Herman Nelson gas heater that was being used for pre-heating. Once the doors were shut and engines started, however, it cooled off noticeably and remained quite chilly until the engine heaters kicked in.

En route to McGrath, the plane made a stop at Lake Minchumina. Here, mail and freight had to be unloaded. A passenger and I unloaded all the cargo and mail while the pilot kept one engine running to keep the cabin warm. Another stop to drop off two passengers was required at the Tatalina, a radar site fifteen miles from McGrath. Again the pilot kept the engine running while they disembarked. Finally we arrived home at 5:00 P.M. greeted with a temperature in the –50s. "Welcome back!" a few hearty souls were shouting as we came down the steps of the plane with our new baby wrapped in blankets like a cocoon. We didn't stop to chat but rushed home only to find another dilemma—a house full of oil soot.

Prior to our departure for Fairbanks, we had installed a new forced hot-air furnace in the cellar to replace an old oil-pot floor heater. That heater and oil stove were all that had been installed when the large two-story house had been built and were never adequate to keep it comfortable. After much pleading to the administrative folks in Juneau, they had finally agreed to purchase a properly designed furnace. After it was installed, it worked like a charm, blowing heated air throughout the house, and we were anxious to enjoy the new system on our return. The week after we departed, however, the hot water coil in the stove burst while our house sitter, Harley King, was attending the local movie one evening. When the coil burst it blew out the oven door, and soot, water, and oil flowed through the kitchen and living room into the basement. When Harley returned he said he didn't know whether to lie down and cry or close the door and leave forever. Instead he hired a woman to help him, and together they cleaned and mopped up the biggest part of the mess.

Did you ever try to clean up oil soot? You can't wipe it up or sweep it since it only floats around or smears. The only thing that will remove it is a vacuum cleaner. Elsie and the two children settled into the downstairs bedroom while I tackled the mess. Each time the furnace blower came on it was like a black snowstorm in the kitchen and living room. I kept vacuuming each time the blower shut off and little by little the black snowstorm diminished. After that it was complete washing of the ceiling and walls in the kitchen, which, as I recall, I finished just as day was breaking. The next day, Elsie was able to help, and together we got most of it cleaned up. Meanwhile Renee, our number-one daughter, played on the floor and ended up looking like a chimney sweep.

Elsie never complained, but I knew that inside she had many reservations about this new life I'd introduced her to. Now we can look back and laugh about it all, and the children love to hear the story of mother and the soot. I like to remind Michelle of how inconsiderate she was choosing that cold November to enter the world and how it had cost me a frostbitten nose and ears that peeled like onions for weeks afterwards.

The story Elsie likes to tell the most about her McGrath adventures involves the year that I appointed her as the local beaver-tagging officer. That year no one was available in town to tag beaver when I was traveling, so I persuaded Elsie to do her part for wildlife conservation and the "good ol' Fish and Wildlife Service." There was only one problem: because she was my wife, I could not pay the ten cents per skin that I paid the other tagging officers. She reluctantly agreed, calling me a government cheapskate!

Every time I returned from a trip, she gave the details of the trappers who visited and laid out their skins on our living room floor to be tagged. The pungent odor wasn't offensive, but it was different and lingered for hours after the greasy hides were taken away. Then, too, trappers always arrived at the most inopportune times, such as when she was feeding the baby or when she was serving dinner. I kept telling her how important she was, what a good job she was doing, and how she was performing a service that only a few other privileged people in the world were authorized to do. Someday she would be able to keep audiences spellbound with her stories!

"All well and good," she would say, "but if I'm so important, why don't you pay me, and by the way the total now is $26.50." All I could say was that someday I would reward her. When she became pregnant again, she advised me that she could do without my rewards.

In July we had a visit from the Regional Director Clarence Rhode and several other chiefs who were flying around inspecting the districts. They had dinner with us and stayed overnight. This was another of Elsie's McGrath duties—entertaining visiting dignitaries and coworkers. This she also did with grace and diplomacy, never complaining. During dinner, however, she mentioned the beaver-tagging operations and her cheap husband. I replied that I agreed it was unfair, but the administrative officer had informed me that I could not pay my spouse on a government check. Clarence looked up and said, "Sure you can, and I so authorize it; pay Mrs. Tremblay."

My mouth dropped, and then I sheepishly said that the books were closed for the fiscal year. There was no way of paying an obligation of the past year from this year's funds. The look I got from Elsie said it all: I was in a world of hurt for $26.50. I've heard about it ever since and have paid my pound of flesh many times over for that administrative mistake. It did no good to tell her I was only following the orders of the fiscal officer in Juneau. The chief had said she should have been paid and that was good enough for her. Oh well, her other rewards have been many, and after three more children she agrees that it was worth it. Our six children also agree, and we can talk and laugh about the Fish and Wildlife days and the $26.50 that Dad still owes Mom.

All of the other Fish and Wildlife Service wives have their tales of what it was like in the pre-statehood days and of the many hardships they suffered while their men were out managing and protecting Alaska's wildlife. These women were truly the unsung heroes of the service and unfortunately, they were never officially recognized. Without their patience and understanding, we would never have been able to accomplish our missions. Alaska's wildlife owes them a great tribute. Those of us who are indebted to our dedicated wives will never forget. One of the old-timers in Nulato remembers and always calls Elsie "Mrs. Game Warden."

Chapter 9

BALANCING ACTS

*I*n February 1957, I received an anonymous letter at my McGrath office, telling me about three moose that had been killed during closed season by villagers at Pilot Station, a small village on the bank of the Yukon River. "Get here right away while the evidence is still available," the writer advised.

I flew the two hundred and fifty miles to the village in a ski-equipped FWS Cessna 180 and was met by several village elders who wanted to know the purpose of my visit. "I want to discuss the illegal killing of moose that I have heard about," I told them. "Will you stay the night and meet with the men of the village?" they wanted to know. Of course I would, and was then given a place to stay, after which I secured the plane for the night. My gear, including the oil drained from the engine of the plane, was moved to my assigned cabin by a couple of willing young boys pulling a small dog sled.

When there was a problem of this magnitude, which involved all the inhabitants, a village meeting was held in the largest building of the community. Often this was the school, a meetinghouse, or occasionally, the village bathhouse. These bathhouses were built of log and covered with dirt, and were at least twenty-by-twenty feet. There was a low tunnel entrance usually covered by a bearskin, and after crawling all the way through you stepped down onto a floor that was made from peeled spruce poles. A fire pit about six-by-six feet was in the middle. It contained large rocks, and had a smoke vent directly overhead. A single bench was built around the perimeter of the log walls.

A communal bath usually preceded community meetings. A large fire was built in the pit in order to heat the rocks. When all was ready, the naked men all filed in and poured water on the rocks and sat in the steam-filled room. They discussed village problems, hunting, trapping, or whatever the current topic might be. After the men finished, the women took over, and I assume they discussed their own particular problems. Later, when everyone had finished with the steam baths, the meeting would be held.

I was not invited to join in the steam bath that night, but was sent for after the men had finished their ritual. Crawling through the tunnel,

I went from a −40°F outside temperature to a steamy 120°F inside. This required the immediate shedding of clothes down to a T-shirt. The chief of the village introduced me and acted as interpreter. This was customary in most villages since the majority of the older people spoke little or no English.

I felt it necessary to explain the job of the FWS and the reasons for game regulations, because a meeting of this kind had never been held in this village, according to the chief. I also explained that we were very concerned with the moose population, for moose were just beginning to extend their range into this region. Moose were only occasionally found this far west, but due to a healthy build-up of the Interior populations, the animals were beginning to show up on the tundra in increasing numbers, feeding on the willows along the many streams and rivers. A few had even been seen along the Bering Sea. They were eventually shot by hunters who had no idea what kind of an animal it was. They learned they were very tasty, and moose were on shaky ground from then on.

How do you explain population dynamics and game management principles through a translator to a meat-hungry people who depended on hunting to live? Whenever one of these hunters found a moose track, it was followed until the moose was killed, no matter the distance or the hours and days it required.

The tenacity of these hunters is recorded in my field diary of December 1956: "One Native at Tuluksak, who is partially blind but considered one of the best hunters in the village, earned his moose the hard way during the second season. He traveled up the Tuluksak River with his dog team until he crossed fresh moose tracks. He then tied up his dogs and took off on foot following the tracks. Twenty-three and a half hours later he got close enough to kill the moose, a young bull. After butchering the animal he went back for his team and hauled the meat 35 miles back to the village. All of this in temperatures of −25°." Village teacher, Phil Pentecost, verified the occurrence.

After I had explained the reasons for protecting the growing moose population and the need for their cooperation, I tackled the problem at hand—the three illegal moose. A lengthy discussion ensued, and the chief explained that there was little food in the village due to a poor fishing season. Any game taken, whether it be a ptarmigan, grouse, rabbit or, in this case, moose, is divided among all the families, with the older people and families with children receiving the biggest pieces.

When the talks were finished, I was taken on a tour of every home and what was left of the meat was displayed in pots and pans on stoves or in the entryways of the cabins. Each family had received about twenty pounds of meat, and every bit of the moose was consumed, including the intestines. Here was a true example of people living off the land and having to endure a difficult winter because of a failure of their main crop—the salmon run. There was some welfare in the village, which was also shared, but not enough to cover basic food needs. I gleaned this information from the schoolteacher and the priest of the Catholic mission at St. Mary's, located downriver from Pilot Station.

It was decision time for me, so the next night another meeting was set up in the bathhouse. We discussed the moose population problem again, and the consequences of killing off the animals before they were able to establish themselves in this area. I also lectured them on the laws, how they were formulated, the purpose they serve, and the consequences of violations. They listened intently as the chief translated back to the Native tongue. I told them I would not take any legal action on the three moose, but that in the future I expected that they would consider the implication of killing off a population of animals that would be of great benefit to them and their children in future years. They thanked me, said they would cooperate, and hoped they would be able to supplement their food supplies with small game and the fur animals they trapped so they wouldn't have to break the law again. I departed on this note, feeling I had accomplished my mission, vowing to continue these meetings in all the remote villages.

Upon my return to McGrath, I found two local trappers awaiting me. They had quarreled over the ownership of beaver houses and wanted me to mediate. After listening to both, I advised them that neither of them could claim exclusive trapping rights to any beaver houses, regardless of how many years they had trapped the area.

They both trapped on the North Fork of the Kuskokwim River; about two days by dog team from McGrath. They had already lost more than a week of trapping, and I suggested that since they were the only two trappers in that part of the country, they split the houses fifty-fifty and go back to trapping. They accepted my solution (one they should have reached by themselves) and left the next day to return to their cabins. What started out to be a blood feud with each trapper threatening bodily harm to the other ended amiably with each getting his legal limit of ten beaver.

Another patrol finished and I was now faced with the paperwork. Reports and more reports. I often wondered where they ended. Today I find that many are the basis for ongoing wildlife studies providing insight into an era that is gone, never to return.

A district that encompasses thousands of square miles and receives heavy resource use requires year-round patrols by the game warden. Realistically, he knows that he will apprehend only a small percentage of game law violators. However, he also knows that if he can get the respect of the people, they will help him protect the wildlife so vital to their welfare. As people almost entirely dependent upon fish and game for their livelihood, most were aware that without the wildlife agent, game warden, fur warden, Bush cop, fish cop, or whatever his designation in the particular part of Alaska he worked, fish and wildlife numbers would rapidly diminish.

Taking an extra moose from a small herd, a few extra beaver from a limited watershed, or an extra net full of fish from a spawning stream will not in itself significantly impact the population. But one successful poacher is enough to encourage a multitude of others, and that's when wildlife gets in trouble. Even more serious problems can develop when this indiscriminate taking is joined with one or two severe winters causing natural die-offs.

History has documented the demise of the buffalo, the passenger pigeon, and other targets of man's greed. With that blueprint of history, such decimation shouldn't be repeated. However, I'm convinced that man, left to his own devices, will reduce wildlife to the last mammal, bird, or fish to satisfy his own needs, be they monetary, personal gain, ego, or a misguided idea of ethnic "right"!

The only effective management tool to balance wildlife stocks is enforcing sound laws and regulations. The warden must gain the respect of the public and the judicial system that determines the guilt or innocence of those accused. An added burden was placed on those of us in the Bush during territorial days. Not only did we initiate complaints before U.S. commissioners, we also acted as the prosecuting attorney and made recommendations on penalties.

Federal judges appointed U.S. commissioners in Bush Alaska, and many selections were not based on competency. It was tough to find a village resident willing to accept the position. New commissioners often needed instruction on how to conduct an arraignment, and to ensure they gave the proper instructions to the accused on their rights to a fair trial. The job didn't pay much, and commissioners were not afforded any special office or equipment, except for a safe to protect official documents. Arraignments, coroner's inquests, and trials were held in the commissioners' homes, which were often one-room cabins.

One bachelor "commissioner," who was not the best housekeeper to begin with, commonly had to clean off his kitchen table of dirty dishes and food to have enough room for his typewriter before convening court. Imagine yourself entering this courtroom to be tried for a violation of federal law.

Under such conditions, wardens had to work closely with the commissioner in their district, because they held the key to their enforcement endeavors. It was important that the people understood the judiciary system and the reasons for invoking penalties. We tried to impress on the Native people at these hearings that we (the wardens) were representing the wildlife that were illegally taken. Our goal was voluntary compliance by hunters, fishermen, and trappers—first through education, and when that failed, the courts.

Violators were usually flown from their village, trapline, or camp to the commissioner. At times this required several hundred miles of flying. After the hearing, we would fly the offenders back to where they were picked up, unless the commissioner imposed jail time, in which case they were flown to Fairbanks or Anchorage. At times we flew the commissioner to the village where the offender lived and held the hearing in the school or any suitable building so other villagers could attend. What better way to educate them about wildlife laws and regulations with the consequences for the illegal activity?

It may not have been the best possible system, but it worked most of the time as long as everyone did his part. I spent a great deal of time with the commissioners in the McGrath District explaining the reasons for the regulations, which to the uninitiated appeared capricious or at times ridiculous.

For example, new commissioners wondered why the Alaska Game Commission outlawed fish traps and nets for taking fur animals. To anyone familiar with this method of taking mink in the Yukon–Kuskokwim Delta, it was an obvious attempt to stop the loss of animals in untended traps. Without experiencing the problem, though, the regulation made little sense.

Alaska blackfish are found only in western Alaska and eastern Siberia. In Siberia the fish are known by the scientific name, *Dallia petorallis*. They are finny critters that burrow into mud and lie dormant when chilling arctic air freezes the tundra habitat solid. Schools of these prehistoric fish are capable of keeping the ice from freezing around small pools by their continual thrashing.

Long ago, local Natives learned that mink entered their blackfish traps in search of food, and they were more easily taken in this way than with steel traps. The fish traps were originally built from willow strips woven into the typical fyke trap, which has a tapering funnel entrance—easy to enter, but difficult to get out. The blackfish trap is about thirty-six inches long and about the diameter of a basketball. These traps are set under the ice in back eddies of rivers or streams connecting lakes where blackfish congregate in large numbers.

Area Natives trap the fish as food for themselves and their dogs. They are also a source of food for mink—and Yukon–Kuskokwim Delta mink are the largest, darkest, and best-furred mink in North America, according to fur-buyers. When the trapper sets his blackfish trap, it becomes self-baiting and a one-way enclosure for these valuable furbearers. So far, no problem; whoever caught the first mink by this method probably felt he had discovered the ultimate trap, and he was close to being right. Eventually these traps were made out of hardware cloth, and it was not an uncommon sight when I patrolled the delta to see loads of them stacked on trappers' dogsleds leaving the village bound for the trapping grounds.

Concern over these devices was not with the traps themselves, but rather in the way they were attended. Tundra blizzards have a way of changing the treeless barrens, challenging even the most experienced in locating landmarks and trails. As a result, many of the traps were lost. Often trappers lost interest in fighting the elements, especially during and after the winter holiday season, and many would not pick up their traps. Unfortunately, the unattended traps continued to self-bait with blackfish, and consequently mink continued to enter them in pursuit of food. The result was wasted mink.

I received complaints from villagers and traders about lost or abandoned traps they had found that contained the rotted carcasses of mink. One reported three carcasses in one trap. That kind of waste brought about the Alaska Game Commission regulation and made fish traps illegal for taking fur animals.

In the 1939–40 regulations, the law required a built-in escape hatch for mink but not fish, thus making it a true fish trap. This failed. Trappers weren't interested in letting mink escape, and it was difficult for wardens to locate traps and identify the owners. Finally the game commissioners outlawed them altogether. Nets were used in the same manner, and they were also deemed illegal.

I held many meetings concerning the traps, all to no avail. They were too efficient and easier to use than steel leg-hold traps. They are still used extensively. Since no one has ever devised a method of controlling abandoned traps, the loss of mink is presumably still a big factor.

Explaining these and other regulations to the commissioners, district court judges, and U.S. attorneys was a challenge at times, but it had to be done. If they didn't understand the purpose of the regulations, they would often dismiss cases, which we felt were important to fur management.

The conflict between the territorial legislature and the FWS concerning the bounty on wolves, coyotes, wolverines, and bald eagles was another sticky problem for the Bush warden. While the FWS had no problems with the bounty system for wolves and coyotes, it objected to a system that subsidized trappers for taking bald eagles, our national bird, which had complete protection in the Lower 48 states. Why a bounty of two dollars on eagle legs? Because they killed and ate spawning salmon. Would you believe there was also a bounty on Dolly Varden because they ate salmon eggs? Two bits a tail. Seals were also treated to the bounty system. Even brown bears were considered at one time.

In 1956, as a means of combating the undesirable bounty on wolverine, the Alaska Game Commission included the wolverine in the regulatory trapping season with mink, marten, land otter, fox, lynx, and weasel. As a side note, eagles came under full protection of the Migratory Bird Treaty Act after statehood in 1959.

Having much of the year closed to wolverine trapping caused problems, especially in rural areas where Natives had trouble understanding the logic of regulations anyway. To claim bounties, trappers had to submit the hide of the animals with the left foreleg attached, along with a signed affidavit giving the date and place the bountied animal was taken. Since there were no territorial wildlife officers, FWS agents were delegated to certify bounty claims. We did this by checking out the affidavit, removing the leg bone, and signing off that we had completed the check. Most of the certifications were taken care of in the villages or at trappers' cabins as we traveled. Others were mailed to our offices where the leg bone was removed, the affidavit certified and sent to Juneau. The hide was then mailed back to the trapper.

The rub came when an unknowing trapper sent the hide of a wolverine, with the affidavit, to the regional office in Juneau. Often the date given for taking the animal was not within the legal season. While it didn't matter to the dead wolverine or occur to the trapper doing his part in removing predators that there was a problem (why else would there be a bounty?), it did to the administrators. The hide and affidavit were sent to the agent in charge of the district where the animal was taken as an "open case"—an illegally taken animal. We had no choice but to locate the trapper and have him sign a release to all claims to the bounty, and to the wolverine hide which became the property of the U.S. government.

Most of these honest but illegal claims were sent from remote villages where many of the older people still had a great sense of pride in their way of life. The majority shunned welfare, feeling that the land provided their living and that give-away programs were for the lazy.

This was one of the most difficult and unpalatable parts of my job. The letter of the law had to be enforced; yet it seemingly served no useful purpose. The older Bush people were basically honest, and they filled out all government forms as truthfully as possible and with pride. They were caught between two opposing philosophies, one dealing with wildlife management, and the other a political measure (the bounty system) that was nothing more than a welfare system that had little effect on predator numbers.

As an example there was no way to tell the difference between a wolf and a dog even though the leg bone was required with the pelt as proof. Many unscrupulous trappers found this out and submitted sled dogs for bounty. We had no way of knowing and had to take the affidavit on its merit. I often wonder about the legality of all the "wolf" pups I bountied that were supposedly taken from dens.

An insight into a typical summer patrol was included in Peter Matthiessen's book, *Wildlife in America,* published in 1959 by Viking Press. Mr. Matthiessen was the guest of the FWS in 1957, and traveled throughout the territory with our agents to view firsthand the status of wildlife in Alaska. He flew with me for several days, making observations and taking copious notes. We made one stop at the village of Eek on the lower Kuskokwim River to take care of an improperly bountied wolverine skin. Here's what he wrote:

"The Service, especially in the law enforcement branch, remains woefully undermanned. The game agent for the western Interior, for example, must patrol alone an area larger than New England, including the whole Yukon–Kuskokwim Delta, and a sketch here of a typical mission in his ceaseless surveillance of the regions will give some idea of the task confronting wildlife agents in Alaska. One must keep in mind that, in addition to their ordinary duties, these men perform the functions of the game wardens in the older states.

"The delta formed between the mouths of the Yukon and Kuskokwim is a remote foggy world of dark tundra, pools, bleak, faceless shore, and isolated volcanic peaks rising mysteriously above the waste; its wilderness of water rivals the sloughs and potholes of the Canadian prairie provinces as the great North American nesting grounds for waterfowl, though only a relatively narrow strip behind the beach is heavily populated by the birds. While the Canadian grounds favor ducks over geese, the reverse is true of the Yukon-Kuskokwim, and emperor, white-fronted and cackling geese, in company with large numbers of whistling swans, are the dominant birds. There are black brant, too, and a variety of ducks, including such sea ducks as eider and old-squaw, as well as innumerable lesser sandhill cranes, shore birds, jaegers, and gulls.

"The land, relentlessly monotone in all but a few summer weeks of feverish flowering, is almost uninhabited. The distances are so great that the game agent must fly endless rounds in suitable weather if he is to touch at each scattered Eskimo settlement and fishing camps even once a year. Much of the work can be done only in season, when the waters are free of ice. On the rare clear days the fishing camps on the outer deltas may be detected by the red racks of drying salmon and the flapping of white canvas tents, but at other times there are no landmarks, only the black faces of the ponds shifting evilly in the Bering mists. Poor flying weather may ground the agent for many days at a time.

"Nor are the Natives always glad to see him. They line up silently on the riverbank as he sets his pontoons on the roiled waters, the ceaseless wind stirring the fur trim on the parkas. The agent singles out the village leader and tells the purpose of his visit. Gently, insistently, almost apologetically, he confiscates a wolverine pelt submitted for bounty out of season, then lectures the round-faced, resigned group on the waterfowl laws which preserve sport shooting for the white man in faraway America. Since the waterfowl, for them, may mean survival, they cannot be expected to understand the laws, and the agent does not really expect them to obey. Apologizing in their turn, they tell him again as they had told him the year before that they must take the geese in early spring if they are not to starve before the great silver king salmon makes its run in from the sea. One says he is proud to be an American and to obey the American law, but that his children must be allowed to eat; he offers to tell the agent how often the law is broken here, if that will be of service to the government, but he repeats, that it will be broken. The agent counsels them obliquely against waste, repeats the letter of the law, and smiles.

Immediately the fishermen smile, too, and remember the [broken] English they had forgotten so long as his presence posed a threat. One asks him in a singsong voice, 'Why is it the birds go away so many in the fall of the year and come back so few?' And the agent patiently explains, using his hands. Like all the Service personnel one meets in remote places, he is dedicated, and does not begrudge his time."

I found Matthiessen's unbiased view rewarding, especially his comments on confiscating the wolverine skin, which I considered a routine but unjustifiable part of the job.

The Yukon–Kuskokwim Delta has experienced a human population explosion since I patrolled. Today there are about 30,000 persons, mostly Yup'ik Eskimos, living in thirty-five villages there. The delta is relatively productive of wildlife, in common with deltas the world around, but hunting and fishing pressures, high in the 1950s, have today reached almost unbearable proportions. Almost any moose that wandered onto the delta then was immediately shot, however, today with strict state enforcement, the populations are increasing. Spring hunting and egg-taking is having a serious impact on certain species of waterfowl, including cackling, emperor, and white-fronted geese, and brant.

The state is now embroiled in an Alaska-wide "subsistence rights" controversy that promises to separate Alaskans for generations to come. What was once simple is now complex. One wonders if the wildlife will survive until a decision is made over who has the rights to its use.

Unlike the two trappers and the beaver houses, it seems we cannot split anything fifty-fifty any more. It's all or nothing.

Chapter 10

THE QUIET MEN

A man of very few words, and even those I found hard to hear." That's how ecologist F. Fraser Darling described Dave Spencer in his book *Pelican in the Wilderness*. I can't think of a better description of "Silent Dave," the supervisor of U.S. Fish and Wildlife Service refuges in Alaska. He was one of the most respected wildlife biologists and the recipient of many conservation awards. Dave is no longer with us, but because of his unequalled contributions to the refuge system in Alaska, the FWS named a portion of the Kenai Wildlife Refuge in his honor.

One of Dave's pet projects was keeping a tally of the musk ox on the National Wildlife Refuge of Nunivak Island, in the Bering Sea. This included the number of newborns and those that died since the previous year. He accomplished this by making annual aerial counts of the animals. While I was stationed in McGrath, I assisted him with these surveys on several occasions, which usually took about five days of flying, depending on weather.

Nunivak Island is about twenty-five miles off the coast of Alaska southwest of Bethel. Residents of the island live in the village of Mekoryuk, on the north end. In the 1950s the villagers were dependent on a hunting-and-fishing economy, supplemented by seasonal work with the Bureau of Indian Affairs, the agency that administered the reindeer industry on the island. Today the villagers own the reindeer business. They are also involved in commercial fishing, guiding musk-ox hunters, trapping fox, and carving walrus ivory.

Musk ox once roamed Alaska's entire Arctic Slope, but Eskimos near Barrow killed the last indigenous animals between 1850–60. Thirty-one animals were obtained from Greenland and introduced to Nunivak Island in 1935 and 1936 as a preliminary step in reestablishing them in their former range. Nunivak was selected since it was relatively accessible, free from predators, and permitted confinement on a large area of good habitat.

The plan was set in motion during the summer of 1930, when a total of 34 animals were captured in Greenland. The count included 8 male and 9 female calves, 7 male and 9 female yearlings, and 1 subadult female. On September 15, they landed in New York and were held in quarantine

*Dave Spencer and I check the vitals on an anesthetized musk ox
on Nunivak Island in the Bering Sea, July 1959.*

until October 18, then shipped to Alaska, arriving at College on November 5. No animals were lost in transit. All were held in a wooded pasture at the Alaska Agricultural College and School of Mines (now the University of Alaska) until they were released on Nunivak in 1936. At least 19 calves were born at the college, but predation by black bears and other losses reduced the herd to the 31 prior to release. The herd fluctuated in size until 1947 when it numbered 49 animals. Since 1947 the herd has increased at a nearly constant annual rate of 16 percent.

FWS personnel made several counts of the animals on foot and by dog team in 1942, 1947, and 1948. Dave started the aerial surveys in 1949, at first using a Grumman Widgeon amphibian aircraft, a smaller version of the Grumman Goose used so extensively by the service in Alaska. Later, in 1958, we started using the Cessna 180 because it was capable of slower flight and made a better survey plane.

Today there are at least six well-established musk-ox herds on Alaska's mainland, all transplants from Nunivak. The original herd now numbers 500 to 600 animals. Transplants continue and the state now conducts permit hunts, allowing hunters to take a specific number of bulls each year.

One very noticeable characteristic of the Nunivak musk ox is their low mortality rate. During the surveys of the 1950s, traveling Natives most often found any dead animals when they were out trapping, hunting, fishing, or herding reindeer. The locations of the carcasses were noted and always forwarded to Dave by mail. Any heads recovered were stored until Dave arrived; at which time the Yup'ik Eskimo finders were paid five dollars for their services.

Full skeletons of the deceased musk ox were in demand by museums. Curators and biology students studied the bones, and they also went on display. With this in mind, Dave kept track of dead animals, allowing a year or more of exposure for the bones to weather. Marked on the map were those accessible for collection during the annual survey.

One such carcass had been found on the 1956 aerial survey and marked on Dave's map for pickup. It was a few miles up a drainage stream that emptied into Nash Harbor. The terrain sloped gently upward from the shallow bay into a series of grass benches. The skeleton was atop of one of these benches and several parties of Native hunters had checked them during the spring of 1957. They said the bones were dry and could be easily picked up, so Dave suggested we make the collection during the July survey.

On July 12, I met Dave in Bethel. I had spent several day there distributing hunting and fishing licenses and discussing mutual enforcement problems with Deputy U.S. Marshal George Guilsher, who was being transferred to Fairbanks. With Dave were two Swedish scientists conducting a research project on arctic flora. We landed in the harbor at Mekoryuk, on Nunivak Island, and taxied up on the beach. As usual, most of the villagers walked down to greet us and help pack our gear to the cabin we would be using. These people were always willing to lend a hand.

Later in the afternoon, a resident brought in a musk-ox skull that he had found months earlier. He was rewarded with Dave's five dollars. These Eskimos protected the musk ox as their own, and Dave took the opportunity to ask who was familiar with the location of the musk-ox carcass behind Nash Harbor. The man named a young hunter who'd been to the place several times and would be glad to guide us there the next day.

According to my field diary, we left at 8:45 the next morning with the two Swedish scientists, the young Eskimo guide, Dave, and me. We circled the grass-covered bench where Dave had marked the carcass on his map, and we counted three creeks that we would have to cross to get there. High grass made it impossible to see the musk-ox remains from the air.

We landed in the harbor and beached the plane at 9:05. Each of us grabbed a packsack and headed up the right side of the narrow river running into the bay. It was a beautiful day for an outing, and Dave set a brisk pace for the rest of us to follow.

After crossing the three small creeks, we climbed to the top of the hill, and found it as flat as a tabletop stretching westward several miles toward the coast.

Dave lined us out and we began walking five abreast in a westward direction searching for the bone pile, but they were well hidden in the deep grass. We walked back and forth, east to west, then west to east, working our way along the bench in one-half mile swaths. There wasn't much conversation; rather, we all seemed to be enjoying our own thoughts and gazing at the beautiful scenery in all directions.

Sometime around 12:30, Dave called a halt for lunch. One of the Swedish scientists, an expert on lichens, had been collecting samples so at least her morning had been profitable. She produced some excellent cheese from her packsack to share while she explained some of the differences in the lichen plants she had collected. Dave, in his usual manner, said very little and the Eskimo had not talked since we had left that morning.

We finished lunch and were basking in the sunshine when Dave said to the Eskimo, "I thought you knew where this musk-ox carcass was?" The Native replied, "No I don't know where this one is, but there's one over there" and pointed over to the next bench.

We looked at one another in disbelief, picked up our packs, and started out in the direction he had pointed. When we arrived on top of the next ridge our guide walked through the grass for about three hundred feet straight to the musk-ox remains. Dave shrugged and started dividing up the bones for each of us to pack back to the plane.

As we started back, I thought to myself that I had finally met a person more quiet than "Silent Dave." The young Eskimo had been willing to go along on our trip to locate a dead musk ox that he had seen several times while herding reindeer. Dave was relying on him to get us to the exact location. Knowing the approximate position of the animal, Dave had led the way thinking that our Native friend would take over as we approached the area. When we arrived on location, the Native assumed we were looking for a different animal and went along with the hunt without question until Dave finally asked for his help.

We arrived back at Mekoryuk at 2:30 and spent the remainder of the afternoon packing the bones for shipment to the National Museum. Feeling I should test the ability of the specialist, who would be putting the skeleton together, I threw in several reindeer bones for good measure.

Later that evening I asked Dave what he thought of our Native guide. Silent Dave answered, "He doesn't say much, does he?"

Chapter 11

WHAT HAPPENED TO CHARLIE WOODS

*C*harlie Woods was typical of many old-timers who had lived a life of adventure in Alaska and chose to live out his senior years alone in the solitude of the wilderness. Most of his breed refused to submit themselves to retirement homes. They sought no help from anyone, suffered the chronic aches of aging in silence, and were most comfortable while living in the peace and quiet of the big woods.

Like many others, Charlie grew a garden in the summer, enduring the myriads of mosquitoes to produce a year's supply of vegetables. His eyes were failing so he was not always successful at moose hunting, but someone always dropped off a piece of meat for Charlie before freeze-up. He had an old boat and motor for his annual hundred-mile river trip to McGrath each summer for seeds, clothing, and staples. He stayed a few days to visit a friend, cash his pension checks, gather up his mail and supplies, and head back again for another year.

In the summer of 1957, however, Charlie didn't show up in McGrath. No one was too concerned, because he never had a specific date for his trip. Then in late August, several Indians from the village of Telida came to town with disturbing news. They always checked on Charlie when they traveled the North Fork of the Kuskokwim River, as his cabin was midway between their village and McGrath. They reported to U.S. Commissioner Pete Egrass that Charlie's boat was tied up in front of his cabin all loaded for a trip, but no one was around. They checked inside the cabin and noticed that the last day marked off on the calendar was August 10, and there were no recent signs of occupancy. They searched the area surrounding the cabin but found nothing. Now the folks in McGrath were concerned.

Pete Egrass notified the Territorial Police at Fairbanks, and on August 21, Lt. Bill Trafton and Sgt. Emery Chapple arrived in McGrath to make an investigation. After talking with local people who knew Charlie and gathering information, they came to my office seeking assistance. Would I fly them to his cabin so they could conduct a search? This was no problem since the Cessna 180 was all gassed and ready to go. We departed after telling Charlie's friends that we'd be back if we needed help conducting a search.

The river in front of Charlie's cabin was long enough for a landing and subsequent takeoff, so after eyeballing it carefully for driftwood, I touched down and taxied alongside his boat. We were able to tie and use the boat as a dock, which was a break since the river was quite swift with a steep, muddy bank, making it unsuitable for beaching a floatplane. With the aircraft secured, we began our search for clues to Charlie's whereabouts.

Everything was as the Indians had described. Charlie's boat was indeed ready for a trip—all equipped with gas and food. It was a large riverboat, more than twenty feet long, which Charlie hauled out each year with block and tackle and launched in the summer using greased poles, ropes, and pry bars. His camping gear was stored under a seat and his sleeping bag was in a waterproof box along with extra clothing. It appeared ready for an immediate departure.

In the cabin we looked at the calendar, which had an X through each day through the tenth, a common way for people living alone to keep track of time. The dishes were clean and in place, and everything indicated that he had been leaving for McGrath on the eleventh when he met with some misfortune.

After searching the surrounding woods and trails without success, we turned our attention to the river. We theorized that he had been loading the boat and had fallen into the water because of a slip or possible heart attack. We searched downstream; checking driftwood piles and eddies for any sign of a body, all to no avail. So it was back to McGrath to make arrangements for closing up the cabin and storing his property. Lt. Trafton and Sgt. Chapple departed the next day for Fairbanks leaving the final details to Commissioner Egrass and me, in my capacity as deputy U.S. marshal. They submitted a report listing Charlie Woods as missing and an apparent victim of drowning. Everyone in McGrath accepted the theory and said it was bound to happen someday.

Two days later, on August 22, I took Commissioner Egrass and a McGrath resident back to the cabin. Together we made another effort to find Charlie's body, without success. We gathered up his belongings and loaded them into the boat. After closing up the cabin the two men started downriver in the boat while I flew the Cessna back to McGrath. Charlie had disappeared, another in a long list of strong-willed loners who'd chosen a hermit's existence rather than the confines of a settlement.

During the next few months, the subject of Charlie was brought up at a gathering or in the local pubs, and it always ended with the same question, "Wonder what really happened to him?" The old-timers accepted the passing of one of their group without a great deal of remorse—they had all lived full lives—but they liked to know how the end had come. When they sat around reminiscing and telling stories on the ones who were gone, there was always a big void at the end if the person had just disappeared. It was forever an unfinished story. It's the same with all of us; we like to bury our dead, and when they end up missing we can never be sure that they're really gone. So the talk continued about Charlie throughout the winter months.

Then on March 4, an Indian from Nikolai sent a message to the commissioner. He had been trapping north of Charlie's place and his trail passed behind Charlie's cabin. On a return trip he had found a hip boot that had been dragged out and left by animals on his dog-team trail. A bone protruded from the end of the boot. He reported that he had not touched it, nor had he looked for any other remains.

The next day, I flew Commissioner Egrass back to Charlie's place. We landed on skis on the frozen river. The snow was deep so we strapped on snowshoes and followed the dog-team trail past the cabin. Sure enough, about three-quarters of a mile behind the cabin there was the hip boot with a leg bone inside. Charlie had been wearing the boot folded down and the bone was broken off just below the knee joint. Only the powerful jaws of a wolf could have been responsible for this. They made numerous tracks around the area, and by backtracking the most-used trail we located more human bones. Further examination produced a pelvis, ribs, and a skull. I took pictures and we tried to reconstruct what had happened, with little success due to the snow depth.

Two things were obvious: first, this had to be Charlie, and second, the wolves had nothing to do with his death. They had evidently devoured most of the already dead body in early fall, and were now making rounds of their territory, checking for any old scraps. Some of the bones were probably carried off to other locations. We collected all the remains we could find (the second boot was never found) and returned to McGrath.

When we catalogued the remains, we cleaned the skull and noticed a small-caliber hole in the skull just above the location of the right ear, which was marked as evidence.

Several days later, at the request of the commissioner, I convened a coroner's inquest. Charlie's remains, with all the information gathered so far, were presented to a local six-man jury. The jury concluded that the cause of death was from a self-inflicted bullet wound. Before the book on Charlie was closed, however, the weapon needed to be located, if possible. When Lt. Trafton, Sgt. Chapple, and I had made the inspection of Charlie's cabin the previous August, we had found an empty box on one of the shelves that had contained a .22 caliber Harrington and Richardson automatic pistol. We had searched the cabin and the boat for the pistol without success. Now the pistol became an important part of the cause of death conclusion, and the jury asked that we return after breakup and try to find it.

The Cessna 180 was not on floats until the middle of June that spring because I had been involved in some long patrols along the Arctic Coast to Point Barrow. Finally, on Sunday morning, June 22, Commissioner Pete Egrass and I, in my marshal status, returned to Charlie's homestead for the last time. We walked to the place where we'd found the skeletal remains and searched the surrounding area. Sure enough, right where the bones had been was a rusted H&R pistol. Pete checked it carefully and determined that it was fully loaded except for one empty round in the chamber.

Thus ended the "Saga of Charlie" except for the big question, "Why?" Why was his boat ready for the annual trip to McGrath? What was he doing back in the woods, and did he always carry the .22 pistol with him on his walks? Did he go back there to commit suicide?

Everyone familiar with the story had his or her ideas and theories. Most agreed, however, that Charlie was not planning suicide, but something had occurred that caused him to end his life unexpectedly. The best theory follows simple logic. He went back into the woods to cut some poles to help in beaching the boat and met with some accident. It could have been a broken leg, a severe cut with the ax, or a stroke, or heart attack. Once incapacitated, he knew the consequences of lying seriously injured, alone, with no help forthcoming. He would have two choices, end it all, or lie there suffering until the end came.

To a man in his late eighties the choice was simple, and he chose the quick and easy route.

Whatever the reason, he ended his life as many others living in seclusion have. He was happy, lived the life he wanted, and stayed until the end in the country he loved. A time to live and a time to die. Charlie had picked the one place in the world he loved for both, and he did it on his own terms.

Chapter 12

LAWLESS VALLEY

*M*y report to the regional office of the McGrath District operation for March 1958 ended with this paragraph:

"A short trip to Fairbanks was made with U.S. Commissioner Dave Leach of Aniak, to confer with District Court Judge Vernon Forbes. We assisted the judge and clerk of court in determining a new boundary for the Aniak precinct. I conferred with U.S. Marshal Al Dorsch about 'Lawless Valley,' a name given the Kuskokwim River area. The residents are again without a deputy marshal at either Bethel or McGrath. Mr. Dorsch suggested this agent accept an appointment as honorary deputy marshal, but the offer was declined as it was felt that the new uniform (we had recently been issued uniforms which were not very popular with the agents, hence a little dig) would sag and bag under the weight of two badges."

I had been detailed to McGrath in June 1956 to take charge of that district, which included all the drainages of the Kuskokwim and Yukon Rivers south from the village of Kaltag plus all of the coastal area from Unalakleet south to Goodnews Bay, including Nunivak Island. At that time there was one deputy marshal stationed in McGrath and another at Bethel to cover the same district.

In territorial days, the marshal's office handled most of the major crime problems and transportation of prisoners from the outlying areas. There was some overlap with the Territorial Police; however, the area in question was so large there were seldom any jurisdictional problems. Also the Territorial Police had a limited budget and were happy to have the marshals handle most of the crime in the Bush areas of Alaska.

Compared with today's standards, the area was quite peaceful, with relatively few major crimes. There were occasional murders, rapes, and disorderly conduct, mostly alcohol-related, but for the most part, the marshals had it easy. We often worked together and coordinated patrols, so I became familiar with their mode of operation. They

From the air, we could follow dogsled trails to check on activities of trappers and hunters. Most were cooperative as I searched their possessions, May 1960.

did not have any aircraft and had a limited budget for chartering local air carriers to respond to criminal complaints. Often they would call for assistance in hauling prisoners or to transport bodies to town from remote areas, especially at the end of the fiscal year when they were really low on operating funds.

By 1958 the Territorial Police were assuming more responsibility for responding to emergency complaints in the villages. The marshal's office stayed busy in the larger cities as court bailiffs, process servers, and escorts for prisoners transferring to federal prisons outside of Alaska.

The Territorial Police were now having major problems since they were saddled with more responsibilities but without additional money. They could only respond to major complaints and emergencies. None were stationed in the villages, so there was always a delay in getting to the troubled areas due to travel restrictions. Their budget was even more limited than the marshals'.

Here again, I made myself available and assisted whenever needed. The regional office had approved this and we were encouraged to assist any other law enforcement agency so long as it didn't interfere with our other duties. In effect I was the only law enforcement official in that part of Alaska. Cooperation was necessary and many times I had to rely on them for help.

U.S. commissioners were appointed by federal judges for each judicial district and were ex officio justices of the peace. As mentioned earlier, some had a room set aside in their home to hold court, but others used the living room, kitchen, or any other available room. The commissioner from Aniak traveled with me when there were large numbers of trappers taking beaver illegally. Most were taking more than the legal limit of ten. The trappers involved would pay a fellow villager who had not trapped that year to falsify an affidavit stating they trapped the skins. Sometimes by checking trapping camps I was able to count the number of beaver taken before the trappers returned to the village. Any illegal beaver skins were seized, and I filed a complaint on the spot. Court was held in the trapper's tent or cabin. At times we just used a convenient log or stump as a bench.

Most often when there was a major problem in a village, the commissioner was transported to that location. He or she would organize an investigation into the facts of the complaint and hold court. In the case of a serious crime, a jury was selected and the local school or meeting hall was used for the proceedings. Justice was usually fair and seldom did anyone complain of their treatment. None of the commissioners I knew had law degrees or any formal law schooling, but all had a great deal of common sense, which prevailed when they imposed a sentence.

The enforcement officer made the investigation, filed the complaints, and acted as prosecuting attorney. If jail time was a part of the sentence, the officer was required to fly the person to Anchorage or Fairbanks. Compared with these days of complicated laws and court proceedings, the system was simple, effective and respected by most throughout the Territory.

A typical request for assistance came from Sgt. Emery Chapple, Territorial Police at Fairbanks, who needed help and transportation to the village of Kaltag to investigate a rape complaint. Emery was a well-respected Trooper who later became commissioner of the Alaska Department of Public Safety after statehood. I left McGrath in the FWS, float-equipped Cessna 180 and flew to Galena, a large village on the Yukon River. An airstrip and hangars were built there during World War II, and were then used for refueling aircraft en route to Russia. It was now a base for Air Force fighter planes on alert during the Cold War. Northern Consolidated Airlines also used it as a hub for distributing freight and passengers to neighboring villages.

I picked up Emery when he arrived on the mail plane. From Galena we flew to the village of Ruby, forty miles upriver, to pick up the commissioner. We then flew to Kaltag, about ninety miles downriver from Galena. What followed was a typical example of Bush justice characteristic of the Troopers in those days.

Emery talked to a girl who had filed a charge of rape against a friend in the village. With a great deal of diligence, Emery explained to the girl how serious the charge of rape was and asked her to explain what had occurred. As I recall, the encounter occurred behind her cabin where she had been intimate with him previously; however, on that night she had not welcomed him. Emery was very patient and let her tell her story. After listening to everything she had to say, he delicately asked if it was rape or more like poor timing on the man's part. She agreed to the latter and said she would drop the charges if the Trooper would talk to the man involved and make sure he left her alone when she didn't want his advances. Emery complied with her wishes and we departed with everyone friends again. What a negotiator. No wonder he became commissioner in later years. The other villager wasn't quite as fortunate and was sentenced to jail for assault he committed during a drinking bout.

The U.S. commissioner was pleased with the outcome and happy to fly back to his home in Ruby. Emery and I then flew to Koyukuk for the night. The village is located at the mouth of the Koyukuk River where it joins the Yukon River. Here Dominic Vernetti, an Italian immigrant, had a store and small roadhouse. He had arrived in Alaska as a prospector during the Iditarod gold rush days. He and his beautiful part-Indian wife, Ella, were gracious hosts and it was always a pleasure to stay and visit with them.

I felt fortunate that we had landed before dark because the rivers were extremely high, with a considerable amount of drift, including debris trees and stumps that had been cleaned off the banks by the high water. Most of it was choking the mouth of the Koyukuk

River in front of the roadhouse. I found some slack water and landed without incident.

With a long day behind us and the plane secured, we settled in for a nice evening of socializing. We enjoyed one of Dominic's specialties that evening—spaghetti with homemade sauce and lots of meatballs. Later as we were enjoying a good bull session, a man came to the store with a split-open foot. He had done it with an ax while chopping wood. It was a nasty wound and we agreed he needed to go to a doctor, or at least a nurse with suturing capabilities. Oh joy! Here it was getting dark and we would have to take off and land in the debris-choked river. Not the most pleasant way to end the day.

The closest facility was the military base at Galena, fifty miles upriver, so we packed him into the plane and departed. Taxiing through the debris in the Koyukuk, I found some slack water in the Yukon River for takeoff. We radioed Galena, advised them of the medical emergency, and requested assistance when we arrived. By now it was quite dark, so I landed in the Yukon River on the opposite side of the village to stay out of the main channel and avoid any logs. We taxied in slowly, threading our way through the rubble with the use of the landing lights. When we were beached, we transferred the patient to a waiting vehicle. With that part of the operation successfully accomplished, we now had to get back to Koyukuk, because there was no place along the river to park and protect the plane from the high water.

By taxiing back through the main channel, I was able to find the same slack water we had landed in, and we took off. Landing in the Koyukuk River was a different situation, however, because it was much narrower and there was no slack water. I made a long approach with the landing lights on as I dragged the water looking for an opening in the drift. Finally, I plopped it in and we held our breath hoping we wouldn't hit a big log or tree stump. We lucked out and taxied to the bank in front of the store, where we pulled up the tail of the floats as far as we could and tied down with the help of several of the villagers. If we were pleased with the first landing earlier in the evening, we were elated with our good fortune this time. Two happy campers went to bed that night.

The next morning we said our good-byes and accepted the thanks of the family of the young man we had taken to Galena. We were to fly back to Kaltag to pick up the prisoner from yesterday's trial. He was in the custody of a paid guard. I would be taking him and Emery to Galena where they would fly to Fairbanks on Northern Consolidated Airlines and I'd return to McGrath. After warming up the engine, I added power to slide off the bank and taxi out for takeoff. The plane began tilting to my side and the left float started to go underwater. A hasty turn and we were back to the bank wondering what was wrong. A quick inspection revealed a hole in the float that surely wasn't there the night before. *How did that happen?*

The culprit was an old engine block that had been thrown over the riverbank to help stabilize the embankment from erosion. In the dark, we hadn't seen the large chunk of metal and had set the float down on the block, which was hidden underwater. This was a major setback, since there was no way to take off without patching the hole, and that meant getting the float out of the water.

In those days, one thing that was always available in the villages was assistance, so we didn't lack for help. Planks and timbers showed up, and with several men pushing and others pulling, we slid the damaged float out of the water where we could work on it. After drying the damaged area with a blowtorch, a temporary patch was applied. Good old duct tape, inside and out. When the float was set back in the water, the patch held, but a very slow leak was still evident. Pumping the float was required before each takeoff to complete the trip. Emery and his prisoner were delivered to Galena in time to catch the commercial flight to Fairbanks.

I headed back to McGrath for a change of clothes and a brief hello to my family. After another float-pumping, I flew to Anchorage for a permanent patch. As I left, my wife reminded me that it might be nice if I stayed home long enough to introduce myself to the children again so they wouldn't forget who I was. My answer was simple: get Marshal Dorsch to put some deputies at McGrath and Bethel and allow me to just do my job as a wildlife enforcement agent!

When I sent my report into our headquarters at Juneau, I received a reply that said something to the effect that while we were willing to assist the Territorial Police with their efforts in the Bush, it could be damned expensive at times.

Chapter 13

WOLF CONTROL

*O*ne of the most controversial programs of the U.S. Fish and Wildlife Service in the 1950s was the killing of wolves by the Division of Predator Control. The policy of the Service was to control (never to exterminate) wolves in designated areas, to build up herds of moose and caribou that were being depleted or threatened. Wolves were taken by aerial shooting and by the use of poisons, both strychnine and cyanide. Most of the hunting fraternity agreed with the need for control and supported the program. Others were apathetic, feeling that the FWS knew what they were doing and shrugged it off as "their business, not ours." Preservationists were a relatively small, elite group and any opposition from that quarter had little effect. The use of poison, however, was a different story and was either reluctantly supported or violently opposed. There never seemed to be a middle ground and there still isn't.

The very word "poison" is enough to throw a fear into the majority of people and rightly so. The fear of the unknown is born into all of us, and I must confess that even though I was instructed in the use of poison baits and cyanide guns, I was never comfortable working with these lethal chemicals. The strychnine crystals were about the size of a peanut and were shipped in small cardboard cylinders. They were prepared for use by forming a spoonful of lard into a ball about one inch in diameter and pushing a crystal into the center. The ball was then rolled into a brown, dry scented mixture of ground seal meal, giving it an attractive smell to the carnivores. They were then packaged in small paper bags with about twenty to a sack. These were set out at bait stations, usually at a location where wolves had killed a moose or caribou.

Cyanide powder, on the other hand, was placed in a .38 (or .357) caliber cartridge covered with wax to keep it intact and weatherproof. The shell was placed in a triggered metal cylinder set in the ground. A baited tube was the only part exposed. When a wolf or coyote grabbed the bait and pulled on it, the shell was fired, forcing the poison into its throat. These were summer baits, and the lard balls were winter baits.

Back then the Fish and Wildlife Service in Alaska was understaffed in every division, so we all wore several hats. Thus, as an enforcement agent I helped tag fish with the sports fish biologist, made game counts, creel censuses, assisted in trapping live animals, collected jaw bones with the game biologists, and counted migrating salmon with the commercial fish biologists, as well as other "duties as assigned." One of the other duties was assisting the predator agents to control wolf populations.

When I first took over the McGrath District, I had help in Harley King, who was with the Predator Division. There were not enough agents to make this a two-man station. For six months he assisted me with the enforcement program, and I helped him with the wolf program. When he terminated his job no replacement was hired due to lack of funds. I was alone doing both jobs for two years until another enforcement agent, Chuck Heimier, was hired. Together we carried out all the duties as required, including the wolf program in designated areas.

The control program was well thought out at the highest level and with the full support of the Alaska Game Commission. I never did hear any objections from any of the commissioners during our meetings in February. The following facts are submitted as best I can remember on the way the program was conducted. The reader can draw his or her own conclusions as to the merits of the methods and means used then.

The word "control" is important because it directed the policy and guidelines under which we operated. I have heard many accusations over the years that the Fish and Wildlife Service killed wolves by scattering poison indiscriminately out of airplanes over most of Alaska. That's pure hogwash. For one thing, ongoing studies conducted by trained biologists dictated the areas needing a balance between game animals and wolf populations. Wherever a large build-up of wolves was preying on low stocks of moose or caribou, the plan called to reduce the wolf numbers in favor of game animals. Prime target areas were those supporting game required by subsistence users and the more popular hunting areas of urban hunters. The control programs were not annihilation schemes, but an attempt to remove surplus predators and allow the moose, caribou, and sheep numbers to recover.

Shooting was the number-one method of taking wolves. Most hunting was conducted from Super Cub aircraft using Winchester Model 12 shotguns firing magnum loads of No. 4 buckshot. These were special shells loaded for the FWS and contained 41 pellets instead of the usual 28. The gunner sat in the rear seat of the tandem aircraft and opened the side window for shooting—shooting to kill the running wolf without hitting either the prop or wing strut. But even experienced hunters in the heat of a chase occasionally put shot into props with varying effects on the aircraft.

It took good teamwork to be effective. The gunner had to completely trust the pilot's ability to keep the plane from stalling or hitting trees while he concentrated on shooting. Hitting a running wolf required a negative lead because the plane was going faster than the wolf. This could prove tricky since the animals seldom ran in a straight line. We had gunners who were capable of taking several wolves in one pass under the right conditions, which is no easy feat while hanging by a seat belt.

The pilot, on the other hand, had to trust the gunner completely. He didn't have time to worry about stray shots hitting his prop, or more seriously, the wing strut, which could cause the wing to fail. His job was to fly low and slow, dodging obstructions as he made passes over the running wolves. At times, especially when deep snow caused the animals to run in a single trail, a good gunner would take as many as seven wolves before they dispersed. Other times on hard-packed snow and in timbered country, several passes might be necessary to kill one wolf as it dodged and ran into tree cover.

The most successful hunters were the pilots who could track. Seldom did we find wolves by randomly flying around the countryside, but rather by identifying wolf tracks or trails and systematically following them to the animals. This was rarely easy, as wolves in search of food are capable of traveling up to fifty miles in a twenty-four-hour period. Once a track was cut and the direction of travel determined, the chase was on. If the tracks went through dense timber, we could spend lots of time finding where they exited. Other times they might became obliterated in a maze of moose or caribou trails, and the pilot would have to circle and sort through the sign to figure out which way they'd gone, or where a kill had occurred. Kills were often found by observing ravens, which took over possession of dead animals once the wolves finished gorging. On and on, the tracking continued with much banking, turning, and other maneuvering, requiring an iron stomach on the part of the gunner.

Once the shooting was over, the next task was making a successful landing so the kills could be retrieved. This was not always easy, especially in mountainous or hilly terrain. Often we had to snowshoe several miles to kills. In especially difficult terrain, kills occasionally had to be abandoned. Every effort was made to get to the animals, however, since this was an important part of the job. We skinned the wolves (later sold at auction), not a simple chore in cold weather, and collected biological data. We took measurements and weights whenever possible, and we sacked and labeled the skull and stomach contents for further study. Then it was back to camp to fuel the plane and tie it down with wood blocks or poles under the skis to keep them from freezing in place. We drained the oil and slipped on wing and engine covers so all would be ready for another flight tomorrow. This went on day after day until the wolves were either thinned out of the target area or the weather closed in.

There were times when I did the shooting; usually with Bob Burkholder as pilot. Bob was a master tracker and flew a Super Cub like a World War I ace. That is, he compelled the plane to do things it was never intended for—things that would have made the Piper folks shudder if they had watched him fly. He was like a bird dog when he was on a wolf track and was one of the few who could follow a trail through a heavy concentration of caribou hoof prints and pick up the wolves at the other end. Sitting in the back was not comfortable, however, because the plane would be doing low-level chandelles, negative G turns, and at times dodging between trees. He never lost sight of the wolves once he had them spotted.

Once we were hunting the Innoko River drainage in February. It was damned cold as I recall, in the –40s. Temperatures like that aren't exactly conducive to hanging out the side of a Super Cub and making a shot at a passing wolf. About an hour after leaving McGrath, Bob picked up the trail of a lone wolf. After about fifteen minutes of tracking, he located the animal in heavy timber. Now it was up to me. Bob had a suggestion. Why not slide the side window open on the left side of the plane and shoot out that side instead of opening up the two panels on the right side? It also should be easier for a right-handed shooter to sight and get a shot off, being extremely careful not to hit the prop or strut, of course.

As usual I was using an issued Winchester Model 12 pump-action shotgun loaded with the special No. 4 magnum buckshot. I had the magazine full and the chamber empty for safety purposes. I opened the window and stuck the barrel out trying to pump a shell into the chamber. No luck. The action was frozen, and the feeding mechanism wouldn't operate. Meanwhile Bob was shouting, "Hurry up and shoot! He's going to get away!" Finally, out of desperation I pulled the gun inside the plane and fed a shell into the chamber manually. Then it happened. As I pumped the shell forward, it went off. Fortunately, I had the barrel pointing out the side of the aircraft. Even so several pellets bounced off the frame member supporting the windshield.

When we landed, I saw where one had hit the ball in the needle and ball instrument dead center. No problem, Bob never used that instrument anyway. But the noise was deafening. What was worse, it went off next to Bob's ear. I'm sure to this day he has a permanent hearing loss in his left ear. I was completely mystified as to why it had fired. Bob was sure I had my finger on the trigger when I worked the pump even though I told him I was positive I hadn't.

When we got out we checked the shotgun and found the difficulty. The firing pin was frozen in the firing position, and when I slid the pump action forward, it forced it into the primer firing the shell. Bob kept working on it, but it was impossible to thaw out in that temperature even by holding it under his armpit. So he came up with a plan. We would take off again, locate the wolf, and I would operate the shotgun by putting a shell in the chamber and fire it by sliding the pump forward. How's that for dedication? That's exactly what we did. On the second or third pass, I was able to make the shot using Bob's suggestion and that was the end of the hunt. That is, except for landing and skinning out the animal, not the most fun in the cold that prevailed that day.

That evening Bob said he'd never had that happen before and was sure I'd mishandled the shotgun. I answered, "Hey, if there's one thing I'm careful of, it's handling a shotgun in a plane. After all I'm usually the pilot, and I'm constantly harping on my shooters to be extremely careful." He said, "WHAT?" So I went around to his right side and repeated what I had said. "Yeah, okay," he said. "I guess I lost some hearing in that ear, but we got the wolf, right?"

Now that's a real wolf hunter . . .

When we used strychnine baits, we brought several of the sacks along on each flight, and if we found a wolf kill, we baited it. We'd land in the vicinity, if possible, and study the kill site to determine the number of wolves in the pack, and the age and condition of the dead moose or caribou. Baits were then carefully distributed around the remains. I say carefully because the errant notion is that we just threw baits all around that would eventually kill everything in sight.

First, the fact was, we knew the wolves would be back, because they always return to kill sites time and time again as they made rounds of their territory. Even after there's nothing left but bones, they will make a visit to check their "property." We knew, too, that they are extremely inquisitive and like any canine have an extremely well-developed sense of smell. They would find the baits no matter where we hid them. So we would hide them away from the actual remains and under pieces of hide or hair so they wouldn't be so obvious to birds and small mammals.

There is no denying that other game besides wolves were killed. Foxes were the most frequent fatalities. However, since foxes live their entire lives within a territory of about five miles, it stands to reason that only the few living in the immediate vicinity would become victims. Birds were a different story, and ravens and magpies were frequent losers; however, when adding the pluses and the minuses, the loss of these other predators had to be considered as the cost of doing business.

There were always unjustified complaints from people who were completely opposed to any killing or the use of poison. I'm not talking about the right to disagree, or oppose the policy of wolf control, or the use of lethal agents, but about spreading falsehoods to the news media. This accomplished nothing except to create a mudslinging contest; however, any documented cases of impropriety by Fish and Wildlife employees brought results and changes in operating procedures.

Also, as public attitude changed, so did the entire program, and during the last few years prior to statehood there was more research going on than actual killing. An example is the study of the Nelchina wolves. After taking most of the wolves from that area to allow a buildup of the caribou herd, aerial surveys indicated that there was only one pack of nine animals left. For the next two years Bob Burkholder spent most of his time following the pack and documenting their travels and kills.

The program ended with statehood except for some continued control work around the reindeer herds on the Seward Peninsula. This was done under an agreement with the Bureau of Indian Affairs and the Alaska Department of Fish and Game at the request of the herders who were losing many reindeer to wolves. Also, at the time of statehood the big game populations were in the best shape they had been in for the past twenty years. Was this because of the wolf-control program? There are those who believe without question that was the case; others, including some game biologists, do not.

Predator control was stopped because of the feeling that wolves were important in cutting out the sick and the weak, a needed component in "nature's balance." Years later after a large buildup of wolves was competing with hunters for diminishing numbers of moose and caribou, ADF&G biologists initiated another control program. Some members of the public, including school children, met this with great resistance. Lawsuits were filed that stopped the control program. Today the controversy continues on a much larger scale, and it's difficult to find anyone who doesn't have an opinion on the subject.

The program approved by the Alaska Game Commission and administered by the U.S. Fish and Wildlife Service was not without merit and was highly successful. It was not an all-out destruction program, but one based on sound scientific evidence conducted by employees who had a great deal of respect and admiration for the wolf. This can be verified by the fact that the wolf population rebounded so quickly after the program ended.

Somehow wolf numbers will have to be controlled again if a healthy population of moose and caribou is to be maintained. The biggest challenge and obstacle is to somehow educate the public and gain support. This seems to be impossible in this day and age of "ballot box" game management with the final decisions being made by politicians.

Another state program is underway. Again a boycott is in effect threatening the tourist industry. Getting complete public support for thinning wolf packs in areas of heavy predation seems to be impossible.

Subsistence hunters aren't the only ones losing; moose and caribou are paying the price for the so-called "balance of nature." Those looking for this fabled land today might also look for the "fountain of youth." Who knows? Maybe they exist together.

Chapter 14

DOG SHOOTS MAN
& OTHER WILD ANIMAL STORIES

*P*rior to statehood, each fall the FWS commonly established game-check stations on roads leading to popular hunting areas. I always enjoyed working along the Steese Highway and the Fortymile Road (now known as the Taylor Highway) during this time of year. Road patrols were a break, too, from the hours of flying that I was always committed to in the fall. Small camp trailers were then manned by both biologists and enforcement agents. All outgoing vehicles were stopped and hunters checked. We used our authority under the Alaska Game Law to search vehicles for illegal animals or parts. It always amazed us how ingenious some people could be at secreting illegal game in car trunks, under seats, and in compartments of recreational vehicles.

A great deal of good biological data were obtained at these stations by collecting the lower jaws of moose and caribou, and most hunters gladly gave up that part of the animal to further enhance game management. The biologists had tripods set up to measure and weigh caribou. Most hunters enjoyed stopping and sharing information. They usually went away more knowledgeable about the work of the biologists and with a better understanding about the future of hunting in Alaska.

The check stations were open twenty-four hours a day. We took turns working with a biologist. One enforcement agent was on duty at all times to handle the traffic. Many folks were miners or others who lived along the highway and were just traveling to town. They didn't appreciate waiting in line to be checked since they considered themselves nonhunters; however, more than one had illegal game stored where he thought it was safe from observation. On weekends, additional agents would join the crew, and even so it wasn't uncommon to have thirty or forty cars backed up after a weekend of hunting activity. We also had help from the military. Army personnel who were working as game wardens on the military bases were detailed to assist us during the hunting season.

When they weren't at the check stations, agents patrolled the road system. Regulations required hunters to be at least a quarter of a mile off

A caribou is weighed at the Taylor Highway check station, October 1955.

the road to take big game, and there were two major caribou crossings on the Steese Highway where the hunter had to be at least five miles off the road. These protected five-mile zones allowed caribou to cross the highway without being molested and gave nonhunters a place to observe the animals without fear of being shot. Additionally, the Alaska Game Law prohibited taking cows and calves of moose and caribou. This posed no problem with moose. However, it was a different story with caribou as both males and females have antlers. While management biologists did not agree with the law, there was little the Alaska Game Commission could do since only Congress could make the change.

Patrols involved driving along the road system and walking into the hunting areas checking licenses, legality of kills, and acting at times as referees when ownership fights of downed animals broke out. I once held the rifles of two combatants who duked it out because one had observed the other tearing out floorboards from an old emergency cabin, which he used as firewood. I doubt if that individual ever tore up cabins again.

The "quarter mile from the road" regulation was an attempt to create a safety zone for nonhunters and motorists. Ray Woolford, my supervisor, had an interesting contact one day on the Fortymile Road. Numerous bands of caribou were crossing the road, tempting some hunters to chance a kill from the roadway. They usually hoped to remove the kill unobserved. Ray was driving down the highway in an unmarked vehicle. As he drove around a curve, he came upon a hunter leaning over the hood of his car taking aim at a caribou several hundred yards off. Ray shouted, "Hey, you can't shoot from there."

The hunter quickly answered, "Yes, I can. I've got a scope." And with that he squeezed off a round, killing the animal. Ray said, "That's not what I meant," and proceeded to write him up for taking a game animal from the highway. The chagrined hunter had to butcher the animal, pack it out, and turn it in at the check station.

A few days later I was parked at a vantage point along the highway observing several bands of nice big bulls moving along a river bottom. There were several vehicles parked in the vicinity, so I felt these animals would probably be taken before long. Sure enough, a barrage of rifle fire opened up about a mile off in that direction. It sounded like a war had begun, and I lost track of the number of shots fired. I decided I'd better check this group out. We had been finding many dead animals that were the result of herd shooting. Novice hunters will at times shoot into a group of animals rather than pick out one animal to kill. This resulted in crippled animals. Usually the hunter would take one and leave the others. A shameful loss of a beautiful animal to stupidity.

When the shooting stopped I headed in that direction, whistling and making a great deal of noise so that I would not be mistaken for a caribou in the event the hunters had any ammunition left. I introduced myself to two hunters who were trying to gut a nice bull. I asked how many animals had been taken and was surprised when they answered only three. They explained that the third member of the party had gone back to the car for packboards. When I questioned them about the number of shots, they meekly said this was their first hunt and pointed out that they were poor shots. One said he fired six shots and the other said he shot at least eleven times at his animal. They went on to say that Bob, the other hunter, had used a full box of ammo before getting his animal. I found this difficult to believe, so after checking the three dead caribou, each having several bullet holes in the carcasses, I scoured the surrounding area looking for additional kills or cripples. After thirty minutes of searching I found no evidence of additional animals, so I had to accept the story. I went back and found the two men still working on the first caribou.

After watching the proceedings for a few minutes, I made a suggestion. It was obvious that the other two animals were beginning to bloat and needed immediate attention, so I recommended that they open them up and pull out the paunches. This would stop the bloating and then they could take their time with the rest of the butchering. They agreed and as we walked over to the nearest carcass they told me they were bartenders from Fairbanks. I sat on a log to smoke my pipe and watch the proceedings.

One of the men held onto a hind leg while the other grabbed his knife in both hands and said, "Well, here we go again." With that he plunged his knife into the abdomen cutting upwards causing the gas to burst out and spray both men with the stomach contents. I could not believe my eyes, nor could I sit and watch any longer. The way they were going about it would cause most of the meat to sour and be unfit for consumption. I asked them to walk with me to the last animal.

As they watched I took my knife and in a matter of minutes showed them how to open the cavity and remove the entrails without puncturing the paunch. When I finished, the fellow who had plunged the knife into the second caribou said to the other "See, I told you there had to be a better way!" I just shook my head and said good-bye.

One year we put a check station at Fox, just north of Fairbanks, to monitor the kills from both the Steese Highway and the Livengood Road. Not many caribou were being taken that year, but the moose hunting was fair and quite a few kills were checking through. We were also experiencing a high population of ptarmigan and many hunters were bagging their limits of fifteen a day.

On a beautiful sunny September day during the middle of the week, my good friend Max Bruton stopped after a day of bird hunting with his dog Lucky. Lucky was a hardheaded Labrador, a great retriever and just as stubborn as Max. Earlier in the season Max had trained Lucky to flush ptarmigan and retrieve them after they were shot. Retrieving was no problem for Lucky, who was great in the duck marshes, but staying close to Max while flushing the birds within shotgun range was more difficult. He just wasn't an upland game dog. On one occasion Max became so frustrated when Lucky roamed too far out that he gave him a blast of birdshot in the rear end. Max agreed it was a stupid and unfortunate incident in a fit of temper and was damn costly in veterinarian bills to have the shot removed.

Lucky and Max stayed buddies, however, and here they were back from a successful hunt. Max was all smiles as he led me to the back of his station wagon to show me his day's take. His shotgun was on the floor pointing aft and the birds were piled in the corner. As we approached the rear of the vehicle Lucky, who had been sleeping, came to life and started bouncing up and down, anxious to get out. As Max started rolling down the back window of the station wagon, Lucky became more exuberant and one of his feet contacted the trigger of the "presumed" unloaded shotgun. There was a loud explosion and a load of birdshot blew a hole the size of a silver dollar through the tailgate, passing between Max and me and catching the pocket of Max's hunting jacket. In the pocket of this jacket were three shotgun shells, which were discharged by the force of the shot, causing burns to his thigh. We were both temporarily in shock realizing how close we had come to being seriously injured.

Max was humiliated, but Lucky wasn't bothered at all; he just wanted out. A week later the story was out, written up in the *Fairbanks Daily News-Miner* and it later became national news. The headline was "Man Shoots Dog — Dog Shoots Man." Wonder where they got that story? Both Max and Lucky are gone now, and for those of us who knew them, we hope they are in the happy hunting grounds, still sharing adventures together.

Later that same week I was patrolling the Livengood Road on a beautiful Saturday morning. You get used to seeing strange things during hunting season patrols, but even so, I was dumbfounded as I drove down toward the Chatanika River. There was a Jeep coming up the hill carrying a whole bull moose. I mean the entire carcass, legs, head, antlers and all, with only the entrails removed.

I turned my vehicle around and stopped the jeep, which was badly overheating from the climb out of the valley. Four soldiers got out. I looked, amazed, at the carcass that covered the entire cab, windshield, and hood with the head and horns hanging over the radiator and asked how they had managed to get it in place. Apparently, some buddies had helped them, and being young and strong, they felt this was the best way to haul it out. I asked who had shot the animal and one of them took credit, producing his hunting license. He told me how and where he had shot it with his partners confirming the story.

As was our usual procedure I wrote "one moose" and the date with my initials on the back of his license. This would indicate that he had taken his limit of moose and was not entitled to another that year. It was not uncommon for successful hunters to go out again to bag another if they hadn't been checked. We didn't have harvest tickets in those days.

I then pointed out that the animal would sour rapidly if they didn't get the hide off and cut it into quarters for cooling soon. They told me they were camped down in creek bottom of the next mining road and would be taking care of the meat as soon as they arrived. I shook my head, turned around again, and headed toward Livengood.

Later in the day I was headed back to the Fox check station and was waved down by two men standing by a flatbed truck. One was very excited and explained that he had shot a moose early in the morning and had gone back to Fairbanks to hire a truck to transport it home. When he returned, the moose was gone. I asked him where he had shot it and how big the animal was. After he described the location and the size of the animal I thought about the moose, the jeep, and the soldiers.

I invited him to accompany me, and we drove down the old mine road where the GIs were supposed to be camped. We located them staying with an old-timer in a dilapidated cabin. The moose had been skinned and the quarters were hanging on a meat rack. I gathered everyone together and asked the four military men again about the taking of the moose. This time the story differed from the first account. After further discussion, they admitted they had not killed it, but found it shot and lying in the woods. I said obviously then this moose belongs to this man who shot it, cleaned it, and then went for a truck to haul it back to Fairbanks. No, they said it couldn't be his because this moose had been recently killed, but had not been gutted.

Scratching my head, I turned to the hunter who was standing by my vehicle and asked, "You did gut it, didn't you?"

"No" he said, "I didn't have a knife with me at the time."

I stared at him in disbelief and questioned him further, "How long did it take you to get to town, hire a truck, and get back to the kill site?"

He looked sheepish and said he had been gone about six hours.

"Jeez," I said, "that moose would have been soured by the time you returned. As far as I'm concerned, it belongs to these men who salvaged it."

I marked his license with a moose taken, ending his hunt for the year, and told him he should thank these hunters for saving him from getting a citation for wanton waste of a game animal. I also lectured him about not hunting again without the necessary equipment to take care of any animal he might kill.

You think you've seen them all, but on these hunting patrols it was just one surprise after another.

Many hunters stopped at the check station for advice on the best areas to hunt and requested information or a clarification of the regulations. One individual came into the Fortymile check station wanting to know where he could go to shoot a wolf. How do you answer that one? The predator control boys had reported only a few wolves in the area and a recent flight made with Frank Glaser had revealed no wolf kills in the area. Also, how often does anyone ever see a wolf in the wild? Very seldom in those days. But being very professional, I pointed to a large river on the map that was mostly dried up that year. I suggested that many times wolves travel along dry river bars while hunting, and by positioning himself on a high point of land he might be successful.

He left thanking me and I went back to work helping to weigh a bunch of caribou that had just arrived. The day was a busy one, and along toward evening I had taken a break to cook dinner when in popped the wolf hunter with a big gray wolf in his pickup. He had gone where I told him to, found a good location, and sat on a log were he could see in both directions. Sure enough, after several hours of patiently scanning with his binoculars, a wolf came loping down the river bar and he nailed him with one shot. His comment to me was, "That was great, now can you tell me where I can go to get another one?"

How do you figure it? To him, I was the greatest guide ever, and to me, he was the luckiest hunter of the season.

Chapter 15

VICTIMS OF CIRCUMSTANCE

*I*n addition to hunting wolves as an enforcement agent, I was also required to do other types of control work. My rifle and shotgun became just as important to this job as they were when I was a professional trapper. These assignments included taking rogue bears, crippled or diseased animals, and collecting museum specimens. Some of the kills were a challenge, requiring precision shooting, while others were just a matter of walking up and dispatching a crippled animal with a well-placed shot that put it out of misery.

Moose that were crippled as result of collisions with cars, trucks, or trains were always given a priority to minimize this suffering. Unfortunately for us, it seemed that at least 90 percent of these occurred at night and usually during extreme cold spells. Most of the time the moose had broken legs and were not far from the site of the accident. Occasionally they wandered off and had to be tracked down. This was not always easy, especially if there was little or no snow and only a light blood trail. Throw in temperatures of −40°F or lower, and it becomes about as unpleasant a job as anyone wants to have. If we located the moose, we had to determine the extent of the injuries and decide whether or not to shoot the animal. If it had to be killed, we positioned ourselves for a quick brain shot to end the suffering immediately.

I learned early in my career that the issued .38 caliber revolver was next to worthless for such work. The massive bone structure protecting the small brain cavity of a moose can cause the bullet to change its course even at close range, making the shot ineffective. This occurred with my first road-crippled moose that was on the side of the highway with two broken legs. At least twenty people had collected at the scene when I arrived. I walked up with great poise, drew my service .38, and placed five shots where I felt the brain should be, all to no avail. Imagine my chagrin, as I had to walk back to my vehicle for a shotgun to finish the job. A hero I was not, but I had learned a valuable lesson and never used a .38 on a crippled animal again except when there was no other weapon available. We were eventually issued .357 revolvers, which were much more effective, but still not as lethal as a shotgun. I also found that a better technique was to have a partner keep the animal's attention while approaching from the rear, placing the bullet in the area where the cervical vertebra joins in the back of the skull.

I had my last problem with a .38 caliber revolver years later, trying to dispatch a black bear that was caught in a snare. This occurred at Ohtig Lake, about thirty-five miles northeast of Fort Yukon. I was in charge of a crew banding flightless ducks. This was part of a study to determine the effects to wildlife of the proposed Rampart Dam on the Yukon River. Over a period of six days we built a trap that was a hundred feet long by twenty-five feet wide and captured more than ten thousand diving ducks, mostly scaup, golden eye, buffleheads, and canvasbacks. It took three days to remove, weigh, measure, and band the majority of the birds. We never kept them in a trap for more than three days because of the food shortage.

Meanwhile, we were plagued by two black bears messing up our equipment and munching up the few weakened ducks that were recuperating in our sick bay. The bears became so brazen they walked into camp while we worked, prompting us to declare war before someone was hurt. We set a snare made from parachute cord on the incoming trail, not really thinking about what we would do if a bear got caught. Within fifteen minutes we were faced with a serious problem. The larger of the bears came into camp, placing his head directly in the noose and was immediately captured. He became enraged and started tearing up all the terrain within his reach. It was then that we checked our equipment only to learn that no one had a weapon. We had carried in so much equipment for this project that we hadn't even considered a firearm. "Didn't need one last time." These words were coming back to haunt Jim King and me.

One of our crew was a local trapper hired for the project. He indicated he had a .38 revolver in one of his line camps on the Porcupine River not far from our location. I loaded him in one of the floatplanes and flew him to the cabin. We returned with the well-used, rusted weapon to find the crew watching the bear from what they considered a safe distance. Since I was the crew leader and the most experienced with firearms I was undemocratically elected to take care of our newly acquired team member. As I approached, he became very alert and after several circles it was evident that I would only be allowed a front-on head shot. A carefully aimed shot between his eyes did not even knock him down. It just infuriated him.

Watching him go into action, tearing up the remaining willows and stunted spruce trees within his reach, was chilling to watch. I have no idea why the nylon cord didn't break, though I can attest that parachute cord is damn strong. Fortunately, he wasn't a large bear, probably weighing only 250 pounds, or the outcome would likely have been different. I was finally able to work my way to his blind side and place another shot behind the ear, which finished the job. With a great sigh of relief we went back to work and completed banding late that night.

We butchered the bear and took the meat to the closest Native village where it was gladly accepted and divided among some of the more needy families. Later we boiled the skull and checked it carefully to determine the damage caused by the two shots. The second had entered the brain causing instant death. The first, even though it entered the front of the skull in line with the brain cavity had been deflected by the thick bone, and angled out the side with little effect except to give him a giant headache. That was the last time I used a .38 for anything except target practice. There may be a message here for those who pack revolvers or pistols for protection against bears.

That was a particularly bad year for black bears. Apparently there was a high population of bears coupled with a shortage of adequate food, especially berries. One miner was killed and eaten in the Manley Hot Springs area and one of our biologists, checking study plots adjacent to where we were banding, got chased up a tree and had his foot badly chewed up. There were several other attacks that summer, including two campers mauled in a tent.

Blackies can be dangerous, although many people disregard this fact, including the miner who had lived in Alaska all his life. From all appearances, he had tried to chase the bear away from his cabin with a broom and ended paying with his life. They may not have the nasty temper of a grizzly, but pound for pound a black bear can be just as mean under the right conditions.

Like oil and water, bears and people just do not mix. One of the best ways to prove this is to put in an open-pit dump next to a military site and leave it unattended. It will become a five-star restaurant and attract bruins from miles around to feed on the exposed garbage. If the food supply runs low, the ever-hungry bears will follow their keen noses to the kitchen area of the camp, and sooner or later will break into buildings searching for something to eat. One military baker was badly mauled while working in the kitchen of the Tatalina radar site. Then you can add to this scenario curious onlookers, who will attract bears closer for good pictures by offering choice pieces of food. Eventually, someone either gets mauled or the camp commander has to account for all the funds he keeps spending for replacing doors and windows. The next step is to call the nearest wildlife agent and ask him to get rid of the bears.

At McGrath I answered many such complaints from the several radar sites located in the district. Mostly they concerned black bears, but occasionally the offender was a grizzly. Sometimes the problem could be solved through radio communication, advising the commander to have his men use scare tactics with flares and other pyrotechnics. This worked occasionally, but if the bears had become well established, it was only a temporary solution. Eventually I would have to make a trip to the base and spend a few days sizing up the problem.

The first requirement was a tour of the compound checking the buildings, established trails and, of course, the dump. Neglected dumps became havens for these carnivores and had to be covered or burned daily. Most base commanders were generally concerned and took the appropriate measures. However, some showed little interest. If on subsequent trips no improvements were made, or if more complaints were received, the matter was usually taken to the headquarters at Elmendorf Air Force Base in Anchorage. This always brought results, and I then received all the cooperation I needed.

Usually I spent a night at the base showing a few wildlife movies and giving a lecture on the dangers of feeding wild animals, illustrated by slides of mauled victims. Also, I warned about making pets of the cute foxes found at camp kitchens, followed by a talk on rabies and the painful treatment required when bitten. I always ended with a discussion of my job and responsibilities, making the point that although I was a wildlife protector, I was now being forced into the role of wildlife destroyer because of the indiscretion and neglect of a few.

The final task was killing the problem bears, which might take one day or several, depending on the number of animals. If there was no dump involved, I located the trail where the intruders entered the compound and picked out a spot to shoot from that would assure there wasn't any danger to any of the equipment or buildings. After that I questioned those who knew the most about the bears' habits and positioned myself on location during the most opportune hours. When the bruin showed up, a well-placed shot ended his military career. It was unfortunate because they were simply victims of circumstance, being in the wrong place at the wrong time, but there was usually no other way, and death was the reward of trying to survive in man's environment.

There were times when the bears were so numerous it seemed the entire population for hundreds of miles was concentrated in one area. Such was the case one summer at Tatalina, an Air Force radar site located about ten miles from McGrath. The military ran a sloppy dump that year, and large numbers of black bears were feeding on the raw garbage that was disposed of daily. When I received the call for help, I surveyed the problem with several high-ranking officers from the Alaska Command in Anchorage. I explained that trying to capture and move the bears would be costly and time-consuming. The FWS had no funds for these programs. After outlining what was entailed, including manpower, cost of traps and crates, plus airpower required to move the animals to another location, the officers agreed it was not within the military's budget either. There was only one solution, and it was not in the best interest of the bears. I was assured complete cooperation and a promise that the military would butcher and distribute some of the bear meat among Native villages.

My biggest problem that year was getting transportation to these sites. My assigned Cessna 180 was on floats, and Tatalina, like all radar sites, was accessible by wheel aircraft only. Fortunately, a local air-taxi operator owned several aircraft and he made a Cessna 195 on wheels available for my use whenever I needed it. There was the proviso that I would fly trips for him occasionally in my "spare time"! The Cessna then became my main mode of transportation for the "bear eradication program."

The dump was about a mile from the base, so I didn't have to worry about rifle shots endangering buildings or electronic equipment. Bear trails entered from several different directions like the spokes of a wheel, so I made myself a blind out of packing crates where I could view the entire area. There I waited throughout the day and night dispatching every bear that made his appearance. By the next day I had killed fourteen blackies. This must have been the biggest part of the dump population, since on several subsequent trips only two more were taken.

The largest animals were butchered. Several weighed more than five hundred pounds. It was interesting that when we examined the stomach contents of the bears they contained every type of garbage imaginable. We found waxed paper, labels, tarpaper, nails, and pieces of metal, leather, wood, and of course a variety of undigested foods. Some were so fat that their stomachs appeared to drag on the ground. A few showed scars from breaking and entering buildings on the base, the cause of this one-sided war. There could only be one winner, and unfortunately for the lords of the forest, they would be losers even though their domain had been invaded.

After I finished my part of the operation, the military went to work by burning and covering the dump daily. Regulations were directed to all military sites requiring that all dumps be covered regularly and all personnel were prohibited from feeding wild animals under penalty of a court martial. Other sites occasionally had problems and an infrequent bear or two had to be removed, but none were as bad as Tatalina.

The military and its equipment caused other problems for wildlife, which in turn added to our workload. For the most part, commanding officers were very cooperative, especially when one of the troops violated the game laws. Not only did the GI face a civilian court, but in many cases they were also required to face a court martial. Such was the case of a captain assigned to fly helicopters in Northwest Alaska. A picture of the officer, his helicopter, and a dead Dall sheep was anonymously sent to our office in Fairbanks. I took the photo of the commanding officer at Ladd Field and explained our concern of taking a sheep out of season with the use of a helicopter, especially a government helicopter. He had the picture blown up, identified the officer, and had him removed from duty until I arrived in Kotzebue. The captain pleaded guilty before the U.S. commissioner and received a substantial fine. He told me later that in addition to the court fine, he lost his captain's rank and was removed from his unit to a desk job. Other cases ended in much the same way.

Bombing ranges took their share of game even though the military took precautions to prevent any unnecessary killing. One such instance involved bombing practice by the Air Force at Big Delta. The target was a bunch of old oil drums located on the Delta River. The planes started at high altitude and dove on the target releasing five-hundred-pound bombs from a predesignated height above the ground. Unfortunately during the early morning hours, a group of buffalo moved out on the gravel bar in the general vicinity of the drums. One of the planes zeroed in on the buffalo during a high-speed dive, thinking they were the target drums, and released his bombs making a direct hit.

As I recall, six or seven animals died instantly and an unknown number were wounded. Several of us were sent to the area to check for crippled buffalo and try to verify the number involved. The seriously injured were to be dispatched immediately and survivors observed to determine if there was any chance of survival. We spent a week in the area tracking and locating six that were dragging broken legs. These were mercifully shot. Only one was fit for human consumption. We saw a few others that showed signs of having sustained injuries but appeared to be capable of surviving. These were photographed and we made our report to the regional office.

Several days later I was back in the area on a different investigation and found another cripple, which had to be shot. This one had a gaping hole in its side and was trailing part of its intestine. It was in terrible shape and obviously suffering. I dispatched it immediately. We found it difficult to believe the animal had lived ten days in that condition. Another case of wildlife and man not living well in harmony, and as usual the animals were the losers.

During the fall of 1954, I was given the assignment of killing one of the old male bison from the Big Delta herd. It was to be made into a full mount and displayed at the University of Alaska Museum. Since I didn't have any experience in skinning and preparing an animal that size for a museum, I requested, and was granted, the assistance of my good friend, Frank Glaser, whom I have mentioned before.

Frank was with the Predator Control Division and the old-timer of the outfit, having lived in Alaska since 1915. He had been a professional

We bagged this buffalo in October 1954 for the museum collection in Fairbanks. It is still on display at University of Alaska Museum.

hunter making his living in the 1920s by providing wild meat for the Alaska Road Commission crew at Black Rapids. They were building the Richardson Highway from Valdez to Fairbanks at the time. He was paid twenty-five cents a pound for moose and caribou, and fifty cents a pound for sheep. All of the kills had to be packed on his back to a designated location where they were picked up by horse and wagon and delivered to the camp.

Later he became a trapper at the Savage River country near what was then Mount McKinley National Park. He had worked on special projects for the old Biological Survey—forerunner of the FWS. In 1937, he became a full-time employee as a wolf trapper. One winter he was sent to Nunivak Island to make a count of the musk ox by foot and dog team. Other assignments took him all over Alaska, and he kept us younger guys entertained with his yarns of the "good old days." It was my pleasure to spend many days with this venerable hunter. He was the last of his breed, and I cherished every day I spent with him. In 1998, outdoor writer Jim Rearden wrote an award-winning and a most interesting book on Glaser's life titled *Alaska's Wolf Man: The 1915 Wilderness Adventures of Frank Glaser.*

On this particular assignment we spent several days driving around trying to locate a solitary bull beyond breeding age that would fill the requirements of the permit. Elsie was able to join the expedition as the official photographer and scribe. Once we killed the bison, copious measurements had to be taken both before and after the skinning. These measurements had to be accurate and recorded on several different forms.

After three or four days of combing the area, a fine specimen was located and taken. The skinning and measuring required many hours, with Elsie recording all the information with both pencil and camera. It was an excellent training session for me by the master, which I put to use many times in later years. The standing mount has been on display ever since and is viewed by many visitors each year.

In 1958 I was sent to Nunivak Island to collect a large solitary bull musk ox for the same museum. This time the animal was located from the air in late March from a ski-equipped Cessna 180. The weather was clear and cold, fortunately, considering the fact that high winds and poor visibility are very common in that part of Alaska.

I landed as close as I dared to the animal without scaring him off and walked to his location about one-half mile away. He was easily taken and I returned to the village of Mekoryuk to pick up two Natives for the skinning job. The needed measurements were taken in accordance with instructions from Jonas Bros. of Denver, the taxidermy firm that mounted all the important wildlife specimens for the university. They gave explicit instructions of the critical dimensions since the firm had never handled a full mount of a musk ox and wanted this to be a perfect specimen. This was not an easy task in the subzero weather with a steaming carcass to work on. The Eskimos were a happy crew, however, having butchered many hundreds of reindeer from the island's herd and they took it all in stride. They also knew they would have an opportunity to eat some fine steaks from the animal.

The head was the most difficult part of the operation because of the way the horns angle downward, close to the skull. Knowing this would take several hours in itself, the hide was removed with the head attached and the job finished inside a heated building. Additionally, the pelvic bone plus a complete leg bone, both front and back, had to be cleaned and shipped with the hide to assist in building the body form. The meat was then distributed to the needy families in the village. One of the families invited me to dinner, and I tasted my first musk-ox meat. It was excellent and I could understand why they were so heavily hunted in the early 1900s.

The salted hide, skull, and bones were boxed and shipped according to instructions, and six months later the completed specimen was on display beside the buffalo.

Other smaller animals and birds were taken for museums and universities in the course of my duties. Geese and ducks were collected from different parts of the Territory to help determine the range of species and subspecies. Most were skinned and preserved before shipping. Diseased animals such as rabid fox were killed whenever they made an appearance in a village, providing we could get there in time. Otherwise we gave permission to someone in the village to take the animal. The head had to be removed wearing rubber gloves and shipped out for examination. Not a pleasant job.

All things considered, and being a hunter by nature, I felt that this part of the job had its compensations. No one likes to see animals suffer, and being in a position to put crippled wildlife out of misery had its rewards. It was never satisfying having to kill and remove animals just because they did not fit in man's environment, but it was and still is an unavoidable fact of life.

There is no such thing as the utopian balance of nature as preached by some, and as long as man and wildlife must coexist, it will have to be by man's standards. To believe otherwise is to foster mass losses of wildlife to starvation and disease. Removing surplus stocks by sound management and controlled killing is as necessary as stocking depleted populations.

Chapter 16

SEARCH AND RESCUE

*O*ne phase of our job never detailed in the manual or by policy was our participation in search-and-rescue missions. It was not the responsibility of the Fish and Wildlife Service to search for missing planes, boats, or persons, but because of the size and remoteness of the Territory, we responded to local calls for assistance without hesitation. The unwritten policy allowed us this prerogative, but if a search went on for a more than a few days we had to back off and turn it over to the military. After that we assisted only when authorized by the regional office.

At the McGrath headquarters, appeals for help were usually relayed by radio or word of mouth, and most often involved someone overdue on a trip. If it was a missing plane the Civil Aviation Administration (CAA), forerunner of the Federal Aviation Administration (FAA), was usually involved and would have either a flight plan or knowledge of the pilot's route of flight. We received information on missing boats or dog teams (there were no snowmachines in those days) from families or friends. Both commercial and private pilots donated their time without hesitation, knowing full well that they could be the objects of the next search. This alliance gave pilots a comforting feeling. It was nice knowing that if you had to make an emergency landing, someone would be out looking as soon as the alarm was set off.

Sometimes the search involved friends and became very personal. Such was the search in 1958 for Paul Tovey and Phil Pentecost, two schoolteacher acquaintances, who were overdue on a short trip in Paul's plane. They had departed the village of Minto during the Christmas holidays for a day of wolf hunting and had not returned. Phil's wife, Dorothy, sent out the alarm with a request for an immediate search because of the severe cold weather. I was briefed at the McGrath CAA flight station and told that Dorothy had indicated they had planned to hunt the Kantishna River country. I was familiar with that country and advised the coordinators in Fairbanks that I would land and check with the trappers in the area to determine if they had seen or heard the plane.

Paul Tovey had worked a few years for the U.S. Fish and Wildlife Service as a biologist. The Pentecosts were close friends, and I had spent many enjoyable evenings with them at their home when they were teachers at Tuluksak on the lower Kuskokwim River. Phil was an avid hunter, and we talked many times into the wee hours of the morning about rifles and bullet velocities. I knew that he and Paul were both capable of taking care of themselves in the wilderness. However, if there were any injuries involved, it would be difficult at best to survive in the extreme cold.

My field diary indicated that I departed from McGrath on the morning of December 29 with the temperature registering –42°F and only one magneto firing the Cessna 180 engine. Normally I would never have contemplated a trip in that temperature with a faulty ignition system; however, friends' lives were at stake. I searched the Kantishna and Toklat River areas and landed at several trapline camps to talk with the trappers. None had seen or heard any aircraft flying around during the past four days. The cold spell had them holed up at their main camps. Because noise carries greater distances in the cold dense air, they felt they would have heard any aircraft engine cruising the area. They had all heard my Cessna for several minutes before I came into view. With darkness arriving by 3:00 P.M. on those short days of December, I went on to Fairbanks and had a mechanic work on the magneto.

The next morning I was off again with the temperature registering –46°F degrees, but this time the ignition system was working properly. I flew to areas that, according to search headquarters, had not yet been searched. This included watersheds of the Teklanika and Toklat Rivers to their headwaters, then back to the Moose River, Birch Creek, McKinley Fork, and Lake Minchumina. I landed and talked with several more trappers who indicated that on the days in question it had been snowing hard with low ceilings and not suitable for flying in that part of the country. This information was passed on to the control center and the locale eliminated from the search plan. I returned to McGrath.

The weather got colder and the only flying was by the military with multiengine aircraft at night, looking for campfires. I was very upset at not being allowed to participate, but policy dictated no flying at below

–50°F. Rumors abounded and I remember going into depression on New Year's Eve when one of the CAA communicators said that he had heard their frozen bodies had been found in a cabin on the Kantishna. That was my search area, and I felt completely let down, thinking that I must have missed seeing evidence of them that might have saved their lives. The information turned out to be false, however, but I kept having a nagging feeling that I had missed them somewhere.

After the weather moderated, it got nasty, and heavy snow fell for several days, eliminating any search efforts. Everyone knew the chances of finding them alive now were remote. The search continued for several weeks, and I continued my efforts by searching the Nowitna River watersheds, locating several big bands of wolves, but no aircraft. Finally the remnants of their aircraft were found. It had crashed and burned just a few miles from Minto, and they had been killed on impact. It was a sad day, but at least their bodies were found and the matter laid to rest.

There are times however, when lost planes are not found, causing added grief to relatives and friends when the fate of a loved one is unknown. Such was the case of my brother-in-law, Johnny Sommer. In November 1954, he flew his Piper Pacer from Nulato to Koyukuk, then departed later that evening for Ruby, a distance of only forty-five miles. Accompanying him was his friend Phillip Huhndorf, who was getting married the next day. They never arrived at Ruby.

We conducted a search effort that lasted for more than a week and were unsuccessful at locating any clues to the fate of the two men. Both were experienced woodsmen, having lived all their lives along the Yukon River, and we knew that if they had survived a crash, they would endure for a long time, even though the temperature was well below zero. Based on this, the effort ranged well beyond what should have been just a straight-line search between the two villages, all to no avail. The conclusion: they had been forced down onto the river and disappeared through one of the many sections that had not been completely frozen.

John Sommer, Johnny's dad and my father-in-law, was more than eighty at the time and could never accept the fact that his son was gone. Neither could his wife, Agnes, nor the rest of the family. Had the two men been found and put to rest the family would have been at ease; however, there was always the nagging feeling they had possibly survived and were suffering somewhere in the wilderness. It was a constant vexing source of grief to John until he passed away, never knowing what had happened to his son.

Five years later, the pilot of a small plane approaching Galena caught the glint of sun reflecting from metal in the thick timber not far from the runway. A search party went out and there they located the wreckage of Johnny's plane. It was in a direct line from Koyukuk to Ruby, completely hidden by dense spruce trees. Galena is halfway between the two villages. Why it crashed no one will ever know, but the heavy timber had closed in over the demolished aircraft and concealed the men's fate.

There have been many aircraft that have disappeared and never been found in Alaska. Many have been concealed by timber just as Johnny's was. Some have been covered by glaciers and others are probably resting at the bottom of an unknown lake.

There was also the famous search for Clarence Rhode, the regional director of the Fish and Wildlife Service, his son, Jack, and Stan Frederickson, the game management agent in charge of the Fairbanks District. Little did we realize that the fate of the plane, a Grumman Goose, would be concealed from us for more than twenty years. An account of that search is detailed in the next chapter.

Occasionally we were involved in a search that not only had a happy ending but provided some humor as well. One that had an interesting ending occurred at the village of Old Crow, Yukon Territory, Canada. I went with Fred Woldstad, chief of the State Fish and Wildlife Protection Division, to Old Crow in January 1961 to fly a joint patrol of the Canada–Alaska boundary with the Royal Canadian Mounted Police. We had a mutual problem of trappers crossing the border back and forth, hunting and trapping in violation of both countries.

On the day we arrived, the temperature plummeted to –50°F, and a dense ice fog covered the valley preventing any more flying for a while. Staffing the post were Constables Jim Lambert and Duane Crosland, who proved to be gracious hosts and provided us with many interesting insights into the problems of policing this section of the Arctic. The Mounties were still using dog teams to patrol this district, which included the villages of Fort McPherson, Arctic Red River, and Hershel

Island on the coast, plus all the country in between. The previous year Constable Lambert made a patrol to all these villages, logging more than eight hundred miles in nineteen days. Prior to his assignment at Old Crow, he had been stationed at Hershel Island, patrolling more than five thousand miles a year with the use of dogs.

At the time, Old Crow and all the other villages in the Northwest Territories were dry, meaning liquor could not be legally sold or brought into town. The police kept a tight rein on the consumption of alcoholic beverages, and consequently there were few serious problems. This was certainly refreshing to Fred and me as we shared with them the serious liquor problem that was occurring in Alaska's Native villages. At this settlement anyone who was arrested for violating the drinking ban was detailed to cutting and splitting wood for the Mounties' house and barracks. There weren't many repeat offenders.

The ice fog dissipated on the third day even though the temperatures remained in the –40°F range. Sgt. Jim Lambert approached us at breakfast asking if we would be willing to conduct a search. One of the Native women in the village was concerned about her husband, who was away trapping on the Whitestone River. According to Jim, sometime around Christmas she had found dead mice in her cabin—an ominous sign that, according to the Athabascan belief in that region, indicated someone in her immediate family had died. She had every reason to believe it was her husband. It was the responsibility of the RCMP to respond to these requests whenever possible, and if our plane was available, he would supply the gas to check out the situation for the worried woman. We agreed and prepared the aircraft for takeoff.

After heating the plane, Jim arrived with his survival gear and the village chief, Charlie Peter. Charlie would be our guide since he knew the location of the trapline in question. After takeoff from the ski strip on the river, we climbed to five thousand feet and found a temperature inversion with warmer air to fly in. It took about an hour to fly to the main trapline cabin located on a bank of the river. We could see dog-team trails leading in several directions but no signs of life at the cabin. The dogs and sled were gone, indicating that our trapper was traveling. I decided to make a low pass to determine the feasibility of landing on the river and decide which trail was the most recently used. This could direct us in the right direction, saving time and effort.

As we descended in slow flight to treetop level, we immediately learned two things. First, the snow was very deep. The depth of the dog-team trail was all the evidence we needed. A takeoff out of the narrow river would be extremely difficult with the load we were carrying. Second, it was damn cold. I eased the throttle into climb power and the engine balked momentarily from the super-cold air running through the carburetor. We had to follow a few bends as we gained full power allowing us to climb back into the warmer air. Looking back after we gained altitude we could see a vapor trail over that part of the river we had just flown. The temperatures had to be in the –60°s down there—not a place to land, we all agreed. Later, when we were discussing the flight at the barracks, Jim indicated he had become quite "shook up" when the engine coughed, and was preparing himself for a forced landing. He was more than happy to give up any thoughts of checking out the cabin.

We followed what we thought was the most recent dog-team trail across open meadows, along sloughs, and through spruce thickets in an easterly direction for about forty-five miles. It ended up at the mess wanigan of an oil-exploration party that had been proceeding north with five tractors and sleds. The dog team was tied up outside and the trapper was obviously inside enjoying a warm meal and companionship. There was no landing site available so we flew back to Old Crow to report our findings to the trapper's wife. Jim indicated that she would have mixed emotions about our findings and the fact the dead mice had lied. The search was recorded in the journals of the RCMP as another successful episode in the annals of the famed northern police organization.

Then there was the interesting search and rescue of the mysterious Richard Hartley in 1959. I was in my McGrath office on April 14 doing beaver sealing reports when one of the local Bush pilots advised me that he had just completed a flight to upper Big River to drop off an outsider, who, with his meager outfit, planned to prospect that area. The pilot said the man told him that he planned to build a raft after breakup and float down to McGrath. I wondered if the man had enough supplies for what would be at least a month in the foothills of the Alaska Range, so I checked with the clerk at the Northern Commercial Company. She listed his purchases as:

8 lbs. beans	1 lb. rice
3 lbs. dried apples	1 lb. salt
2 lbs. sugar	1 can pepper
3 lbs. Crisco	1 lb. tea
1 lb. margarine	Assorted candy bars

Since he was camped in good mountain-sheep country and had a rifle, I thought it wise to contact him. Certainly since he was a non-resident, he didn't have a valid hunting license, and I wanted to make sure he knew it would be illegal for him to kill any game to add to his meager food supplies. His plight would not qualify him for emergency "taking" under the game laws.

On April 20 I landed at Hartley's camp. He was living under a small tarp, and his cooking kit consisted of a small frying pan and pot. The snow was three feet deep and, having no snowshoes, he could not extend his trails more than a few hundred yards from camp looking for firewood. After introducing myself and advising him about the game laws, he said he was aware that he could not legally shoot game, but was not worried. He had camped a few winters in the Black Hills of North Dakota with limited supplies and felt he would be able to make out okay. Hartley did admit, however, that he had not counted on the snow being so deep or the weather being so cold. I asked if he was familiar with these mountain rivers in the spring and he said, "No!"

I decided he could not make it here until breakup and, because he would not consider returning to McGrath, I moved him downstream about eight miles to an unused cabin. This would at least afford him good shelter from the heavy wind and rains. I estimated his total outfit, including food, rifle, ax, Swede saw, and sleeping bag weighed approximately sixty pounds. He was wearing a wool jacket, ski cap, wool pants, and shoepacks. Temperatures had been recorded down to −20°F during the nights at Farewell, about sixty miles away.

By May 28 no one had heard or seen Hartley, so I made a trip to the cabin on Big River to see how he was doing. The Cessna 180 was now on floats. The river where the cabin was located was not suitable for a landing, so I had to be satisfied by checking it from the air. It appeared vacant, so I flew the river to its mouth on the Kuskokwim and then downstream to McGrath. There was no trace of him.

On June 6, Hartley still had not shown up, so I made another trip up Big River. Len Jones, the Weather Bureau station manager at McGrath, agreed to go along as observer. There was no sign of Hartley on the way up, but on the way back we saw him waving frantically from a sandbar, where he had stamped out the word "HELP." He had heard the plane as we made our way upriver. At the time he was walking in the brush and not visible, so he knew we had not seen him. He had quickly prepared the signal in the event we made a return flight over his location. We made a difficult landing in the narrow, swift glacier river choked with debris and fallen trees.

Hartley was hardly recognizable from weight loss. His clothes were torn, and his shoepacks were worn through. His rifle was all that remained of his outfit. He said he had lost three rafts and for six days had been making extremely slow progress. Walking the game trails along the riverbank and through dense growths of willows, alder, and spruce was taking all his strength. Without insect repellent, he had been plagued by mosquitoes and was a mass of bites and sores. The only food he had eaten for more than two weeks were two squirrels which he had shot and cooked on a stick. He told us that he had just about abandoned any hope of walking out to any settlement. As we flew back to McGrath over the route he was trying to follow, we agreed that he probably would never have made it.

Later the clerk told me that as Hartley was buying a new outfit of clothes he kept remarking that he was happy to be alive and pleased because he found what he had gone out looking for. No one ever knew what it was he had "found," and to my knowledge he never returned.

He was one of the lucky ones, though. Many newcomers have disappeared, never to be found again. Others were found, but only after it was too late, and all we could do was ship their bodies back to the families.

For my efforts in the Hartley episode I received the Department of Interior's Valor Award. As the commendation was being read at the Department's award ceremony in Washington, D.C., I could only think of how closely related the circumstances are that make you either a champion or a failure. Had I wrecked the aircraft during that delicate landing, I would have received a different kind of award, but because I was successful, I enjoyed a bit of recognition. Like most, I'm convinced everything in life is connected to timing, and in this case, my timing was right, and so was Hartley's.

Chapter 17

ENGINE FAILURE

$J$was stationed in McGrath when, on August 23, 1958, I received instructions to fly to the Brooks Range and do a route search for Grumman Goose N720. Our Regional Director Clarence Rhode was the pilot. Aboard was Stan Frederickson, game management agent from Fairbanks, and Clarence's son, Jack. They were on a reconnaissance sheep patrol operating out of Porcupine Lake and were to return to Fairbanks on August 22. The weather had been bad and radio signals nonexistent. I flew the route he was supposed to have taken from Porcupine Lake back to Fairbanks, where he had a speaking engagement that evening. No trace of the aircraft.

On the 25th, search efforts were put under the direction of the 10th Rescue military search-and-rescue group in Fairbanks. The northern half of Alaska was sectioned off into numbered grids, and search pilots were assigned a specific area each day. As many as twenty-eight planes were involved during the first few weeks as we searched an area of more than 300,000 square miles (about twice the area of California). More than 2,000 flying hours were totaled, with 260 people involved, all to no avail.

For my part, it was a frustrating effort with many tight-jawed turns in fog-shrouded canyons trying to check every nook and cranny that might conceal a black-and-orange Grumman. This was our chief who was missing, along with a fellow agent, and a young college student who had but six hours of course work to complete before receiving his degree. Each day we started out full of enthusiasm, especially if the weather was good, which was not often, thinking that this was the day they would be found. After several weeks, as we began retracing search areas for the third and fourth time, however, we all knew the chances of finding them alive became more remote.

Interestingly, when the military took over the search efforts, they were having trouble with radio communications caused by the solar disturbances prevalent at the time. The Fish and Wildlife radio network we were using was made up of World War II vintage equipment the military had decided was obsolete. We had our own high-frequency channels of 5907.5 and 3027.5. Our planes had Lear T-30 radios with a tunable antenna. We had set up two of our search bases at Bettles and Porcupine Lake and were able to set up a good radio communication network with our Fairbanks office. All of our position reports were made every half-hour to the secretary.

When the officer in charge of the search found out how effective our radio network was, he decided to set up his headquarters at our Fairbanks office. This worked very well, much to the chagrin of the military brass. I marveled each time one of the military planes had to relay his coordinates to my Cessna 180 and request that I forward them to headquarters with my small Lear T-30 radio.

Then there was the day I wished I didn't have such a good radio. One of the military DC-4s flying above the overcast had spotted what appeared to be a wrecked aircraft. They were circling a hole in the cloud deck and wanted a small aircraft to identify what they were seeing. I was north of Bettles, so they gave me the location and asked me to check out the Atigun Pass area. I flew east under a solid overcast of 2,500 feet, cutting across the headwaters of creeks to get there as soon as possible. Big mistake, because after a short time I had no idea what watershed I was on. Not lost, just misplaced. I received several radio calls asking for my position, and I did my best to tell them where I was, explaining that I was having to make several weather detours.

Finally, I located the right river and started talking with the pilot of the DC-4. He tried to direct me but without visual contact, it was impossible. Nothing to do but proceed up through the overcast and join him. I flew north out of the mountains and spiraled up into the clear. He circled the area and moved so I could take a look. Yup, there was something down in the snow at the head of a creek. It looked to me like a snow slide, but positive confirmation was necessary. Back down I went underneath the cloud deck and made my way to the drainage.

When we were on the right creek, we could tell that whatever it was that we'd seen was in a cirque with very little maneuvering room for the Cessna.

"Okay, here's what we do," I instructed my observer. "I'm going to fly up the creek and make a turn at the head of the canyon, and you identify the object."

Simple, right? Sure! Flying up to the head of the stream at slow flight with twenty degrees of flap, making a tight turn to get back down again was going to take all my concentration and abilities. I made the first attempt and the observer said I was banked so tightly he was unable to see enough to make a determination. So it was back again, this time making a turn in the opposite direction. He said he was sure it was a snow slide but would need one more pass to be positive. Jeeeez! We did it though and he made it official. It was just rocks that had come loose and slid down the side of the mountain taking the snow with it. I radioed in the news and learned that all radio communications had been on hold waiting for my report. After I flew back to the main river and was able to relax, I realized I had chewed up my gum and swallowed it on one of the turns. Damn. And I didn't have another stick. That one was definitely a pucker factor of 10.

On a later flight I was sent to search one of the six-mile square areas on the north side of the Brooks Range. According to an overflight made by a military aircraft, the area was supposed to have searchable weather. Sig Olson was my observer, and we left Fort Yukon early in the morning. There was a heavy overcast and as we made our way up the Junjik River, there was a very strong wind flowing through the mountains from the south. I chose the pass that took us into the headwaters of the Ivishak River. The head of this pass was just fifteen miles east of the one that Clarence had taken on his fateful flight.

A heavy overcast seemed to be lowering as we headed up the East Chandalar to the Junjik River, which would then take us through the low pass in the mountains to the search area. With the thickening clouds, there was a strong south wind funneling through the passes, causing a great deal of turbulence. As we approached the summit, we were a little apprehensive. The weather was getting worse.

I knew we had to negotiate a tight turn to get through to the valley before we could tell how bad it was on the other side. Once I committed we'd have to go through because the canyon was too narrow to turn around. I tried to slow up for a look at the point of no return. The strong tail wind and turbulence, however, made it impossible, and before we could say "yea" or "nay" we had no choice but to fly to the other side. Sort of like threading a needle the morning after the night before. I was amazed the wings managed to stay on in the severe turbulence.

The only choice now was to fly east along the foothills, passing three miles south of Porcupine Lake. I had the lake as my ace in the hole in the event we were unable to get back to the Junjik. After what seemed like an eternity, but was in fact only about eight minutes, we came to the Canning River and the low pass to Spring Creek, which led to the Junjik and out into better weather. We called headquarters, gave a weather report, and received coordinates for another search area. Over the assigned sector, we began a detailed search of the heavily wooded countryside with few landmarks to guide us. Sig Olson was trying to keep track of our progress on his map, but we could never agree as to our exact position.

Then it happened. The cabin filled with smoke and the oil pressure gauge started fluctuating. Unbelievably, we were over a nice round lake with plenty of room to make a safe landing. I say unbelievably because we had been flying over nothing but timber for quite a while and there, underneath us, was the only lake available in that section of the world. We were at five hundred feet, so there wasn't much time to do anything but shut the engine down and land. The smoke was thick, and even with both side windows open, visibility was restricted. The landing was tense but uneventful. When we came to a stop we each stepped out on a float. I asked Sig to open the cowling on his side so we could assess the problem.

From where I stood, I could see oil pouring from the underside of the cowling. At first it appeared to be a broken oil line. While I looked for the source I heard a strange banging noise coming from the other side. I asked Sig if he knew what was causing the banging.

"Man, that's my knees shaking against the side of the plane. And I can't get them to stop," he answered.

After laughing I decided we had to get to shore. Sig, being an old canoe man, grabbed the paddle that was tied on the spreader bars and began making like a voyageur stroking for the nearest beach. After every ten or fifteen strokes he would cup his hands and yell "HELP!" at the top of his lungs. We both laughed and wondered who besides the two loons at the far end of the lake would hear his plaintive call out here in the middle of nowhere. That didn't bother Sig. He kept yelling anyway.

Once ashore I found that the source of the leak was a ruptured oil cooler. I had Sig string out the radio's trailing antenna, and we had our second piece of luck. We were unable to talk to Fairbanks but our Anchorage aircraft office, more than five hundred miles away, came in loud and clear. I apprised them of our problem and in no time Tom Wardleigh, assistant aircraft supervisor, was en route in a Grumman Goose with Jerry Lawhorn, the chief mechanic, and replacement oil cooler and oil.

We removed the rest of the cowling and oil cooler, then all we could do was sit and wait. We couldn't help remarking what a beautiful day it was and how fortunate we really were. Earlier we had been flying in very poor weather over some of the worst terrain one could ever encounter. Had the oil cooler chosen that time to rupture, we would have been in a real emergency situation. Making a forced landing in that rocky topography and in those turbulent conditions could have been catastrophic. Then with additional luck the engine decided to malfunction over a lake suitable for landing instead of having to put down in the heavy timber, which could have caused injuries and severe damage to the aircraft. So I ask, "Who was in charge of that flight?"

The only thing I can take credit for is making an acceptable dead stick (no power) landing. I'm a firm believer in God and am convinced he definitely intervened in our behalf. A lake was provided along with good weather and fantastic radio conditions. You can't beat that.

Several hours later Tom arrived with the cooler and oil. He had been unable to locate a gasket, but had a sheet of gasket material and began tracing out the pattern and cutting one out. With everybody working together we soon had the new oil cooler on and all the bolts safety wired. A test run showed everything was working normally, so we all shook hands and went our separate ways.

After twenty minutes of flying toward Fort Yukon, the oil temperature started to climb. I was in radio contact with Tom, who was returning to Anchorage, and told him I would have to land if it got much higher.

There was a long pause and he replied. "That gasket is made like a square figure eight and I'll bet we left out the middle section allowing the oil to bypass part of the cooler, causing it to overheat. You'll have to take it apart and check it out."

We landed in a lake about twenty miles northeast of Fort Yukon to let the temperature cool. We finally limped into the village just before dark. We would wait until morning to tackle the oil cooler again.

Next morning we removed the oil cooler and found that the gasket indeed had been cut wrong so we went to work cutting out another one. This was a trial-and-error process with many choice words as we labored on the muddy bank of the Yukon River, trying to keep from dropping parts, bolts, and screws into the murky waters. Being a mechanic was not my bag, and patience was not my virtue, so the pressure mounted. After attaching the cooler, we again safety wired the bolts holding it in place. This required threading a long piece of stainless wire through a hole in each bolt head and making the necessary twists and turns to keep it from coming loose. My knuckles kept getting barked from scrapes along pieces of metal. All this time Sig was making with the smiles and cheerful remarks as he handed me tools and parts.

Just as I was about to try another shortcut, he stopped and said, "My Grandmother use to say, 'Be the job big or small, do it well or not at all!' "

This broke the ice and we stopped to have a breather and chuckle before putting the cowling back on and replacing the many screws that held it in place. Before the job was finished, that phrase was repeated several times and became the theme for the remainder of the search.

Not until twenty-one years later was the mystery of Clarence Rhode and the missing Grumman Goose solved. On August 23, 1979, two women hikers traversing a 5,700-foot pass at the head of the Ivishak River spotted the wreckage of an aircraft. At first they thought the patch of orange was lichen against the dark grays of the ridge. A closer look revealed an airplane smashed against the mountainside. They found significant evidence, including the flight logs, which were turned over to the National Transportation Safety Board. An investigator identified the plane as the missing N720 at 68.34N and 147.15W thus ending the mystery of our missing leader's fate. He was exactly where he was should have been crossing that pass into the Wind River. We can only guess, but perhaps the visibility was too low to allow him to cross into the next valley and he was unable to make the necessary turn in the narrow cirque to get back down the Ivishak.

I had checked that pass several times, first on the route search and later as the search intensified. I wondered how I could have missed the wreckage until I talked to Jon Osgood, the NTSB investigator. He said on the first attempt to reach the wreck with a helicopter they could not locate it. They had to return and get one of the hikers to join them, and even then they had difficulty locating the plane.

How many patches of orange lichen or dwarf birch with orange and red fall colors I checked during the search, I'll never know. It was considerable. Also the wreckage was scattered in small pieces over a rock and shale formation, making it extremely difficult to see. Under these circumstances it would have been a chance sighting at best, and unfortunately no search plane had happened over the right spot at the right time. Also a light snow had covered the entire area shortly after the search began.

Today, hanging on a wall in my house, is a reminder from Sig that takes me back to those days in my memory. It is one of his famous cartoons showing a pilot working on an airplane engine. Nuts and bolts are flying in every direction and the pilot is obviously very frustrated. It is captioned, "Be the job big or small, do it well or not all." The frame is made from sloppily cut molding fastened together with bent nails. It's a cherished possession, a reminder of a memorable occasion and a good friend.

Chapter 18

LEGAL BEAVER

*T*he best example of good wildlife management and law enforcement working as a team has to be the reestablishment of Alaska's beaver population. This, the largest member of the rodent family, was heavily harvested for its valuable fur, and in the early 1900s was brought to near extinction in the Territory.

No animal played a bigger part in the history of North America than the beaver. Fur trappers and fur companies, such as the Hudson's Bay Company, pushed across the continent seeking beaver pelts and laying the foundation for future settlements from coast to coast. For years hat makers used only beaver fur for felting material in Europe, and thousands of pelts were shipped to this market annually in the eighteenth century.

The famous Hudson's Bay Company extended its fur trade routes as far as Fort Yukon in Alaska. Trade goods were transported from England to Montreal by ship, then canoes, and on the backs of voyageurs across Canada to the confluence of the Porcupine and Yukon Rivers, the farthest west of that company's stronghold. It took several seasons for goods to arrive at all of the company's Canadian forts. The same brigades returned east with the beaver pelts, which eventually landed in England. In the American west it was the Rocky Mountain Fur Trade, and mountain men pursued this valuable fur animal throughout the uncharted country. This unsatisfied search for beaver pelts opened up the country for future settlement.

It was not the steel trap, but the rifle that caused the overharvest of this furbearer in Alaska. Shooting swimming animals after the winter ice melted off in lakes and rivers was the easiest and most common way to take beaver. It was also the most wasteful. After spending six months under the ice and snow, these animals become quite tame after breakup. The hunter had only to paddle around the lakes and streams at his leisure watching for the telltale V in the water, which marked the swimming animal. A well-placed bullet did the rest. Spring was the time to harvest both beaver and muskrats.

Unfortunately, not all bullets were well placed, and therein was the problem. If the beaver was not killed outright before he expelled

From left, trapper Nick Mellick Sr., U.S. Commissioner Dave Leach, and, standing, fur-buyer Sam Applebaum look on as I'm sealing beaver at Sleetmute, April 1957.

the air in his lungs, he would sink and was lost to the marksman. Early trappers I talked with admitted that losing three out of five beaver they shot was not uncommon. It was this method of harvest that was the demise of the beaver, and by the 1920s the population was at an all-time low.

The Alaska Game Law of 1925 provided the basis for wildlife management in Alaska. It set up a game commission of five appointed members, one from each of the four judicial districts and the fifth from the Bureau of Biological Survey (later to become the U.S. Fish and Wildlife Service). The commission had the power to set the seasons and bag limits for the taking of game, fish, and fur animals, and employ game wardens for enforcement of the act. It set up provisions for licenses, permits, and a record-keeping system for recording the numbers of game taken. Under this authority the commission authorized a system for marking legally taken beaver skins before they were sold.

To stop the excessive killing, the first action was to close the season completely. The 1925 regulations stated: "Beaver and marten— No open season and may not be taken at any time." (There was also a concern for marten, which were heavily trapped. Later a limit of ten was imposed.) Then for the next three years, beaver season was opened for the month of May with a limit of twenty. Shooting with a rifle was permitted, but not by shotgun. The seasons for 1929–31 were entirely closed. The season opened again in 1933 in the upper Tanana and Yukon River watersheds from January 1 through March 31 with a limit of ten.

Also introduced that year was a new provision under the methods and means of the definition of "taking," which read, "Beaver may be taken only by the use of steel traps, but such traps shall not be placed within twenty-five feet of any beaver house or den." (This was to avoid taking the young, or kit beavers, as they are called, that didn't swim very far from the house.) "No beaver may be taken by or with the aid of a rifle or shotgun or other firearm."

In 1933–34, the season opened with a limit of fifteen. It closed again in 1935; however, for the 1936–37 season, the commission changed the methods and means again to allow for the use of rifles. When the season opened again in 1937–38, the limit was set at ten, where it remained until 1954, when the numbers of beaver started increasing again.

In 1940–41 the commission took another big step. The seasons had been closed as needed in those districts where the populations remained low without the desired results. The commissioners were aware that shooting was a problem; however, there was considerable pressure by the trappers to continue that method of harvest, so they wisely chose another course of action. They limited the taking of beaver to the early spring months while the lakes were still frozen. This was the most effective measure taken because it excluded shooting completely and forced trappers to learn to trap under the ice. The season opened in February and closed on March 31, except for a few areas that closed on April 10. With the rifle eliminated and a limit of ten beaver, enforced by the use of an intensive sealing program, the animal made a spectacular recovery during the next fifteen years.

My own experiences with the beaver program were both interesting and rewarding. Traveling to the Native villages during and after the beaver-trapping season to seal the pelts was the highlight of the year's activities. As the spring days became longer and warmer, flying was more enjoyable, people on traplines became more active, and there was a general feeling of accomplishment by everyone after the short, cold days of winter in the Interior. When the trapping season ended on March 31, people congregated in the villages, which was a time for holidays. Each village had own its Fur Rendezvous, with dog-team races, snowshoe races, and dances in the evenings. It was a time to renew friendships and hold family reunions after a winter of isolation for most.

Prior to the season, we hired a tagging officer in each village (as I did with poor, underpaid Elsie), usually a schoolteacher or postmaster. The ten cents per skin could amount to one hundred or one hundred and fifty dollars a season in the bigger beaver-trapping villages.

There were two ways for a trapper to legalize his beaver skins. In either case an affidavit had to be completed stating his name, address, and license number, the location where the beaver were trapped, and the number of skins being presented. (Natives were not required to have a license prior to statehood.) If it was a tagging officer handling the skins, he or she would fold the affidavit into an envelope, place a special string through a leg opening of the hide (or hides if there was more than one), through a grommet in the envelope and pass the ends through special holes in a lead seal. The lead would then be squeezed together with serial-numbered pliers. Only FWS agents were allowed to remove the affidavit or cut the strings for sealing. Once sealed, the pelts were then legal to sell or transport within the Territory. Usually the trappers would tag their beaver and sell them to a local trader or store owner. The trader would hold them for sealing, after which they could be legally shipped out of Alaska. Most went to the Seattle Fur Exchange and were sold at auction.

The seals we used were metal, similar to those used on railroad boxcars. They were numbered in sequence with one hundred to a bundle. One end had a locking device, and the other end was perforated. The seal was passed through a leg hole, one to a skin, and pushed into the locking device. Once the locking pin was in place, the seal could not be removed without breaking it or cutting the seal. Each seal number was carefully recorded on the affidavit of the trapper who had taken the beaver. At the end of the season, the seal numbers were recorded on a special form beside the trapper's name, a tedious job for us non-office types. The forms and affidavits were sent to Juneau for filing; thus there was a complete record of each beaver taken by trapper, date, and locality.

While I was working out of the Fairbanks office in the early 1950s, the biggest concentration of beaver was taken in the mid-Yukon and Koyukuk River watersheds. We usually operated out of the village of Koyukuk, which was centrally located within this vast area. Trader and store owner Dominic Vernetti usually bought more skins than any other trader in Alaska. Weather permitting, we made the rounds of the villages every two weeks, sealing all the beaver that had been purchased, thus enabling the buyers to ship them to market.

It was not uncommon to walk into a trading post in late March and find several piles of tagged skins, five to six feet high, stacked along a wall. Whenever I looked at one of these piles, representing the limits of many trappers, I thought about the fur trade of the eighteenth century in Canada. In those days the value of a six-foot-long musket was a pile of beaver skins stacked alongside the upright gun until they reached the tip of the barrel. You can well believe the trader compressed them by standing on them or by any other method until as many pelts as possible could be stacked. That's a lot of beaver, and the result of a great amount of labor to trade for a weapon, which was usually of the lowest quality being produced at the time.

Two of us would situate ourselves beside the pile of skins with a box to write on. One cut off the string, removed the affidavit, and called out the number of skins that had been tagged. The other agent counted out the number of seals needed and read off the first and last number. While these numbers were being recorded by the one ciphering, the other attached the seals. The process would last anywhere from a few minutes to several hours, depending on the number of skins. Once in a while someone tried to slip a beaver past us that had been shot. These were seized and usually a complaint was filed against the trapper.

We would also patrol traplines making sure traps and snares were the legal distance (twenty-five feet) from beaver houses. Those that were too close were pulled and the trapper contacted. If the violation warranted action, he would be taken before the nearest commissioner. If he was found guilty, after he made restitution, we flew him back out to his trapline or home. The usual fine was fifty dollars for the first violation. Many times the commissioners paid the fine for those he knew personally, fully expecting to be reimbursed. This way the trapper could return to his trapline and not lose the entire season.

We also sealed as many beaver as possible while on the traplines. This prohibited trappers from accumulating more than the legal limit for sealing by other non-trappers that never left the village.

There were trappers in the villages that asked us to come to their home to seal their beaver. Most of the time it was because they were in debt to the trader and rather than turn the skins in on credit they shipped them out for a better price.

It was not unusual for an entire family to be out on the trapline. The Bureau of Indian Affairs discouraged this because it took the children out of school; however, the tradition went back many generations and was difficult to change. On one occasion a family of six asked us to visit their home. There they presented us with seventy beaver pelts. It was always interesting to observe the caste system in cases like this. The father presented the ten largest skins, then the mother the next largest and so on down the line until the last child had the ten smallest. In this case there were ten small beaver left over when they were finished. When asked whom they belonged to the father pointed proudly to his pregnant wife and said, "Those for baby inside!" Ummm, whose name do you put on that affidavit? Unfortunately we had to seize the ten and explain that it was not possible to seal beaver for an unborn baby. He smiled and we smiled. It was a good try anyway. Usually small beaver skins were not presented for sealing but held back and used to trim moccasins and mitts.

On one patrol of the Andreafsky River, a tributary of the lower Yukon River, I spotted a beaver house that had at least thirty different traps and snares set around it. Beaver were not plentiful in that area, and apparently several trappers were competing for the few animals that were available. Some snares were set at the legal distance while the remainder were set progressively closer to within a foot or two of the house. Obviously, as each trapper moved in to make a set he had to get closer than his competitor due to limited space available. It reminded me of the Maginot Line (the zone of fortifications erected by the French before World War II) and I wondered how any beaver could swim anywhere in the vicinity without getting fouled in wire and steel.

A dog team was approaching the small lake and I was able to land and make contact with the driver, a Native from Mountain Village. He became uncooperative when I introduced myself and immediately claimed he could not understand much English. This was an old ploy that had been used on me before, so I spoke slowly and used diagrams in the snow to explain my concerns over the illegal sets. He kept nodding and shrugging until I paced out twenty-five feet and pointed out the snares that were set legally and those that were too close to the house. My patience was waning at his games of "me no understand" when it was obvious that he knew exactly what I was saying.

Finally, I asked him very slowly which were his sets. Without hesitation he walked over and picked out several that were the legal distance from the house. So I could only shrug and think, "What the heck—beat again." Then I asked him his name. His answer: Rusty Prunes. That did it. I told him to make sure he advised his friends about the twenty-five-foot regulation as I pulled up all the illegal snares and departed while I still had my sanity.

Later I stopped at Mountain Village and inquired about a man called Rusty Prunes and was told that indeed that was his name. Seems like years back the Bureau of Indian Affairs was anxious to make sure all the Natives had proper surnames. The trader at this particular village helped them pick out and use the names of store goods: consequently, there are families of Beans, Coffees, and of course, Prunes. In other villages, missionaries, schoolteachers, and others helped in this name distribution. Thus we have names like Tommy Fox, Timothy Snowball, and historic names like Lincoln and Washington. My education was continuing by leaps and bounds.

While I was stationed at McGrath, the majority of my work was with Natives, both Indian and Eskimo. In that capacity I likened my role to that of a referee. My main job was to enforce the game laws, which were promulgated to assure healthy populations of wildlife and fish while allowing the surplus to be harvested. Seasons and bag limits had to be monitored. However, there had to be some latitude and reason applied when dealing with people who were completely dependent on the fish and game resources as their major food source. It was then that the role of referee came into play—to assure that all had a fair chance to take the available game without making serious inroads into the populations stocks.

In that capacity I often answered complaints from the villagers who were worried about others killing more than they needed and many times wasting the meat. I kept a few of the letters that best illustrate the problems considered serious enough by villagers to write regarding some of their neighbors. The following was written from a Yukon village on December 8, 1957. (The beaver season did not open until February 1.) The letter is copied verbatim, leaving out the names of the people involved.

Dear Sir:

I do not like to report such things against my neibers, but we all want to play fair with Government by fair hunting and by fair fishing. I have seen with own eyes that the Beaver houses were smashed open and the beavers were killedon the spot by these 3 men (names omitted) and some of the men have dependentmoney from government, that's why I want a game warden to come here this instent to over look at there beaver catch now, and no waiting. I have seen 2drying and 1 not dry'd yet and they were still active in smashing open'd the Beaver houses I have seen 2 Beaver houses been open'd by these 3 men someof these men get money from Government that is aid-dependent money—and they are not supposed to do this bad trick against us and many children who have no parents here and all over Alaska—that's just like trying to destroy money for alaska neibers. If you ever come to (village name deleted) for this investigation please do not mention my name, as a reporter against these men—because I want you to ask me questions in personal, have your interpreter (name deleted) who is always at home—and all the councils know these men who are hunting Beavers at this, But one of the councils have told these 3 men to keep hunting right in front of my open eyes in one room house. This is it I want game warden here now with a looking in a house fur permit—now.

Another from a village upriver is quite lengthy and is quoted only in part.

Dear Mr. Tremblay:

Just a few lines that I feel is my duty to write you thinking you were still our warden around this neck of the woods and know you would be able to catch some of these birds that set their traps right up against the beaver houses and those that chop into the houses. There were two brothers last year that trapped between 80 and 90 beaver last season. In fact when they returned they had theirfather and mother sign up a lot of beaver. He and his wife never left the village.

I think they will in the near future start hauling the traps out and will have them all over the country same as last year. Ray I hate to report this to you but I think its my duty to do so. So kindly do not let anyone know that I wrote you this information. Let me know right away if you received this letter.

Yours truly, (name withheld)

Several letters such as these were received every season from different people throughout the district. Most were from the older people who were genuinely concerned about wildlife because they had been dependent on fish and game for their livelihood before they had such things as government grants and welfare. They had known hunger and had no problem with game being taken out of season so long as it was needed and used. Sharing was also an important part of their culture and dividing up the spoils with those unable to go out was encouraged. What really caused problems, however, were the younger men who would not work and killed whatever and whenever they felt the urge. The answer was always the same: "It was their right!" Even then it took courage for the older people to turn in their own people, but they were concerned, and rightfully so, that overkilling would deplete the very wildlife that many depended on.

I followed up on every complaint. Sometimes it was possible to catch the guilty parties and other times meetings were held with the village councils to get their cooperation in stopping the overkilling. Most of the time they pledged their help and were able to slow down the needless slaying.

It was encouraging to see the beaver make a comeback through our enforcement efforts, education, and good wildlife management practices. They now have expanded their range and are even a nuisance in some areas. I think everyone agrees that the rehabilitation of this animal in Alaska was a milestone in the annals of wildlife conservation.

Like everything else, just when you think your work is finished for the season after traveling constantly to seal all the beaver in the district, you receive a letter like this:

> To Alaska Game Commission
> McGrath, Alaska
> When you were at Nicholai on April 4th to bag beavers you come to soon for me. I come leta that night with my Beaver skins so I don't get my Beaver skins tag yet and I got big family. Beaver prices is bum this year I cant not pay air plane fare to McGrath and I will be in Salmon river and if you want to tag my beavers before brack up you just come to salmon river at the lake will be pretty good for few more days only
> (name withheld)
> P.S. I cant spent Beaver on air plane trip to you.

I made a special trip up to Salmon River and sealed all his beaver. That ended the 1959 season with close to 10,000 skins being sealed in the McGrath District alone during the last year of territorial status. The newly created Alaska Department of Fish and Game took over control of all resident fish and game in 1960.

PART II: THE 1960s

Big Changes in a Baby State

Ray Woolford (right), Sig Olson, and his wife, Esther, pause for a photo. They were in the village for an inspection of the McGrath Headquarters, 1959.

Chapter 19

THE DUCK WAR

*I*n 1961 I was involved in a nasty confrontation in what has been called the Duck War—a conflict that erupted when federal Fish and Wildlife Service (FWS) agents attempted to end spring hunting of waterfowl by Alaska's Natives. Spring hunting of waterfowl in the United States had been prohibited by international treaty since 1916.

"Duck War" describes it well. Shots were fired at agents, including me, and lives were at risk as we tried to enforce the law. Natives who depended upon wildlife for food and whose ancestors had done so for centuries believed they had a right to continue spring waterfowl hunting. But for the young men, it was a sport, not a need.

The Migratory Bird Treaty Act, an international convention with Great Britain and Mexico, created the conflict by requiring a closed season on migratory birds between March 10 and September 1.

When the U.S. Fish and Wildlife Service was the management agency for Alaska's wildlife, enforcing the Migratory Bird Treaty Act had a low priority because of lack of money, equipment, and personnel. But when Alaska as a state took over management and the FWS was relieved of the responsibility, our agents then concentrated on enforcing federal laws.

Natives not only killed waterfowl in spring, they also collected their eggs. The birds often provided the first fresh meat for rural Alaskans after a long winter. This wasn't a serious biological problem in early years because there were relatively few Natives; another reason enforcement of the treaty had a low priority. But, as Native numbers increased in the mid-twentieth century, the impact on ducks and geese increased. The white-fronted goose, the cackler, and the black or Pacific brant went into decline, followed by the emperor goose, and pintail and canvasback ducks.

Removing one female duck or goose from a breeding population, in the view of biologists, equals the kill of several birds during the legal season.

Not only were the Natives shooting waterfowl in the spring, in summer they captured them by driving them into traps. All waterfowl lose and replace flight feathers in summer, at which time they are flightless and commonly gathered in large flocks for about three weeks. It is a simple matter to build a trap with netting and drive the birds into it. Geese can be driven into traps on land, and ducks found on lakes can also be driven into traps. Biologists have used this method of capturing birds for banding purposes.

Dr. Calvin Lensink, a nationally known waterfowl biologist and then manager for the Clarence Rhode National Wildlife Refuge (now the Yukon Delta National Wildlife Refuge), which encompasses the vast Yukon–Kuskokwim Delta, calculated in 1956 that "sixty thousand ducks, geese and swans are killed on the delta each spring. This harvest occurs just before and during nesting season, the period that is most critical to production of young after legal hunting, predators and diseases have already taken their toll."

Lensink added, "The 5,000 to 6,000 swans killed on the delta is a larger number than the legal and illegal kill in all of North America. More geese are killed in spring on the delta than are legally taken in all of Alaska. Spring hunting of white-fronted geese accounts for 15 percent of all legally harvested birds of this species. It would seem that we should consider this harvest of critical species as significant to their continued welfare."

In 1959 the FWS began to inform rural residents of the need for conservation, and of the international treaty to which the United States was a signatory. Meetings were held in schools, National Guard armories, and other public buildings. I conducted meetings in all major villages of the Yukon–Kuskokwim Delta, where Alaska's largest concentration of nesting waterfowl occurred. It is here that the world's largest population of Eskimos, the Yup'ik, also lived in about thirty-five villages.

We showed the movie *Beyond the Flyways* and explained the treaty and the hunting regulations. We also explained that rural residents would have to start observing waterfowl hunting laws and do their part to conserve waterfowl. At the same time we warned that the FWS would be enforcing the laws. I emphasized that they had no special rights to these birds anymore than people living in the poorer sections of the lower states, where the birds wintered.

Rumors of threatened violence against agents and our aircraft spread across the delta. We saw a copy of a letter circulated between

Napakiak and Napaskiak, villages near Bethel, urging people to stick together and to resist enforcement laws so that everyone could continue spring hunting.

On March 10, I showed the *Beyond the Flyways* movie and talked to villagers at Quinhagak. Shortly, the school newspaper reported, "Fish and Wildlife man held meeting and told us we can't hunt geese in the spring; now everyone is mad."

We focused mostly on villages that we felt had little need to harvest spring birds, for they had other resources, including a dollar economy. Bethel was one of these, where we knew cab drivers en route to the airport with passengers sometimes stopped to shoot geese flying over the road. We also were aware of well-paid teachers and commercial pilots, using company planes, who shot birds while accompanying Natives on spring waterfowl hunts.

Hunting was, of course, mainly with shotguns, and many of the hunters used outboard-powered boats after spring breakup. Local stores had long heavily stocked shotgun shells each spring. Thus our effort to stop spring hunting was to have an economic impact on village traders.

On April 28, 1961, FWS Agents Jim Branson, Mil Zahn, Neil Argy, and I flew to Aniak on the lower Kuskokwim River, where we were to headquarter as we began the first concentrated effort to enforce the Migratory Treaty law in the Yukon–Kuskokwim country. I flew a Cessna 180 on skis. They flew two Piper Super Cubs—one on ski/wheels, the other on big wheels.

At the same time Agents Harry Pinkham and John Klingbeil went to Barrow village on a commercial airplane. They depended on local transportation during enforcement work.

I was stationed at McGrath, and the Yukon–Kuskokwim Delta was part of my district, so I was put in charge of the operation on the delta.

The Yup'ik Eskimos on the Delta are expert waterfowl hunters who usually hunt from well-constructed blinds and pits, using decoys made of mud and cardboard cutouts often made by schoolkids. As birds were killed they were propped up in lifelike positions with sticks to entice more birds within range. Hunting took place at all times of the day. Waterfowl, newly arrived from their wintering grounds, had little fear of plainly visible hunters, boats, planes, and dog teams, and were easily killed.

This homemade skimachine predated the era of snowmobiles. It was the first one I'd ever seen—in fact, the only one I'd ever seen. Willie Alexie of Napakiak used it to travel on the frozen rivers of the Yukon-Kuskokwim Delta, May 1960.

As we flew over the delta, we saw hunters everywhere. Some used dog teams to reach the best hunting areas, others just walked on the crusted snow or river ice. One hunter, Willie Alexie, and his sixteen-year-old son traveled thirty miles from their home in the village of Napakiak to the mouth of the Johnson River in a homemade ski machine powered by an aircraft engine and propeller. When observed they were hunting from two widely separated blinds. After we landed they walked out with shotguns and three pintails ducks. The snow sled contained ten more pintails. When I asked the two hunters where they obtained the money for gas, new shotguns, and other equipment, they said they had done well fishing the summer before and had money left over.

We landed near other hunters, and found ducks, geese, and swans in their dogsleds. All the illegal birds were seized and the hunters cited into court.

We saw many hunters at blinds where we couldn't land because of deteriorating snow and ice.

Ugliness erupted near the village of Kasigluk, which lies west of Bethel. With Neil Argy aboard, I landed to check a dogsled for illegally

Dead pintails were propped up as decoys at The Bluffs on the Kuskokwim, May 1961. Using the ducks for decoys was legal; doing it in the spring was not. (Photo by Jim Branson)

killed waterfowl when about thirty people ran out of the village to our airplane. They pulled the doors open and tried to force us out. Several men tried to drag Argy away from the plane, attempting to hit him as they did.

We tried to talk with the crowd, but they would have none of it. One man shouted, "If you circle me, I shoot the airplane down and I shoot you, too."

The crowd demanded an immediate meeting. We were in a no-win situation and needed help, so I started taxiing for takeoff. As the plane moved, several men clung to the wing struts and the tail. When the plane accelerated, they dropped off, and I flew to Bethel where we briefed State Trooper Rod Redston on the incident. We asked him to go to the village to talk with the residents. He agreed and chartered the plane of Ray Christianson, then a state legislator.

Redston told the villagers of the seriousness of shooting at aircraft and federal officers. There were heated arguments, but cooler heads calmed the hunters. Redston made it clear that enforcement efforts would continue, and the wisest plan was to observe the law. Pilot Ray Christianson, an Eskimo and fluent in the Yup'ik language, translated Redston's words for the older residents.

I later learned from a schoolteacher that Kasigluk villagers had planned a more elaborate attack on us had we held the meeting they demanded. They believed the birds belonged them. Our attempts to convince them otherwise had been fruitless.

On the evening of May 1, five miles north of Bethel, Agents Branson and Zahn saw two blinds at a place called The Bluffs, with seven hunters present. Two dog teams were tied nearby. They landed and walked toward the blinds. They hadn't gone far when hunters there started to shoot at them with shotguns and a .22 rifle. At least thirty to fifty shots were fired at the agents, and other shots were fired toward their distant airplane parked on the river. They could hear bullets ricocheting off the ice.

Branson and Zahn weren't hit (nor was their plane), but they quickly ducked out of sight and returned to their plane. By radio, they called for Argy and me to help.

I flew the Cessna over the area and talked with Branson on the radio. As I circled I saw the men running west across the tundra. I continued to circle them as Branson and Zahn pursued them on foot. As I watched from above, several of the fleeing hunters hid in a patch of willows on a ridge, apparently waiting in ambush for the agents.

We had no way to communicate with Branson and Zahn, but somehow I had to let them know of the trap, so I dove the Cessna and buzzed the brush where the hunters were hidden. I climbed, circled and again buzzed the hunters' location. This time I heard a series of thumps from the ground and realized we were being shot at. I yelled at Neil, "I hope those are shotguns we hear and not rifles."

On the third pass I kept the plane at a more cautious level, and Argy saw one of the hunters pointing a gun at us, so I rolled the plane steeply away from him. Fortunately they were using shotguns and .22 rifles and were poor shots. Branson and Zahn had gotten the message about the ambush from the buzz job and hearing the shots returned to their plane. We were at a loss for the drastic action being taken by these so-called hunters. The bottle of whiskey we later found at the blind might have contributed to their behavior.

Walking back to the river, Branson and Zahn found an army rucksack holding about seventy pounds of waterfowl and a gunnysack full of thirty-five pounds of waterfowl thrown into a depression at the side of the trail.

I landed on the river and we decided to leave Branson and Zahn at the blinds for the night while Argy and I flew both planes to Bethel. We purposefully flew over the hunters to give the appearance that we had given up.

When we landed at Bethel we found indentations on the bottom of the left wing and fuselage of the Cessna from the shotgun pellets. Fortunately none of the .22 caliber bullets had struck the plane.

Branson and Zahn found the two dog teams tied up and left behind, and at one of the blinds there was a single-shot 20-gauge shotgun, a Remington nylon .22 automatic rifle, and a 12-gauge single shotgun with the end of the muzzle blown out. Nearby was an H&R 12-gauge bolt-action shotgun, several cackling geese and pintail ducks propped up as decoys, two sleeping bags with cooking gear, and canned food.

At a nearby campsite they found a fox carcass, a fresh red fox skin, a black-bellied plover, several pintail ducks, a pair of little brown crane wings, and a dead gyrfalcon. In one of the sleds were two National Guard issue sleeping bags and ponchos, and a bottle of whiskey.

That evening around 10:40, one man returned to the blinds. He was arrested, put in handcuffs, and questioned. He reluctantly provided the names of his companions.

A team of FBI agents from Anchorage flew to Bethel that day to interrogate the other six hunters who had been apprehended.

One of the hunters was a high school student scheduled to graduate that spring. He was also a member of the National Guard. He admitted to shooting more than thirty birds. His father owned and operated a grocery store in Bethel. He was given a sixty-day suspended jail sentence.

Two other hunters were unemployed National Guardsmen. They received the same sentence. Three of the others were minors and were

Seized as evidence in the May 1961 arrest were violators' guns along with illegal ducks, geese, crane wings, a red fox skin, plover, and a gyrfalcon—they were shooting at anything that came by. We brought in the FBI to the Kuskokwim River with the Grumman Goose. (Photo by Jim Branson)

not arraigned. One said he had taken his father's dog team without permission. His father, who had a full-time job, had warned him not to go hunting because he didn't need the birds.

The ringleader was a twenty-three-year-old unemployed National Guardsman. It was he who first fired at Branson and Zahn, and apparently encouraged the others to follow suit. During his arraignment, when the magistrate asked why he had gone bird hunting, he pled "starvation."

He was sentenced to thirty days in jail. Later that day he was escorted to his home by Agent Zahn to pick up his court-confiscated shotgun, a deluxe-grade Remington pump. While en route he dug a large roll of currency from his pocket and gave several dollars to a youngster on the street.

The last of the hunters was incorrigible. His family feared him, and the father asked that he be jailed overnight. He was the only one of the party who refused to give a statement to interviewing FBI agents and, in fact, attacked one of the agents with a straight-back chair. In more than three hours of interrogation, they pried from him only his name and a wealth of four-letter obscenities. The court sentenced him to juvenile detention.

Over the next week or so, six other hunters were apprehended for taking ducks, geese, and swans, and taken before the Bethel magistrate. Many other hunters were seen from the air, but they were in locations where we couldn't land safely.

After leaving one village, a teacher advised me that the school janitor asked if the game wardens were there to enforce the law against killing ducks and geese. The janitor said he'd always hunted in the spring and he would continue. The teacher asked why he needed them since he was making two hundred and fifty dollars a month. His answer: "That money to buy shells with!"

This attitude prevailed and we couldn't help but notice that most were well equipped with new shotguns, shell belts, goose calls, and all the accessories.

Meanwhile, at Barrow our agents apprehended a state legislator returning from the offshore ice with a shotgun and an eider duck. He first refused to give his name and said the bird was needed to feed his children. He also said the residents of Barrow would stand behind him.

They stood behind him all right. The next day, 138 villagers approached the agents, each with an eider duck and asking to be arrested. Sixty-eight of the defendants listed themselves as hunters. The others were mostly employed as laborers, carpenters, maintenance men, businessmen, cat skinners, and mechanics, an airline agent—and a preacher. It was quite an assortment of "subsistence" hunters.

Col. "Muktuk" Marston, organizer of the Eskimo Scouts during World War II, announced he was collecting guns for the Barrow Eskimos whose firearms had been confiscated. Eventually the matter was turned over to the Justice Department by the Anchorage U.S. Attorney's office.

Alaska's U.S. Sen. Ernest Gruening told the Natives they didn't have to abide by the Migratory Bird Treaty Act. He said they should continue hunting, and if they were apprehended, he'd defend them in court. He believed actions of the FWS were a misinterpretation by an overzealous bureaucrat and his associates with an incorrect interpretation of the treaty.

Unfortunately, this doctrine was widely accepted by Alaska's Natives. State Rep. Ray Christianson published a letter on State Legislature letterhead that was posted in all the villages. It read, "I have been advised by Senator Ernest Gruening that it will be all right to hunt for ducks and geese this spring as long a you use them for food. The Game Warden is not supposed to bother you, but if they do, be sure and let me know right away so that I can get in touch with Senator Gruening and straighten it out."

In 1963 Alaska Gov. Bill Egan attacked the FWS, and me personally, after a reporter quoted me that I would make an arrest if I observed anyone violating the Migratory Bird Treaty Act.

Interestingly, the *Fairbanks Daily News-Miner* came to my defense, saying, "It seems the governor is trying to blame the agent for doing his duty, while overlooking the obvious fault that lies within the treaty itself—a 1915 treaty the agent had nothing to do with. What else was he to say? It is his sworn duty to uphold the law."

The editorial continued, "The entire problem is not a matter of the governor's nor indeed Tremblay's views. It is a sad situation of law, and if the law is wrong, it should be changed."

An Alaska resident living in Anchorage wrote to Pres. John F. Kennedy on July 2, 1961. "I work with the Eskimos in some of the poorest parts of the state and I like them very much. I am sure at times some of them are hungry, but they are not the ones making the noise. There must be a better way to get them food without killing off nesting birds.

"The Eskimos have jobs, washing machines, every one of them had a boat, they get social security, old age pensions, aid to dependent children, free hospitalization and many other things that other citizens enjoy. They are beginning to enjoy the rights of citizens and should learn to accept some of the responsibilities of citizenship. With all their guns and other equipment all the birds would be killed off in a few years. Then where would they be?"

Politics prevailed and the Barrow violations were dropped by the Department of Justice with the usual government verbiage stating, that in the future any violations of the Migratory Bird Treaty Act and regulations will be vigorously prosecuted. Penalties for the Kuskokwim violations and assaults were left intact since they had been executed by Magistrate Nora Guinn, herself an Eskimo. She said she wholeheartedly agreed with our efforts because spring hunting of waterfowl had gotten out of hand. In addition to the penalties she handed down, she gave each violator a lecture about abiding by the law.

The FWS finally took a position that concentrated on trying to save those birds most in danger—and allowing rural residents of the Yukon–Kuskokwim Delta who genuinely needed the food to take a limited number of non-endangered waterfowl in the spring.

Then, incredibly, on October 23, 1997, the U.S. Senate approved subsistence hunting amendments to the migratory bird treaties with Canada and Mexico. On March 5, 2001, the FWS announced that the Alaska Migratory Bird Co-management Council of Native, state, and federal representatives were developing regulations for spring and summer subsistence hunting waterfowl in Alaska. These regulations have been updated and were put in place in 2002.

Give and take—yin and yang. Whatever works. The main thing is perpetuation of the resource and allowing a limited take by those actually in need.

With every right there has to be a responsibility. Now, with the appropriate regulations, those in need will be able to hunt waterfowl species not in jeopardy. The greedy will have to take their chances with federal enforcement agents. A win-win deal for rural residents—and for our valuable waterfowl populations.

As an interesting side note, the stellers and the spectacled eider numbers have drastically declined and are now listed as "Threatened" under the Endangered Species Act. If the decline continues, they may have to be considered as "Endangered."

Chapter 20

CHECK RIDE UNSATISFACTORY

So said the pink slip handed me by the FAA Flight Inspector. It was a flunked check ride for my multiengine land and sea rating. How could this happen? We had not even gone flying, and here I was scuffing my way back to the Grumman Goose I had flown over from the FWS hangar at Lake Hood, only to ferry it back, a failure.

My logbook shows the date as September 23, 1964. Talk about humiliation. How was I going to face all the guys at the hangar who I know were ready to throw me into the lake as part of the ritual of passing any check ride for a float rating? All the smiling faces that patted me on the back as I left, saying "Go show the FAA what Goose flying is all about!" How could I show them when the inspector wouldn't even go up with me?

It had started in the spring when the regional director decided I should get checked out in a Grumman Goose because much of the work I was doing required the use of the large amphibian airplane. To say that I was pleased was like asking a Labrador retriever if he wants to go duck hunting. Aircraft Supervisor Theron Smith and I talked it over and he suggested I should get enough instruction to solo from Al Kropp, the FWS professional Goose pilot. After that I was to accompany Al on Goose trips scheduled that summer that didn't interfere with my regular duties. At the end of the summer when he felt I was ready, I would go for a check ride and my rating.

All went as planned and I had some great training. The first phase required learning the intricacies of flying with two engines and the problems that occur when one quits and you are forced to continue with only one. I also trained on the best speeds and procedures for bringing it in if both engines quit. Instructors will tell you that the engines on an airplane are just to keep the pilot cool. If you don't believe that, just let one quit and watch him sweat.

Then there was mastering runway landings with the narrow-geared Grumman that could eat your lunch if you didn't put it on the pavement squarely, regardless of the crosswind component. Many a pilot learned that the hard way. If the Goose started to drift right or left after touchdown, it was a one-way trip off the runway, usually with considerable damage to the plane. It was a balancing act because of the way the two engines mount high on the wings, causing the weight to shift to the side of the drift. Add a crosswind against the bulky fuselage, forcing itself underneath the uplifted wing, the narrow gear, rubber tires grabbing the macadam, and you have all the makings of a great ground loop.

Next to landing on a surfaced runway in a crosswind, learning to land on saltwater swells had to be the most challenging. Anyone who has operated a boat in rough water knows how unforgiving swells can be if you don't approach them at the right angle. This can be disastrous with a plane. Naturally there are limitations to the size of swells you can land on with an aircraft. It can be difficult to judge the height of swells from the air and many times it's a judgment call by the pilot based on experience.

One thing that can be assessed, however, is the direction the swells are running and then the never-to-be-broken rule has to be applied: always land parallel to the swells regardless of the wind direction. To do otherwise is courting disaster, even if it's a very small swell.

This type of training is a real pucker factor for both the student and the instructor. Picking the right spot to land the plane can be very difficult for the student. It has to be on the crest of the swell, or on the backside and kept under control in the rough water until it comes to a complete stop. Pity the poor instructor sitting there trying to make instant decisions on when to take over the controls if the landing is not going as planned. Having been in both seats, I'm sure the instructor has the greatest stress factor. You have to let the student make mistakes in order to learn, but when do you take it away from him to avert an accident?

Then there was beaching. This entailed driving the aircraft through the surf onto a hard beach above waterline, allowing passengers to get out without having to put on hip boots. Loading and unloading freight on dry land is easier and the ship is in a better position to be secured for a lengthy stay. Having to anchor is avoided if possible in saltwater tidal conditions.

The key words are "hard beaches," for if you misjudge and the Goose bogs down, you may be there for a while. If this occurs in soft sand on the way out, and the pilot hasn't been able to get the plane turned around toward the water again, well, let's just say you're up the proverbial creek. Hopefully there are shovels on board for digging.

The other part of the equation is the tide. Good pilots pay as much attention to the tide books as a boat operator, because if he gets stuck on an outgoing tide, he can be there for a long time. If there are passengers they will become diggers and pushers, and the pilot is the blaster. It's a tricky operation, and even with a great deal of experience you can occasionally pick a soft one. This is not only frustrating, it can be a serious problem if the weather is deteriorating and there's a schedule to meet.

All the training went as planned and I had more than fifty hours in the bird with cool weather fast approaching and freeze-up on the near. Theron decided it was time, and I made an appointment.

The day of the check ride was clear and calm. A good omen, I thought to myself as I taxied out into the Lake Hood for a water takeoff. Merrill Field, where the FAA office was located, is only a ten-minute flight. A short time later I was sitting in front of Elden Gubler's desk. I was to learn later that he was known for failing more pilots than any of the other local FAA inspectors. In fact local instructors who sent students up for check rides that were unlucky enough to draw his name were said to be "Gublerized." At the time he was just another tough-looking inspector priming up to rake me over the coals.

He read all the paperwork, including my certificate and medical plus the certificates for the aircraft. Then came the orals.

His first question was, "What is the Vmc (Velocity Minimum Control) of your aircraft?" BLANK! Nothing came out because I didn't have the foggiest notion what he was talking about. "Well, okay, then," he continued, "what's Vxse?" (Velocity best angle of climb single engine) BLANK! "What's Vyse?" (Velocity best rate of climb single engine) BLANK! It didn't take long for him to realize he might as well be talking Greek to me because I was completely stalled out, so he tried another track.

"Okay then, tell me how you're going to make a takeoff with your airplane if I decide to go for a ride with you." I knew I was in trouble when he used the words "If I decide to go for a ride with you."

Using my best diction I went through the procedure that went something like this: "After going through the checklist reading, each command out loud, and showing you each move I'm making (this is always a good way to impress an inspector), I will line up in the center of the active runway. When cleared for takeoff, I will advance the throttles and when I obtain flying speed I'll lift the plane off the runway, lower the nose until we reach climbing speed and begin an ascent out of the pattern."

He threw up his hands and shouted, "Who taught you to fly, some World War II pilot?" I said, "As a matter of fact, yes." Theron had flown B17s in the big war and was a hell of a pilot. The reason for that particular takeoff procedure was to get off the runway as soon as possible and save wear and tear on the gear. Oh, boy, was that wrong. He lectured me on what the FAA was teaching these days and asked why I wasn't aware of the V speeds that were the bible of flying now? With the advent of small, fast twin-engine aircraft, pilots were killing themselves and their passengers by not holding the plane on the runway until reaching minimum single-engine airspeed before lifting off. If the critical engine failed (usually the left engine on most twins) after takeoff, the other engine will roll the plane over on its back unless the power is immediately shut down.

That was all well and good for the hot twins, but this was a Grumman Goose, built in 1941. It didn't have those nasty tendencies, and I was flying it like they did in World War II! "No good," said the inspector.

He gave me a manual that outlined what the twin-engine check ride entailed, underlining the appropriate V speeds, gave me a pink slip, wrote the failing note in my log book and said, "See me again when you're ready." Not even a good-bye or have a nice day.

That may have been just as well in the mood I was in. How come I wasn't aware of this manual that was available from the FAA on giving check rides? How come I didn't know about V speeds? How come I didn't know how to take off a twin in accordance with the prescribed procedures now being taught? Well, I was certainly going to go find out.

After landing and shutting down I stormed into Theron's office. He was all smiles, thinking I had my new license in my wallet, knowing he had trained me well. When he looked at my face the smile left and he knew all was not okay. My first question was "What's the Vmc speed of the Goose?" BLANK! "What's Vxse?" BLANK! "What's

Vyse?" BLANK! "Well, since you don't know, how was I supposed to know, and I flunked my ride; in fact there never was a ride."

He was as flabbergasted as I, and carefully looked at the exam guide I showed him. "Well," he said, "it's obvious things have changed and we're not up to standards." Right on! About that time the aircraft chief for the Bureau of Land Management walked in. Since the BLM also had several Grummans and he was supposed to be a good Goose pilot, I turned to him and said, "McCormick, what's the Vmc speed of the Goose?" BLANK! "What's Vxse?" BLANK! "What's Vyse?" BLANK! I was beginning to feel lots better.

Obviously we had to go back to the drawing board, and it had to be soon because freeze-up was looking us in the eye. It was decided I would get some instruction from a local instructor, Bud Hardesty, who had lots of recent twin training to his credit. We spent some time on the V speeds, and since the manuals for the Goose were 1940 vintage, we had to come up with our own determinations. After doing a lot of experimenting and calculating, we decided that 85 knots was the Vmc of the old bird. Then we went out and made numerous takeoffs holding the Grumman on the runway to that speed before lifting off. It was a different way to fly for sure. It meant pushing the long nose of the plane down until it was practically on the runway to keep it from lifting off prematurely. The tires were almost smoking, and when 85 knots was finally reached, it fairly well leaped into the air. Not very comfortable, but by the FAA manual. After evaluating it, we all decided it definitely added a dimension of safety, providing the tires didn't blow out.

After spending several hours practicing the new takeoff procedures and a few more making up a manual of V-speeds by flight tests (none existed that we were aware of), I made another appointment for a check flight. I asked for Elden Gubler. I had to prove myself and since he was the inspector who busted me, I wanted him to be the one to reestablish my bruised ego. The first available date was October 15. I could only bite my nails and pray that we would have a late freeze-up and that some of the lakes would remain ice free for the water portion of the check ride.

The appointed day arrived and I told Theron that if I didn't make it this time I would have no one to blame but myself. We hadn't had any hard freezes and the big lakes across the inlet were still open.

It was another nice calm day, but this time as I taxied out I didn't think about omens, just V-speeds and the manual we had so meticulously prepared.

I walked into the building packing all the manuals and books plus every outline that I could find on check rides. I wasn't taking any chances this time. Passing a window I could see Elden sitting stiffly at his desk studying some papers. I decided that those papers must have been part of a manual the FAA provides for inspectors on "ten easy ways to flunk multiengine applicants."

I sat in a chair in front him for several minutes before he finally acknowledged my presence. Then with a smile he said, "Let's go fly your Grumman."

"Wait a minute," I said, "what about all the studying I've done and the manuals we prepared? Ask me some questions."

"I don't have to," he said. "I know you've studied and know all the V-speeds. Now I want to find out if you can fly."

That must have been one of the things he read in the outline on how to keep the applicant off balance for the best impact before flunking him a second time. It was working because I remember as we were walking out to the plane that I had the sickening feeling of a lamb being led to slaughter.

When we got to the plane, he asked me to point out all the features of the Grumman, from the drain plugs to the radio antennas. After that he asked me to take him for a ride. "Give it your best shot," he said. This is what I had been waiting for. A chance to show off the skills practiced during the long summer. Everything went smoothly including the single-engine maneuvers, which are not the Grumman's best feature. After two hours of flying we taxied back to the FAA building, and without further words walked back into his office. He prepared the paperwork and congratulated me as he wrote in my logbook "Multi-engine flight check land and sea. E. S. Gubler AL/FSDO-1."

I didn't need an airplane to fly back to the Fish and Wildlife Service hangar this time, but decided it would be appropriate to return in the Grumman Goose that I was now authorized to legally operate. Now was the time for the backslapping and smiles of the crew that had helped me get the rating. Fortunately, Lake Hood was frozen and I was able to escape the swim promised when I passed the check ride.

Theron was obviously relieved and said, "Well, we all learned something from this. I guess we better get with it and start using some of the new technology."

"Right," I said, "but let's not ignore all the techniques learned through the school of hard knocks on how to operate in the Bush. You write the FWS manual for our operations, and we'll use the FAA bible for check rides and flying on maintained runways."

After all, look at all the old-timers who are still operating in the Bush. All that knowledge isn't found in the FAA manual, and unfortunately it isn't being shared with new pilots any more, right? How true.

Chapter 21

WHAT WENT WRONG?

*D*uring the more than 12,000 hours I flew in Alaska during my career with the FWS and as Aircraft Supervisor for the Alaska Department of Public Safety, there were many incidents worthy of detailing. Many are humorous, some deal with errors in judgment, and others involved skills learned over the years that kept me out of serious trouble. After I retired I gave lectures on pilot safety for the Alaska Aviation Foundation. I found that pilots are more receptive to safety suggestions when I shared with them the mistakes I made. We've all made blunders, and it is always gratifying to hear how someone else fouled up. As we listen we say to ourselves, *Hey, I'm not the only one who can screw up.*

Alaska, one-fifth the size of the Lower 48, has few roads. The only way to get around most of it is by flying. For this reason many agencies and companies have their own planes and pilots. The FWS realized this in the early 1940s and organized an aircraft division. Professional pilots with Alaska flying skills were hired. They hauled personnel, moved freight to remote areas, conducted aerial surveys and flew agents on enforcement patrols. These pilots could not keep up with the demand for their services, so a few qualified enforcement agents with pilots' licenses were selected, trained, and put on flight status. After World War II the Territory grew by leaps and bounds, and the Department of Interior realized that more aircraft were needed to enforce Alaska game laws. By the time I arrived on the scene the aircraft division had a fleet of single and multiengine planes.

Since I had a pilot's license with Alaska experience, soon after I was hired, they sent me to Anchorage for a flight check with Theron Smith. I was then authorized to pilot Fish and Wildlife Service aircraft up to 165 horsepower.

After another check ride in Gullwing N-782 on September 1, 1953, my authorization was amended on October 13 to include aircraft up to 300 HP. On February 14, 1964, after a check ride in a Beaver DHC-2, it was amended again to include aircraft up to 500 HP. Then in 1964, I moved up to 900 HP with multiengine land-and-sea privileges after my flight check in the Grumman Goose G-21. The final flight authorization

The learning curve never ends. I'd landed on the Susitna Flats many times in the fall without incident. But during one spring thaw, I landed on a quagmire instead of a nice, hard runway. I shut it down before the plane went up on its nose—it felt like slow motion. (Photo by C. D. Evans)

was issued verbally after I was issued an FAA type rating in a Douglas DC-3. This was authorized after we conducted a walrus survey with a "Doug" in the Bering Sea. The oral authority was never issued in writing since we never again conducted surveys with a DC-3.

Instead the FWS used a rebuilt Grumman Goose, which had four and a half feet added to the fuselage. It was powered by Garrett turbine engines. The four-man cockpit of this plane allowed biologists to sit behind the pilot and copilot while conducting surveys. The seating arrangements in the DC-3 had always been a problem for the observers. One usually sat in the copilot's seat and the other had to stand behind the pilot.

My career nearly ended on the first official flight I made out of Fairbanks. I was to conduct a patrol west of Fairbanks where we heard that a few Nenana folks were illegally killing moose and selling the meat. It was a blustery, cold day in February when Jim King and I set out in a Piper Pacer on skis. Flying over the frozen muskeg swamps north of Nenana, we spotted the remains of a moose kill. There were many wolf tracks around the area and we wanted a closer look to determine whether predators or illegal hunters had made the kill. I made a low pass over the small lake to get a better look. As I tried to clear the trees at the end of the lake in the turbulent air, I flew through the tops of high cottonwoods. This did considerable damage to the plane. I was able to keep flying and managed to land on a nearby large lake.

We found the cowling crunched around the front of the engine, with many rips in the fabric on the underside of the fuselage and wings. Also, the leading edges of the wings were dented where they hit the trees. Fortunately, the frozen trees were brittle and shattered when we hit them.

We freed the front of the engine cowling and made a few hasty patches to the torn fabric. I flew the plane by myself to check it out before picking up Jim and flying to Fairbanks and reporting the incident to my supervisor, Ray Woolford. Ray checked the damage and made arrangements with Fairbanks Aircraft Services for repair. He then told me to write a memo on the incident.

Here I was, brand new on the job, writing my first memo to the director describing how I had just busted up one of his new planes. The first thing I had to do was reconstruct the accident in my mind and determine what had caused it. Obviously it wasn't pilot error: it was a downdraft at the end of the lake that caused me to fly through the trees. This is what I said in my report. After I submitted the memo to Ray, he checked with a local commercial pilot who had flown in the same area that day. The pilot agreed it was very windy and turbulent, and sympathized with what had occurred. Ray wrote his evaluation of the accident, vindicating me, and giving me needed support. Aircraft Supervisor Theron Smith wrote up his appraisal of the incident recommending that I remain on flight status and receive more training in low-level flight.

The accident committee at the regional office reviewed the case. They recommended I remain on flight status. Years later I learned that the assistant law enforcement supervisor made a strong case to fire me. This would not have been a problem since I was on probationary status having been on the job for only about a month. Fortunately for me he did not get agreement from the committee. On such delicate threads careers sometime hang.

I went over the events of the accident many times as I pursued my career. Downdrafts are often blamed for aircraft accidents and sometimes this is a correct evaluation. There are times, however, when pilots use this weather phenomenon as a scapegoat to cover errors, and I was finally able to convince myself later that is exactly what I did. It was an error in judgment, plain and simple. I focused my eyes on the tracks in the snow too long, and when I looked up there wasn't enough room to climb over the trees. I hadn't fooled Theron. He had written in his report that low-level flying requires a great deal of planning, which is why he wanted to give me more training.

It was a valuable lesson and I was aware of it every time I flew low to evaluate something on the ground. If it was a small area with limited maneuvering space I made several passes at higher altitude to determine the best way in and the best way out, keeping in mind turbulence and wind characteristics. I then made a decision as to the safest approach to check the location. If an observer was on board, he did the looking while I kept full attention to flying the aircraft. Simple, but so important, and it kept me out of trouble through thousands of hours of low-level flying.

I remember vividly one of my early check rides with Tom Wardleigh, assistant aircraft supervisor for the FWS. With a remarkable career of flying in Alaska, working as a flight instructor, and serving as executive director of the Alaska Aviation Safety Foundation, Tom certainly is one of the shining stars in the history of Alaska aviation.

It was Tom who had earlier given me my check ride and upgrade to fly the Gullwing Stinson. He had the ability to relax students while he evaluated their performance for an annual flight check or to amend the flight authorization to a higher horsepower rating. I remember on the Stinson check ride he looked over a few minutes after takeoff and asked why I had the control wheel locked in such a death grip. I had no idea that I was that tense. Later in my career, when I gave check rides, I recalled his way of getting pilots to relax and tried to follow these techniques. A check pilot is always looking for how the student will act under emergency conditions, and a heavy-handed instructor will never be able to really evaluate these abilities. A good flight instructor should be in a position to communicate his or her skills and other knowledge gained over the years to help the student become a more proficient and safer pilot. Tom had that ability.

During a particular winter check flight out of Anchorage, we were flying a Cessna 170 stationed in McGrath. After performing the usual stalls and turns at altitude, Tom pulled the power and I made a simulated emergency landing in an opening of spruce timber. After recovering and getting back to flying speed, he suggested I show him how I conducted a low-level trapline patrol looking for violations. I leveled off at five hundred feet and slowed the plane to a good maneuvering speed with the flaps set at twenty degrees. As we flew along he encouraged me to explain how I would follow a snowshoe or dog-team trail in the snow. After a while, as I explained the types of maneuvers I used, he asked me to slow the aircraft to the point where I felt it was ready to stall. This I did and added full power at the critical point. He then said do it again and wait until it starts to actually stall and recover. This I also did and waited until the plane started to shake before going to full throttle.

After leveling off, he looked at me and asked, "Do you think it's safe to practice stalls at only five hundred feet altitude?"

"Absolutely not," I replied. "It's not only dangerous, but it's scary as hell."

"So then why are you doing it he asked?

"Because you're telling me to!" was my reply.

His next words were, "When you're flying the airplane, you're the pilot in command. Never let anyone tell you to do anything that you feel isn't safe, regardless who it is!"

What a lesson. That advice remained with me during the rest of my flying career and one I passed on to many other pilots . . .

I've heard it said that the second-greatest thrill to man is flying. The first is a safe landing. So when Tom asked me on another occasion, "Can you land shorter using the full-stall technique or by making a wheel landing?" I answered, "A full-stall landing for sure."

Then he bet me a dinner he would land shorter than I by making a wheel landing at the same strip and using the same airplane (in fact the same one I had been flying for the last several hundred hours). Naturally I accepted, thinking it was an easy way to get a steak dinner. I lost! After that I changed my short-landing techniques and was rewarded by landing at places I had previously avoided. It was also the technique we later taught to all the Department of Public Safety pilots.

Many pilots will still argue that full-stall landings are best. I can only say that over the years of training many pilots in landing on short strips, this method proved to be the best and safest.

The approach technique that is generally used for tail-wheel aircraft requires carrying ample airspeed, 1.3 x VSO (stalling speed or the minimum steady flight speed) with full flaps, and power adequate to overcome burbles, gusts, etc. Just short of the touchdown point, you reduce power and land the aircraft positively on the touchdown point in a wheel-landing attitude with the stick forward applying heavy braking until the elevators begin to lose control. This eliminates the hazards of stalls, long landings, and missed touchdown points, and results in shorter landings with the aircraft under positive control at all times. This technique should be practiced on a local strip with markers at known distances and remember the three Ps: practice, practice, and practice.

Naturally whenever a pilot lands, the takeoff has to be considered. It's often necessary to carefully walk the takeoff area and put up markers to determine the "lift-off spot," or the point where the aircraft can be stopped if flying speed is not obtained.

A friend once took me on a hunting trip in his airplane. The trip ended badly and illustrates what can happen when you don't follow through with a well-planned takeoff plan. The area was near King Salmon. It was during the years when it was legal to spot moose, land, and shoot. There was a large moose population in the area, so it was just a matter of flying around and finding the right size animal for the freezer. This was strictly a meat hunt, and we wanted a cow.

After a short flight, we found a group of four animals with a nice plump cow in the group. The area was typical tundra with small tussocks mixed in with the vegetation. Close to where the animals were feeding, there was a relatively smooth spot where my friend chose to set his plane down. It was a beautiful day, and after shooting, we took our time skinning and butchering the moose, which was in prime condition.

When the quarters were all laid out, I mentioned that I would be more than happy to pack them individually to a gravel bar that was about a quarter of a mile away. My friend said no way, he would be able to haul the meat out in two loads and then come back for me. I watched as he walked out the spot he planned for his runway. He methodically paced the strip out and then placed his back seat on the left side of the proposed runway, where he felt he should be airborne. Then he paced off the remainder of the sector and placed the seat back on the side where he would chop the throttle if he wasn't flying, feeling he could get the plane stopped before running into the willows. I watched and thought to myself, my friend really knows what he's doing. I complimented him on his takeoff plan.

We then loaded two quarters into the plane and he taxied to the end of the usable makeshift runway. I stood at the halfway marker where, according to his calculations, he should be airborne. He started his takeoff run, and when he got to where I was standing he was bouncing badly. From my perspective his speed was actually decelerating. I was shocked when he didn't cut the throttle but continued past the last marker. It seemed like everything from that point on was in slow motion. The plane went into the willows at full throttle throwing up brush over the wings. It only went a short distance more and then the wheels hit a small hidden creek, causing the aircraft to completely overturn. I ran to the spot in time to see my friend climbing out of the side of the plane, which was now bottom side up. He was saying over and over, "It was just ready to fly, it was just ready to fly."

Trying not to hurt his feelings I told him that from my vantage point there was no way the Cub was going to fly. The bouncing and rocking was actually spilling lift from the wings and the terrain prohibited him from obtaining any more speed in that short distance. Here was a well-planned takeoff that failed because the pilot didn't adhere to the strategy he so carefully planned.

The rest was like a bad dream. We disassembled the wings and tied everything down, not knowing how the wreck was going to get back to the airport. A plane came looking for us and landed on the nice gravel bar I had eyeballed. He took my friend back to King Salmon and left me some food for the night. I ended up packing the moose to the gravel bar as I had first suggested, and my friend borrowed a plane to fly it out. He went back later with a mechanic. They were able to right the plane, reattach the wings, and fly it back with a new prop. The repairs, which were major, took most of the winter. Certainly a costly lesson but emphasizing that once a plan is made, the pilot should execute it to the best of his ability and not change his mind thinking,

"The plane will fly because I am the pilot, and I am in control." Maybe yes and maybe no!

On another occasion when disaster struck I was checking out a well-known guide's sheep-hunting camp in the Alaska Range. His landing strip, a gravel bar high in the mountains, was exactly five hundred feet long with washouts on both ends. Not a good strip for an unskilled pilot. Our two Super Cubs were parked well off the runway. The guide was expecting a friend to fly over and drop him a note telling him when to pick up his next party of hunters. As we talked, the guide's friend flew up the valley. He didn't bother to drag the strip for a look, even though according to the guide he had never seen it. He flew up the valley, turned, and approached the strip downwind and downhill. It became obvious he wasn't just going to drop a note; he was going to land in his Piper Cruiser. When he was on final, the guide yelled to me, "Stop him! He'll never be able to make it!"

Right. How do you stop a pilot from landing when he's on final, and you're on the ground? I ran up the runway waving my arms trying to convince him to abort. No luck! He was going too fast, and touched down about halfway down the gravel bar. Instead of making a go-around, he started braking, trying to stop in the remaining two hundred and fifty feet. An impossibility. The plane went over the end of the gravel bar and into the wash, tore the gear off, smashed the cowling and turned the prop into a full curl any mountain sheep would be proud of.

We ran down to the plane as the pilot was climbing out dressed in slacks, sports coat, and Jodhpur boots. He was yelling, "What did I do wrong?"

"What did you do right?" the guide yelled back.

The landing was a failure before it started. He never dragged the strip to estimate the length. He didn't make his approach into the wind, as is normal for any landing, and he didn't take advantage of the upslope of the runway. He landed blindly with everything against him. A damn costly error.

After any favorable off-runway landing, there has to be a successful takeoff, as my friend at King Salmon learned the hard way. We always remind pilots at seminars to be aware of density-altitude and the effects of heat, weight, and the length of the runway when contemplating a takeoff, especially with a heavily loaded airplane.

A well-known and experienced pilot once crashed a Cessna 180 at the end of the runway near the village of Eagle. I asked another local commercial pilot who knew about the accident what happened. His answer was brief. It was a hot day and the pilot was hauling parts for a bulldozer. He failed to calculate the weight of his load. Who weighed things in those days anyway? So the explanation was, it was one degree too hot, he was one pound overweight, and the runway was a foot too short.

One of the biggest problems of enforcing game laws with an aircraft is having to land where a violation was committed. Many times illegal guides with stripped-down Super Cubs land where our enforcement planes, equipped with a full complement of instruments and radios, can't. This can be frustrating and has caused numerous accidents when agents or officers try to enforce flagrant violations.

A common method of taking big game is for a guide to locate a large animal from the air, land the hunter at an appropriate location, and drive the animal with the airplane to that location. This is especially true with bears. When aerial polar bear hunting was legal in the 1970s, it's doubtful that many bears were taken any other way.

Illegal guides have been known to pull logs behind their aircraft after landing, preventing anyone else from using the runway. Some guides have painted planes in camouflage hoping they will disappear when on the ground. Two wildlife officers once watched from the air as a well-known illegal guide torched his camouflaged plane after they had found him in a national park with an illegally killed bear.

There's big money in illegal hunting, and guides tear up planes regularly getting in and out of what seems like impossible spots. During my tenure as aircraft supervisor with the State Department of Public Safety aircraft section, we pickled and stored planes that were seized in illegal operations. Not only were several not airworthy, they were junk. Hunters spent thousands of dollars for the privilege of being passengers in these thrashed-out pieces of trash. Ignorance can be bliss, however, and the pursuit of a big-game trophy, especially one that may go in the record book, can cause these killers to forgo any common sense.

How does a safe pilot compete with this mentality? He can't, and that's the message I worked on during my tenure as both the agent in charge of the U.S. Fish and Wildlife Service enforcement division and as aircraft supervisor of the Alaska Department of Public Safety. Trying to compete to make a case against the bad guy has resulted in damaged aircraft and injuries to the pilot and passenger.

During the last years of my career it was Kent Edwards, U.S. District Attorney in Anchorage, who said that the only way we would ever make strong cases against illegal guides was through undercover operations. We were finally able to get congressional funds for covert operations on the federal level, which were later matched by the state. These operations have been very successful and taken the pressure off trying to follow the crazy pilots into crazy places. Planes used in illicit operations are expendable to these jockeys and regarded as a cost of doing business. Wreck one, get another, and at times the big-money hunter provided the necessary capital. There have been fatalities, but then I assume that's just another added cost to making big bucks!

So we taught professionalism to our pilots and tried to get them to use the right priorities. Gone are the days of the daring Bush pilots whose feats were legend. Stories abound about those who were successful, but there aren't many stories about those who were killed trying to accomplish the impossible.

Attitude, attitude, attitude. The macho image that says, "Because Joe did it, I can" is just as wrong as "The Right Stuff" attitude of, "Oh, Lord let me die if I must, but don't let me do anything stupid!" The professional attitude is the one that makes for a safe pilot whether he or she is an airline pilot, commercial pilot, or the private pilot enjoying the wonders of flight. I'm reminded that there are a lot of mechanics out there making a good living repairing Bush pilots' airplanes.

As the old saying goes, "Engines can quit and systems can fail. When they do, the pilot has a choice—remain the pilot or become a passenger."

Chapter 22

A ROYAL PAIN

*D*uring the fall of 1967, I was advised that I would be one of the pilots on a proposed big-game hunt for the King and Queen of Nepal. This was to be a big affair in Alaska, with the Department of Interior and the Department of State involved.

According to information we received, a meeting had been conducted at the Nepalese Embassy in Washington, D.C., on September 25, 1967. At that meeting, attended by representatives of State and Interior, the Nepal First Secretary of the Embassy announced that Their Majesties The King and Queen of Nepal would arrive for a ten-day state visit in the United States about November 1. After the state visit, Their Majesties would then proceed to participate in a fifteen-day big-game hunt in Alaska.

A representative of the Department of State noted that Pres. Lyndon Johnson was also very much interested in this hunting project for the King and Queen.

The letter requesting support of the Department of Interior was sent to the Secretary of Interior from the Honorable James W. Symington, Chief of Protocol, Department of State.

The letter of intent stated:

"... the country of Nepal is an ally of the Western World and is most friendly to the United States. It is desired that this relationship continue. Accordingly, the facilities of the Department of Interior are to made available for the purposes of enhancing the hunt."

Included also was the statement:

"There will be about fourteen members in the party, but hunting will be done only by His Majesty King MAHEDRA Bir Bikram Shah Deva and Her Majesty Queen RATNA Rajva Lakshmi Devi Shah."

A letter in September listed in quantities the species they wanted to hunt—two each of the following: moose, caribou, Kodiak brown bear, elk, mountain sheep, bison, sea lions, and musk oxen. If possible, they also desired to obtain two each of black bear, grizzly bear, deer varieties, and a few wolves, foxes, etc. Quite a shopping list, to say the least, and all this in November, which is notorious for bad weather in Alaska.

The Department of Interior agreed on October 17 to the Department of State's request and issued instructions to the Directors of the Bureaus of Commercial Fisheries, Sport Fisheries and Wildlife and Land Management for their support and cooperation in helping to make the hunt a success. A representative of the Department of the Interior Fish and Wildlife Service and the Department of State Protocol Office were to coordinate the operations.

The selection of a guide was delegated to the Washington office of the Fish and Wildlife Service. Al Burnett of Kodiak was chosen as principal guide to provide the hunting services for the hunt. Burnett realized he could not handle all of the planned hunting by himself, so he hired additional guides as assistants.

The Department of Interior would supply three Grumman Goose aircraft with Theron Smith, FWS flight supervisor in charge of flight operations, and the Department of Commercial Fisheries would make available their Biological Field Station at Karluk Lake, Kodiak, for quartering the hunt party. The Alaska Department of Fish and Game would furnish enforcement officer Gene Tautfest to assure compliance with state hunting regulations. In addition to flying one of the Grummans, I would act in my capacity as U.S. game management agent to make sure federal laws were also complied with. The third Grumman was to be supplied by the Bureau of Land Management and would be flown by Cal Ward.

The Navy and Air Force were to assist with aircraft including, but not limited to, C-54s and C-130s to help move people, camps, and equipment. An Air Force flight surgeon was given the assignment to assist the King's personal physician in the event any medical assistance was needed. Additionally, the Navy supplied equipment such as life jackets, mattresses, sleeping bags, pillows, bath towels, etc. Also supplied was a new bed and springs for the King and Queen with daily fresh linens. Other detailed instructions to the guide required a diet that included aromatic Darjeeling tea, curries and rice, Spanish dishes, fowl, especially breast of pheasant and partridge, meat, hearts of palm and artichoke, hot sauces, and chilies. All vegetables were to be fresh—never canned—and ripe fruits were to be served with all meals. Bristol Cream sherry, vintage wines, Craven-A cork tips, daily newspapers and news magazines, with English candies, were to be at hand. Breakfast was to be served in the room. All meals were to be taken privately. Bovine products were not to be used, nor were pork or mutton, fish, or shellfish. A separate chef was to prepare meals— never by a camp cook. The hunts were to start no earlier than ten o'clock in the morning and were to conclude at three in the afternoon. Sounded a little stuffy and damn demanding, I thought.

Other members of the hunt program were the Nepalese entourage, including the Ambassador of Nepal to the United States, the Deputy Prime Minister, military personal secretaries, personal physician and flight surgeon, plus full first-aid and surgical equipment, the Queen's brother, officer in charge of royal flight, a woman companion for the Queen, and journalists. Included also were the U.S. government personnel, security men, chefs, game skinners, a bull cook, Alaska Air Command officers, Army, Navy, Coast Guard and FBI, plus official photographers, and a representative of Jonas Brothers to prepare the trophies. This was not going to be your average run-of-the-mill Alaska hunt.

Several meetings were held at the Protocol Office of the Alaskan Air Command with most of the participants involved in the actual hunt, or those setting up the logistics. As usual with this kind of an operation, too many organizations and people were involved, which created much confusion. The safety of the King and Queen was given top priority and caused problems throughout the hunt. The military envisioned a search-and-rescue helicopter, which would follow our aircraft, and be on hand in the event of an accident. This was ruled out when I pointed out that this hunt was to be completely legal and a helicopter present in the hunting area would give reason for residents to speculate they were being used for hunting purposes. I also pointed out that every effort would be made to haul out the meat of game taken and we would do our part in making sure there would be no criticism from anyone as to the manner in which the hunt was conducted. It was decided the helicopter would be on standby at a location outside of the hunt area.

The King and Queen with their entourage of seven Nepalese cabinet members, two State Department security agents, and one Department of State Protocol officer arrived at Elmendorf Air Force Base on November 9 aboard Air Force One. I flew to Kodiak with the main party aboard an Air Force C118. A banquet was held in Kodiak at the hotel that evening in honor of Their Majesties. Police were posted at all entrances. I really slept secure that night knowing I was well protected from any bad guys.

At a meeting that evening, the Protocol Officer said Their Majesties requested that they hunt from the smaller aircraft, i.e., Burnett's Cessna 185 and Park Munsey's Cessna 180. Munsey, another Kodiak guide, had been hired by Burnett to help with the hunt on the island. Theron suggested that the Grummans, being twin-engined, would be safer, but he was turned down. This was the beginning of many disagreements that occurred almost daily on how the hunt was to be conducted.

On the morning of November 10, the entire party was moved to Karluk Lake via the Grummans, single-engine aircraft, and a Navy Albatross. During the next five days, there were thirty-six to thirty-eight people billeted at the Karluk Lake facility, including a chef from the TraveLodge and a chef from the Anchorage Captain Cook Hotel.

At first the King had to be accompanied on all hunts by his aide, who was a Nepalese General, along with a State security agent, the principal guide, and a photographer. Accompanying the Queen was a Nepalese Colonel, an assistant guide, and usually a photographer. Back-up airplanes carried the packers, skinners, and additional photographers. One does not need a vivid imagination to realize the difficulty of moving such a large party to a hunting site for the purpose of making a successful stalk and brown bear kill.

On the first day a grandiose party including all of the above, plus the entire Nepalese cabinet, were flown in the Grummans and Cessnas to Three Saints Bay, where a bear had been spotted there the previous day. The King and his entourage climbed up the mountain while the pilots and planes remained on the beach. We were able to watch the procession as it plodded up the mountain, and it was very evident that no bear in his right mind would stay put for that much commotion. Sure enough he did a disappearing act. By the time everyone was back on the beach, the weather had turned sour and we had our difficulties making it back to Karluk Lake. The weather remained stormy and windy for the next several days. Imagine thirty-eight folks holed up in a relatively small bunkhouse with nothing to do while the weather remained inclement. Several movies and a projector were borrowed from the King. These had been rented to occupy Their Majesties when the weather was sour. We had to wait until they weren't being used at the big cabin, referred to by us commoners as "The Palace." Otherwise card games and lots of reading were the order of the day.

On the 15th, I had to fly to Kodiak with a group of people who would no longer stay with the party. The next day I returned with a load of fresh groceries, including pheasants, which had been flown to Kodiak from the Dakotas, or so I was told. Everything went to "The Palace."

Then I was required to make a trip and deliver one of the Department of State officers to Painter Creek on the Alaska Peninsula. This was supposed to be where the next phase of the hunt would be conducted. My instructions were to get back as soon as possible because I would be needed to do some flying. Landing at Painter Creek, we found a large military camp with cooking and sleeping tents set up. Snowmachines, which had been rented in Anchorage, were being driven up and down the gravel runway by some of the military folks. Quite an impressive set-up. After dropping off my passengers, I started back for the Karluk Lake camp.

The weather kept deteriorating as I flew back to Karluk Lake. I worked my way up the Savonoski River and through the pass to Hollis Bay. There the weather was even worse with low-hanging fog, so I took a compass heading and flew at wave-top height across Shelikof Strait. I knew I could climb out and intercept "Blue 27 Airway" and fly instruments to either King Salmon or Kodiak if things really got bad. The heading I was on would take me to Kupreanof Strait, and I was timing the trip so I would know when I should be seeing Raspberry Cape. Everything was going fine when out of the mist there appeared a fishing vessel just ahead of me. I hauled back, and as I went over him, entered the murk. This required an immediate descent again on instruments to make visual contact with the water. The old adrenaline was really pumping by then. I finally picked up the outline of the Cape and was able to work my way along the coast back to Karluk Lake. All the while I'm thinking to myself, *This is really stupid,* and wondering what kind of flying I would be needed for after I got back. I landed and beached the Grumman. Theron came out and asked about the trip, shook his head and said there would be no more flying that day. All that stress for nothing.

I wondered later what the skipper of that boat must have thought when he saw me heading straight for him? That is, if he did see me! What were the odds of a small boat being in my direct line of flight in the middle of a huge body of water like Shelikof Straight? Maybe someone can figure out those odds. I can't, but the one thing I do know is that in another mathematical formula it was a pucker factor of 9.9. Hell, no, an even 10.

On November 17, Al Burnett transported the King to a new hunting site in a Cessna 185. Theron Smith was on standby at Fraser Lake with the Queen and her party. The plan was that the King would kill a bear spotted the day before, return, and then they would all accompany the Queen to the location of another bear.

As the day progressed and no contact had been made with the King's party, Theron flew to a smaller lake and stood by while the Queen shot a bear assisted by guides Park Munsey and Ron Hurst. Upon returning to Karluk Lake, it was learned that the King had also taken a bear with Burnett, which completed the hunt. Al claimed the King's bear had been taken at Kiavak Bay outside the refuge. The bear apparently had not been skinned because of approaching darkness but had been gutted and left at the kill location. The information was given to the press the next day. On this day I proceeded to King Salmon to be available when the party moved.

The plan to use Ugashik Lake and Painter Creek for the second hunting location was canceled because the Kodiak police, Office of Naval Intelligence, and FBI had uncovered an alleged assassination plot. It was determined that the hunt would be conducted from King Salmon utilizing the military Air Force Base for Their Majesties' party and the facilities of the Bureau of Commercial Fisheries for the rest of the commoners.

On the 18th, assistant guide Park Munsey went to the location of the King's bear for the purpose of retrieving the hide and skull. Mr. Munsey later confided to a protection officer of the Alaska

Department of Fish and Game that the bear had not been killed at Kiavak Bay, but rather on one of the drainages of Fraser Lake approximately one mile within the boundaries of the closed area. This was one of the first of several game violations that occurred.

On the 19th, the entire group was flown to King Salmon aboard a military C-130, arriving at noon. Although there were strong winds blowing, the King requested an immediate hunt. For the next two days I made several flights with both the King and Queen; however, strong winds and turbulence prevented the taking of any animals. On one of the flights the King was so sick he was on his hands and knees in the back of the airplane with his personal bodyguard holding a bucket for him. I thought, *Boy, royal upchucking doesn't smell any better than that of any other passengers I've carried.*

On the 21st, the King took a large bull moose in the Mother Goose Lake area with guide Burnett. I assisted guide Ron Hurst in a successful taking of another large bull moose by the Queen in another area not far from where the King made his kill.

The following day Theron and I returned to the kill sites with the packers and skinners and transported all of the meat into King Salmon, where it was shipped to Anchorage via Northern Consolidated Airlines. We then secured the Grummans in a hangar and flew to Anchorage on the airlines to spend Thanksgiving Day with our families. The royal party was also flown to Anchorage via military aircraft.

For the next four days the party hunted out of Anchorage and the Talkeetna area, utilizing the efforts of several more guides and single-engine aircraft. The King took two caribou and a goat. The Queen took no more trophies. It was later determined that the goat was shot in a closed area.

We returned to King Salmon on the 24th and flew the Grummans back to Kodiak to await the arrival of the party for an elk hunt on Afognak Island. Another of the many changes in plans.

The party arrived at Kodiak on the 27th at approximately 1:30 P.M. aboard an Air Force C-130. Their Majesties and party were in hunting clothes and wanted to go to the elk-hunting area immediately. The King and his party were loaded in Theron's plane and the Queen and her group in mine. The third Grumman carried the packers and skinners. The area around Afognak was buffeted by strong northwesterly winds and proved unsuitable for hunting, so we returned to Kodiak. The following day provided us with winds in excess of 40 knots and the group made a local deer hunt, using Navy vehicles for transportation. Upon returning to Kodiak that evening, the hunt was canceled and the party returned to Anchorage via the reliable Air Force C-130.

On the 29th all three Grummans returned to Anchorage. A banquet was held that evening for some of those who participated in the hunt and I was told that the King had made an unsuccessful sheep hunt. The sheep-hunting party had consisted of two guides with fixed-wing aircraft and a helicopter. Apparently the guides attempted to take a sheep with the aid of the helicopter, a flagrant violation of game regulations.

Their Majesties departed shortly thereafter, leaving behind a lot of animosity and unpaid bills. There seemed to be a great deal of misunderstanding as to who was to pay the bills for the hotels, catering, and guide services. The royal party ran up bills of more than sixty thousand dollars. The Nepalese said the costs were too high and refused to pay. According to an article in the *Anchorage Daily News* dated May 4, 1968, they still hadn't paid the bills, and the Captain Cook Hotel general manager said he was at wit's end on how to collect. Apparently the U.S. State Department was an interested bystander. But it had shown no willingness to intervene—presumably because it might hurt Nepalese sensibilities.

I have no idea what the Captain Cook Hotel finally settled for. According to an article in the May 1969 issue of *Today in Alaska,* Burnett was quoted as saying he settled for half and was paying three thousand dollars at a time. He claimed he still was personally responsible for more than twenty thousand dollars. His contract with the Nepalese Embassy required him to sign for all expenses. He even had to pay for purple Hawaiian bananas and orchid centerpieces.

There was a lot of adverse criticism in the form of an undercurrent of grumbling among guides and a few of the sporting goods stores. Burnett was not a particularly well-qualified guide for the operation mostly because he did not have a big enough operation to handle such a large hunt. The fact that he solicited help of several other guides and outfitters to assist in making the hunt a success squelched some of the criticism. There were other more qualified guides with lodges and equipment that could have handled the hunt in a more efficient manner. Never was anyone on the local level of the Fish and Wildlife Service or Fish and Game asked for any input in the selection of a guide or outfitter.

There was continuous friction between the representatives of the Department of State and the Department of Interior as to who had the most authority. The Department of State Protocol Officer prevailed most of the time since he participated in the meetings between the King and guide Burnett. It was apparent that he was as concerned over his own hunting activities as he was of the royal hunt.

The hunt was termed a success even though Their Majesties had not taken all the animals requested. This was due mostly to the adverse weather conditions that prevailed throughout the hunt.

Was the hunt really a success? Depends on whom you talk to. Apparently as far as fostering good relations with Nepal, the President of the United States and the Secretary of Interior were well pleased, although some wondered at what cost.

Were there infractions of the Alaska Game Laws? Definitely.

Who was to blame? Again it depends on whom you talk to. The Department of Fish and Game made several investigations. Even though Burnett and the other guides were told that under no circumstances would game be taken illegally, there were constant rumors, among them: "State authorities were saying 'waive the rules.'" And, "There's room to bend a bit for a King, the state guest of our President." These, of course, were just rumors but some of the guides may have believed them. Otherwise why would they use a helicopter to try to kill a Dall sheep? After many months, Al Burnett's guides' license was revoked for taking the King's bear in a closed area. As far as I know he never reapplied for his license and quit the big-game guiding business.

It's obvious that politics and big-game hunting should never be mixed. This was a prime example of what can go wrong, did go wrong, and several innocent people were hurt in the process. For my part, I received a gift of a jewel-studded (actually cut glass) rhinoceros statue, and if you ask to see it I can honestly say I don't even know where it is.

Chapter 23

SURVEYS WITH THE DC-3

*T*heron Smith had been my mentor since I qualified as a pilot for the Enforcement Division back in 1953. He had a wealth of flying information from years of professional flying, which he patiently shared with his students.

On October 24, 1965, I was just beginning the learning curve of handling the DC-3 while assisting a couple of biologists on a special mission, with Theron again serving as my instructor. While we flew toward the Aleutian Islands, we alternated seats as he observed my flying and advised me on the proper procedures for flying that great bird. When Theron was at the controls, he explained every move he made and the reason for his action. We had many discussions on the electrical and hydraulic systems so necessary to know in the event of any in-flight emergency. It was "Doug Flying 101" with the master.

Our passengers included Dave Spencer, FWS refuge supervisor, and Karl Kenyon, a FWS marine biologist from Seattle. We were instructed to fly to Amchitka, where the military was about to test an atomic bomb set in a 5,000-foot-deep shaft that was sealed with tons of cement. Our job was to conduct a sea-otter survey after the blast to determine any loss to the sea-otter population. The biological part of the trip turned out to be a complete loss because of severe weather. High wind churned the water around the shoreline while we were there, making it impossible to observe otters in the surf, much less count them. Flying out and back, however, was a tremendous experience and provided some excellent Doug training.

After an uneventful trip from Anchorage to Cold Bay, we were held up two days while several violent storms moved up the Aleutian Chain like a set of rosary beads. The biggest reason for the delay was the long hop from Cold Bay to Adak with limited gas reserves. We figured the flight time would be about four hours, depending on winds. The Doug had an eight-hour fuel supply and in the event en route weather prevented us from making Adak, we might have a serious problem returning to Cold Bay.

With that in mind, we made arrangements with Reeves Airlines to "top off" our tanks at Umnak, a small settlement on Umnak Island.

Reeves flew mail and supplies to a sheep ranch on the island in a DC-3, and they kept a reserve supply of fuel there for emergencies. By refueling at Umnak, we would have enough for any exigencies we might encounter.

We departed Cold Bay on October 27. Winds and low visibility made for an interesting landing at Umnak. After taxiing up to the fuel shack, one of the two inhabitants came down to help us take on fuel. Getting up on the wing was no easy task in the fifty-plus knots of wind that were blowing. I was handed the gas hose and told to start fueling. Nothing came out of the nozzle. After about ten minutes, I was told to come down while Theron and the guy in charge of the facilities tried to figure what was wrong. The inside of the shack was a maze of pipes and valves and looked like a mad spider was involved in the construction. Theron, Mr. "Patience Personified," checked each valve and followed each pipe to its source. The guys who lived on the island had no clue. There didn't seem to be any way to get gas to run. Finally he hunched up his shoulders, which was the only way I was ever able to tell when he was frustrated and climbed the ladder to the top of the outside tank. Low and behold there was no gas in the tank.

"Not to worry," says the happy fellow. (He didn't get much company, that was obvious.) "We have that truck over there with more fuel, and we'll just pump it into the tank." When that was accomplished I went back up on the wing and sure enough gas started pumping into the reserve tanks. After topping off I went down and checked the sump drains using paper cups to catch samples. Instead of clear gas the sample was full of dirt and scum. What looked like cobwebs and blotches of "whatever" came pouring out and never cleared. We made a decision to takeoff on the main tanks and after getting on top of the overcast to switch to the rear tanks and make sure the engines would burn what appeared to be very contaminated fuel.

Once on top and in the clear, we switched tanks. After running a few minutes the engines started missing, so did our heartbeats. We immediately switched back to the mains and the radial engines started running smoothly again and helped slow down our pulse to normal again. Now we had no choice but to go on to Adak on the mains and use the rear tanks only in the event of an emergency.

As we got closer to Adak, another problem confronted us. The controllers at the Naval Air Station had set up a series of what were called "gates" to indicate the plane's exact position when approaching Adak. Scores of military aircraft connected to the project were flying in and out of the Navy facility every day. These imaginary positions were located by using Distance Measuring Equipment (DME), which unfortunately we didn't have on this plane. Luckily the tops of most of the mountains were showing above the overcast. By keeping a close track of our location with "time and distance" and tracking the mountaintops that were visible, we were able to do a fair job of locating our position. The one-hundred-mile gate was very close to Korovin Volcano, so we called in that position to Adak and got an affirmative. The fifty-mile gate was close to Kasatochi Island, which although only 1,030 feet high, could be seen through the clouds, so we made that our second position report. No problem with that one either, and we were put into a holding pattern while other aircraft made approaches.

The weather was at minimums, but Adak had a Ground Control Approach (GCA) system in service so all aircraft were landing without any problems. This was my first GCA, and it was most stimulating since the pilot is completely under the control of an unknown person operating the radar. We had to use about a 30-degree track to stay on the centerline, which in itself was interesting, as we came down through the murk. Finally the controller said we were in sight and, sure enough there was the runway. Ah, yes, with all of these modern instruments and ground controllers, how could a person go wrong?

With good fortune we had made it on the main fuel tanks, so now what to do about the contaminated gas? Fortunately the Navy had equipment to purge the gas, which they willingly did for us. So all that chaos at Umnak was for naught and the entire fuel in the rear tanks, which we had paid for, had to be destroyed.

There were other problems at Adak. A Greek ship had gone aground at Great Sitkin Island, and crews were busy trying to contain the leaking oil. Since there had been a delay in detonating the bomb, we spent our time making surveys around Adak to determine any sea mammal loss due to the oil. We were able to find only one sea otter, so Dave Spencer radioed the refuge headquarters at Cold Bay requesting one of the biologists to check on the progress of the cleanup and to verify any other loss of animals and birds.

We received word that the bomb had been detonated and to proceed to Amchitka on the 29th. Being good guys, we took on board a group of reporters anxious to get to the island and report on the blast. This was another instrument flight with a landing on Amchitka into some of the violent winds for which the Aleutians are famous. Storms and high winds plagued us day after day. On the second day the winds were violent enough to tear out the tie-down rings requiring us to chain the wheels down as the only means of securing the aircraft.

The storms continued, making it impossible to do any aerial observations. Our time was spent walking and checking the beaches and surf. We spotted thirty sea otter, four seals, and numerous sea birds, all in good condition and showing no effects of the blast. We did find some eagle parts underneath some of the cliff nests indicating that someone had shot a few of the birds.

One evening Dave Spencer took me aside and told me he overheard one of the officers commenting to a friend that he was leaving on the evening flight with his eagles. Dave suggested I do something about it. I called my assistant agent, Don Combs, in Anchorage and gave him the information, telling him to meet the plane and check out the story. The next day Don called and asked me, "What the hell are you smoking out there?" Seems that the officer was bragging about being promoted to colonel and was going to get "eagles" on his uniform. Thanks, Dave.

Finally on November 8 after checking weather forecasts, we determined it was time to give up and return to Anchorage. We departed at 0940, checked for sea otter around Adak, and refueled. At the request of the commanding officer, we took on a Navy passenger who needed a ride to Kenai due to a family emergency. Another fuel stop at Cold Bay, and then on to Kenai all IFR. This was my leg to fly and I was looking forward to the challenge. It was a turbulent trip across the mountains with severe up- and downdrafts. We were both kept busy. Theron had to keep lowering the gear and flaps as we hit violent updrafts and then retract them while I throttled up to "takeoff power" again as we cascaded on the downside of the wind shear. Once over the mountains, the weather cleared and we could see Kenai from a long way out. A beautiful sight after flying through the turbulent overcast. Our passenger got out with his baggage, and we were off again, an easy twenty-minute flight to Anchorage in clear weather. Then, shortly after takeoff, we lost all the oil in the starboard engine and had to shut it down. The Doug handled quite well at 2,000 feet with one engine and no load to speak of. We landed without problem at 2455. My first night landing on one engine.

Now who was really in charge of that flight? Theron and I were the pilots, but who controlled the engine, which performed so perfectly during all the time we were over the Aleutians with a bad fuel supply? Then in anything-but-nice weather while we were over the Alaska Range on instruments fighting turbulence? Why did we bust the engine on the last leg of the flight within easy flying to Anchorage? We certainly had some guidance other than our flying skills and plain old luck. Being a firm believer, I know that God had a hand in there and took us under his wing or at least controlled the wings of the DC-3. I leave it up to you to decide.

Three years later, I found myself back in the Doug's cockpit with Theron for final training for upgrading my certificate to include a Type Rating in the DC-3. What began as a training flight and wildlife survey turned into a memorable outing that might have had international ramifications.

"When we're back from this trip, I'm confident you'll be ready for your check ride and Type Rating in the DC-3," Theron said.

It was April 12, 1968, and with those words, we took off from Anchorage to conduct a walrus survey of the Bering Sea. I flew in left, or pilot's seat, and Theron was the copilot and navigator.

On the walrus survey, Carl Kenyon, marine mammal biologist, was in charge of the counts, assisted by John Burns, a marine mammal biologist with the Alaska Department of Fish and Game. They would call the shots as to where and when we would fly. The surveys were to be conducted at three hundred feet above the ice or water, and all the walrus would be counted that were within a quarter of a mile of each side of the airplane. This required one of the biologists to sit in the copilot's seat for counting the mammals on the right side of the aircraft, and the second biologist had to stand behind the captain or pilot. Since the stand-up spot was the most tedious, they traded off frequently.

Surveys on good days lasted up to eight continuous hours, which was tedious for both the crew and counters, so Theron and I traded off also. This was the reason the FWS in later years rebuilt a Grumman Goose with a four-man cockpit for over-water surveys. With that configuration the biologists sat behind the pilot and copilot, making for a more comfortable working condition for all concerned.

Our biggest weather problem was fog. When dealing with a survey area covering most of the Bering Sea, the weather can continually change, especially when flying over areas of solid ice, which give way to ice floes and open water. We didn't have any electronic navigation gear in those days, such as GPS or Loran, so we had to rely on the old-fashioned method of "compass headings" and "time and distance." Theron, being an excellent navigator, compensated with his best guess to the drift caused by wind.

Most of the time we hit our latitude and longitude destinations within the limits imposed by the biologists. On occasions we were off course because of the fog or low ceilings. This required the biologists to make compensations on their plots. Several times we encountered fog with visibility as low as a quarter of a mile. We hung in each time, remaining in contact since to punch out and go on instruments would mean the end of the transect with no way to get back to that particular spot to continue the count. This could also require deadheading back to base, costing extra money that the scientists could not afford, so they said.

Most of the flights ended up in Nome, and knowing we might have to return in bad weather occasionally, we practiced instrument approaches on each arrival, much to Carl's consternation. He would scream from the back of the airplane that it was costing him money to fly an extra fifteen minutes and could we be so kind as to do the practicing on our own time and money! Our answer of course was that in the event the weather was down after a long flight he would be very happy that we were proficient with the approach. Most of this was in jest, however, since Carl had been a Navy pilot in World War II and had flown fighters off carriers. He knew very well how necessary precision flying was when making an instrument landing, but then, money was tight for this survey, and he wanted to be able to complete the analysis with the bucks he had.

Then came the day when we ran into fog while flying west into the Gulf of Anadyr. We continued our course and I turned northwest at Theron's direction and started another leg. After the appropriate time on that heading, Theron gave me a new course that took us southeast and we started a new transect. We were still in the fog with about half a mile visibility. All this time we were thinking about the briefing we had received from a captain of Navy Intelligence prior to our departure. He had advised us in no uncertain terms that we were never to fly within fifteen miles of the coast of Russia. We assured them that we had no intention of flying anywhere near the coast and thanked him for the warning.

My notes of that day read as follows: "Departed Nome at 1027 on a heading of 245 deg. to 63:30N and 172:40W then 211 deg. To 63:30N and 174:40W where we hit fog and flew a reciprocal for 10 minutes. We then took up a heading of 260 deg. for 45 minutes and hit fog again. Had to reverse course again for 10 minutes and took up

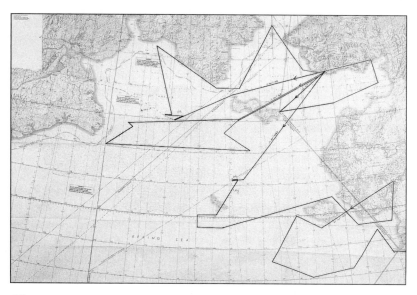

This map shows the route that we flew during the walrus surveys of April 16–23, 1968. We recorded the tracks as we flew them, then transferred the information to a final map so biologists would know exactly where we'd gone.

a new heading of 312 deg. to 64:57N and 176:50W followed by a heading of 109 deg."

After about fifteen minutes of flying east we found ourselves over land and a group of Natives were waving up at us. A quick look at the map indicated we were probably over the small village of Nuntigram built on a peninsula. We had obviously flown too far north of our intended tract and our positions were not as accurate we had hoped. There was nothing to do but continue on our current heading. Soon we were back over ice again still in the fog.

After about another fifteen minutes of flying, we broke out into clear weather. The Russian coast was about fifteen miles north of us so we were okay at this point. Then the MiG arrived.

I don't know who spotted the plane first, but suddenly we lost interest in the survey and gave our full attention to the fighter. He made several circles coming up from behind and buzzing over the top of us. We quickly looked in our flight manuals and located the international signals that applied when approached by a foreign military aircraft. According to the instructions, if the aircraft flew ahead of us and waggled his wings it would mean we would have to follow him or the pilot would not be responsible for our safety. We watched carefully knowing that the Russian air base of Urelik was just north of us. However, after each pass, the MiG made a sharp turn to the right and repeated another pass. Then he disappeared from our view. In a few minutes he came back from the right side all slowed down with his gear; flaps and speed brakes extended. In this configuration he made a pass across the nose of the Doug.

As we were taking pictures, several things were very noticeable. First he was going too slowly for that kind of flying and also how small the pilot appeared. For some reason I had visualized all Russians to be big guys. Interesting the things that go through your mind when dealing with an unknown. Then I had this thought, here was a pilot who had probably screwed up somehow and had been banished to Siberia. If that was so he might want to make a name for himself at our expense. But such was not the case because it was obvious that he was very busy himself taking pictures of the Doug. I thought about the picture of the scantily clad, curvaceous gal painted on the nose of the plane we were flying. It had been leased from Red Dodge, a well-known Alaska pilot, and underneath the picture was the caption "Hello Dolly." I'm quite sure this was the center of his attention.

After he went past the nose of the plane he probably decided it was time to fly the airplane again. We watched in horror as he leveled his wings, applied full throttle, kicked in the afterburner and whatever other power he had and slowly descended while trying to recover flying speed. Remember, we were at three hundred feet, and he didn't have much air space under his jet fighter. We could actually see water spraying from behind the plane as he built up airspeed. Someone remarked, "If he goes in, we'll have a hell of a time explaining that we had nothing to do with it!" After what seemed like an eternity, but was probably only a few seconds, he had enough speed to pull up and was gone.

"Okay, can we focus on walrus again?" mumbled Carl. We conferred and decided that since it didn't seem like the Russians were going to harass us anymore we would continue with the original flight plan and proceed north inside Big Diomede Island to our designated point opposite East Cape.

The rest of the flight was uneventful, with many walrus counted and a return to Nome in time for dinner. Flight time 7.7 hours.

We flew surveys for three more days as far as 179:18W before returning to Anchorage on April 24. The biologists were happy, and Theron and I were also happy that all went so well.

After studying up for the orals with Red Dodge, owner of the Doug, and spending two hours in a Link trainer, I passed my check ride. Red, one of Western Airlines chief pilots, flew as first officer. Since he owned the plane I'm sure he was very interested in not only making sure I passed, but also that I brought the Doug back in one piece. So at last I was a genuine legal DC-3 driver, and my Airline Transport Pilot's license had its first Type rating stamped on it.

Chapter 24

THE GRUMMAN GOOSE

*M*y second love affair with an airplane was with this great amphibian. First built in 1936, it has seen service all over the world. Originally, Grumman built it as an executive and general utility airplane; however, the Navy modified it to government specifications and used it extensively in World War II. With two Pratt and Whitney R-985 engines developing 450 horsepower each, it was the workhorse of the Fish and Wildlife Service for many years, and later with the Alaska Department of Fish and Game. Patrols of the commercial fisheries were conducted with this venerable aircraft, and they were a common sight along Alaska's coastline. It could land on water or land in the most remote regions.

Prior to statehood, the Fish and Wildlife Service had several professional pilots to fly enforcement agents on commercial fisheries patrols with the Grummans. This included putting out stream guards and supplying them during the spawning runs. Guards were temporary hires placed on the important river and stream mouths to protect the valuable stocks of salmon entering the waterways. These fish mill around in river mouths waiting for the right temperature and water level before starting their important upstream migration. Commercial fishermen are well aware of this and the greedy ones would sneak in, complete a quick set, make a big haul, and quickly leave.

While it was impossible to protect every stream, most of the most important ones were protected for the summer. After statehood, the Alaska Department of Fish and Game changed the procedure and placed guards at different locations hidden from the beaches. Fishermen never knew which stream was protected. This stopped a good deal of poaching. There was enough money in this illegal taking that fishermen have been known to shoot into the brush to scare off any hidden guards before entering the stream mouth. During territorial days, stream guards were bribed and a few ended up missing.

The Grumman provided the most effective means of patrolling and supplying camps because of its versatility. As well as landing in the open water, it could lower the landing gear down and climb out on beaches. Fuel drums, lumber, metal roofing, and you name it, were delivered wherever needed. It could haul a ton if the pilot wasn't too concerned with being legal.

One of the reasons I was trained to fly the Grumman during the summer of 1964 was to more effectively patrol the oil rigs in Cook Inlet, which had been accused of operating "dirty." We received several complaints from workers who were genuinely concerned that the industry promoted throwing garbage, including mud sacks, into the water at night. Also according to these whistle-blowers, mud cleanings, which contained oil, as well as old oil from generators and other equipment, were also being discharged into the inlet. The Fish and Wildlife Service had authority to check for any violations under the provisions of the Migratory Bird Treaty Act.

I also became involved with enforcing the provisions of refuge regulations, especially those controlling brown-bear hunting on Kodiak Island. These regulations required that all brown bears taken be sealed and verified as legal. Refuge managers, with the assistance of agents of the enforcement division, conducted an elaborate enforcement program to assure compliance. These island bears were seldom pursued by aircraft because of the mountainous terrain. However, camps were established and supported by planes. Most of the patrol efforts were to assure compliance with the license and permit provisions of the regulations, and to assure bears weren't taken in any closed-to-hunting areas.

Bear camps were mostly located at the heads of bays and landings, and could sometimes be tricky, requiring local knowledge of gravel bars and hidden obstructions. This also made some beaching a challenge. Most of the hunting occurred out of camps of registered big-game guides. They were, for the most part, of a higher caliber than the mainland airplane harvesters, and usually ran a much cleaner operation. This was probably in part due to the type of terrain being hunted.

Patrolling Cook Inlet with the Goose was probably the most challenging flying I did. I mentioned in a previous chapter about the danger of swells. As mentioned, landing in open water required landing parallel to and on the crest or backside of a swell. To forget this basic rule was to court disaster. At times in Cook Inlet there are multiple swells moving in several different directions. Other times the swells weren't as pronounced and these insidious ones could cause serious problems. In open water with no shoreline to use as a guide,

We picked a perfect spot to land the Goose for lunch while conducting an eagle survey on Prince William Sound.

I learned to evaluate them from several different heights and then line up on the one that looked the best and then take a compass heading. When it became difficult to read the swells on final approach I at least knew I was lined up in the right direction.

There was always a big sigh when the old bird came off the step and settled into the water and became a boat. If we had landed because of an obvious sheen, it was now time to take water samples. While the biologists were doing this, I often looked up at the gigantic platform and realized how insignificant and small we really were. A small cork bouncing around in a huge body of water. After the samples were collected, all that was left was the takeoff. Line up with the swell and pour on the power. Climb up on the back and try to build up enough speed to take off on the crest. At times this could be just as exhilarating and exciting as the landing.

In politics, as always a series of compromises, the governor appointed a committee consisting of representatives of the oil companies and executives of both the state and federal bureaucracies having jurisdiction with the industry. The idea was to allow the operators to clean up their act without the consequences of enforcement action. This was big money to the state and they were treading on tender toes.

The chief of the Fish and Wildlife Service enforcement division was a representative, and I occasionally represented him. The committee met quarterly for a show-and-tell session. We would submit the number of oil slicks that had been reported during the period by private commercial pilots or those we had cataloged ourselves. The industry members would then submit a report of any spills they had knowledge of. These included workers inadvertently spilling "some" oil, someone forgetting to turn off a valve or occasionally opening up the wrong one. Then we would compare notes with a discussion on how things could be improved. As with any government committee it didn't last long and very little was accomplished except no violations were filed during that period. In fact the rule was that if one of us observed a spill, we could not report it to anyone except the governor's representative. Talk about a closed shop! My lips were supposed to be completely sealed.

At the time I had a very concerned newspaper reporter who was constantly calling me for information on any oil leaks. My answer had to be, "I'm not aware of any at the moment."

There had to be a better way, so we finally came up with a method that kept me legal. When I located what appeared to be a spill I would call the reporter and ask him if any spill had been reported. If not, he would immediately call back after I hung up to ask me if I had observed any spills that day. Once asked I could not lie and would have to advise him of what I had seen on patrol. If it were significant enough, he would ask to be taken on a flight as an observer and to take pictures. This cat-and-mouse game went on all one summer until there was a noteworthy effort on the part of the industry to clean up the inlet mess. Today it's a relatively clean environment due mostly to the concerns of a few individuals and the fact that the oil industry can't stand bad publicity.

As with the Gullwing, I had my embarrassing moments. I was asked to take some state legislators on a look-see trip of the Cook Inlet oil platforms. On the day we were to make the trip, the hangar crew really gussied up the Grumman. She was all shiny and clean and I was in my best class-A uniform. When the cavalcade arrived I was busy inside crossing the seat belts so everything would be ship-shape. I proceeded out to greet the group and noticed it also included a few women. No problem, but I told myself I had better be on my best behavior. The Grumman has a small two-step removable ladder that hangs from the doorframe for getting in and out. I was wearing a new pair of jodhpurs with leather soles and as I was stepping onto the first step I had my eyes on my passengers as they were getting out of the limos. Not paying particular attention (after all I had done this hundreds of times) my foot slipped in between the steps and the fuselage.

As I lost my balance I knew I had a choice of either letting my foot slide inside the steps with the possibility of causing a scraped limb, or falling forward and then having to try to dislodge it. I went forward in what was a most ungraceful forward dive, landing on my hands. I pulled my leg and the steps loose in one motion. Then from my knees I looked up at the open mouths and said, "Hi, I'm your pilot!" What would you have done? I fully expected to see them all get back into the limos and head back to town, but they were a game group and they all laughed with me. At least I think they were laughing with me. The rest of the trip went well even though my uniform was a mess. Have to keep a sense of humor if you want to be a good Goose pilot!

We hauled everything imaginable in these workhorses. Since we weren't bound by FAA regulations, as long as we could get the door closed it was considered a legal load. I moved Agent Zahn and his family from Dillingham to Kodiak when he was transferred to that district. We loaded up all their belongings and when we were finished it reminded me of Steinbeck's book and movie *The Grapes of Wrath*. All that was missing were some chicken coops hanging from the outside. When it was all stuffed in, I had to climb in the cockpit window to get to the controls.

During the Fairbanks flood in 1967, I was busy making two and three flights a day to and from Anchorage. On the trips to Anchorage I was loaded up with critical parts like carburetors, heater elements, and furnace motors to name a few. On the return it was food and supplies needed to get people started again. I remember on one trip I was loaded with bread, nothing but loaves of bread. All the bread that would fit inside the cabin and in the copilot's seat. A flying bakery truck, I thought, as I departed. It wasn't a very heavy load but it sure smelled good.

Then there were always animals to move. The state decided to establish a herd of moose on Kodiak Island one year in August. The Fish and Wildlife Service was asked to participate with the loan of one Goose. Two Grummans were needed to haul nine moose calves. By August the calves were about three months old and getting quite big. The vet had them tranquilized by the time we arrived in Palmer, where they had been held. We loaded five in my Goose, all hog-tied and lying on their sides. Fortunately my helper was Ken Daniels, chief mechanic of the State Aircraft Division. Ken is a big, strong guy and we found that his strength was needed before we reached our destination.

When we were within an hour of Kodiak, the sedative began wearing off and several of the moose began kicking and trying to untangle their legs to stand up. It took all of Ken's strength to keep them down as he kept tightening up all the ropes. We finally arrived with a big sigh of relief and hastily assisted the biologist, who was there to greet us and unload our unhappy passengers. They all wandered off and we went back to Anchorage with a smelly plane. As I remember all nine moose were killed that first hunting season even though there was no open season.

Sometimes you win and sometimes you lose.

In the spring of 1978, I felt it was time to retire from the U.S. Fish and Wildlife Service. I knew that the state's aircraft section hired temporary Grumman pilots each summer and planned to apply for a position. I had some long talks with my friend Buck Stewart, who was the state's aircraft supervisor. The answer was, yes, I could fly as a summer hire, however, Buck was retiring, and Commissioner of Public Safety Burton had suggested that I should consider being his replacement. I read and reread the minimum qualifications and decided I not only would qualify, but I wanted the challenging job. The qualifications required a current FAA commercial pilot license with multiengine land and sea rating, two thousand hours of Alaska flying experience, FAA-certified aircraft instructor, four years of professional experience in aircraft maintenance and operation, and commission as an officer in the Department of Public Safety. There were other two-thousand-hour pilots who had the flying and maintenance experience; however, being able to meet the state's police standards to qualify for a commission as an officer was the big problem. I sent in my resume and application to the state administration office and was told I would qualify.

I retired from the Federal Fish and Wildlife Service on Friday, April 7, 1978, and then went to work for the State Department of Public Safety on April 10, the following Monday. How's that for a short retirement? One weekend.

When I took over the job, the state had about forty pilots and twenty-nine airplanes. Three were Grummans, 1 de Havilland Beaver, 2 Cessna 180s, 4 Cessna 185s, 1 Cessna 150, 1 Cessna 207, and 17 Piper Super Cubs. There were also 2 Hiller 12E helicopters. A total of nine people worked in the hangar as aircraft mechanics, sheet metal workers, a radio technician, and secretary. The job description stated that I had to plan the section's budget and equipment levels, develop operation standards for pilots and equipment maintenance and operation, check out new pilots for technical competence and maturity of judgment, make or direct periodic check flights to assure continued flight proficiency and compliance with regulations, and designate departmental check pilots. I also would serve as pilot of single- and twin-engine land seaplanes. Quite a bit of responsibility I realized.

The three Grummans had been transferred from the Fish and Wildlife Service under the Statehood Act. One was stationed in Juneau, one in Kodiak, and one in Anchorage. The Juneau and Kodiak Grummans were mostly kept busy with commercial fisheries patrols. The Anchorage plane was used mostly to give check rides, VIP flights, moving freight to the outlying districts, hauling prisoners, and as a backup in the event one of the others had mechanical problems.

Each winter for three years one of the airplanes was flown to Viking Air in Sydney, B.C., Canada, the only Goose repair facility on the West Coast. There a complete overhaul was performed including a new center section, which was also a fuel tank, and retractable wing floats. The original wing floats were a problem whenever the Goose was flown in instrument conditions. Ice formed on the struts and wires, sometimes causing them to snap, which then allowed the float to swing freely. The retractable floats folded up on the ends of the wings, added a few knots of airspeed, and cleaned up the plane against icing. The Grumman is not a great instrument airplane and was only flown in IFR conditions in emergencies.

I really loved my job. The Grummans were my pets and I jealously guarded against any threat to get rid of them. Selling them raised its ugly head many times in the legislature and each time I had to justify their use. They did the work that was required. However, they were a maintenance problem. The last one had been built in 1944, and parts were either hard to get or nonexistent. We had to make our own replacements, which were costly. At the time, however, no other plane was available as a substitute that could do the job required.

One interesting incident occurred that almost ended an early career with the state. The maintenance supervisor, Ken Daniels, knew everyone in the business. He was able to scrounge parts when needed to keep the planes flying. It was a "scratch my back and I'll scratch yours" kind of agreement. We borrowed from other aircraft operators, replacing the parts as soon as we could get them ordered and shipped in. It was impossible to keep an inventory of every part required for a fleet as diversified as ours. In this way the downtime for our planes was minimal. You can imagine how important this was when a plane had a mechanical in outlying areas. If there was an operator in the area, we could always get a part. Conversely operators also borrowed from us.

Emit Soldin, one of the old Fish and Wildlife Service retired professional pilots, came into my office with a request. He was getting a private Grumman ready to ferry to Seattle. It was to be used in a new television program in Hawaii. If I remember correctly, the series was titled *Tales of a Golden Monkey*. The Goose he was repairing needed a set of brakes to get to Seattle. They were hard to come by, and the only ones he was planning to purchase weren't available for the trip south. I talked with Ken, who advised me that we had three spare sets, so it would pose no problem. Emit walked out with the brakes.

Murphy's Law set in on the trip to Seattle. The two ferry pilots departed Anchorage and flew on a direct heading across the Gulf of Alaska. Somewhere off the coast of Yakutat, one engine quit and the other soon followed suit. They were forced to land in some very rough water miles from shore. A "mayday" had been radioed before they landed, so all they could do was sit on the Goose as it bobbed around in the swells, slowly sinking. Eventually a helicopter plucked them off the hull just before the Grumman sank to the bottom of the ocean. Along with the Goose went the state's brakes.

Shortly afterward I had an administrative inspection that required all parts listed on inventory be identified and available for viewing by the examiner. We squirmed our way through the inspection. Many of our parts were on airplanes that were in the field, making it impossible to come up with each piece of equipment listed on inventory. A note was made about the missing brakes so I applied pressure on Emit to replace them soon, sooner than soon. He did, but the inspector wrote up a not-so-nice report on our record-keeping system and storage of parts. The end result came after I retired with the state administrative division requiring that all parts be listed on a newly acquired computer with a paper trail for every piece of equipment and where it was located. This ended the borrow-and-replace system that Ken had going. An unfortunate ending to providing timely service to the maintenance program.

I retired—again—in 1983 and started my own business as an Arctic survival instructor. The Aircraft Section has made many changes since that time. I was able to change the aircraft supervisor position description before I left office and take out the commissioned police officer requirement, which was no longer needed. Ron Samsell, my chief pilot, took over the position and did a credible job and now is retired. The Grummans are gone, replaced with a turbine-powered Cessna Caravan on amphibian floats. It's my understanding that it's doing the job; however, gone is the ability to beach the aircraft, which was a great uniqueness of the Goose. Thus ended a great period in aviation history.

One of the Grummans I flew has been restored to its original configuration and painted in the good old black-and-orange colors of the U.S. Fish and Wildlife Service. It now sits proudly at the Alaska Aviation Heritage Museum at Lake Hood in Anchorage. I can at least go out and look at it and view my name in the aircraft logs. I also have a model sitting on my desk, my memorial to that great airplane.

Chapter 25

THE PROTECTORS VERSUS THE SPOILERS

$\mathcal{U}$p until statehood, the FWS Enforcement Division placed emphasis on intensive patrols during hunting and trapping seasons, investigating violations, and prosecuting violators through the federal court system. During the off-seasons a bigger effort was put forth to control the activities of illicit guides who made a profitable living killing wildlife without regard for the law.

Then there were those who killed because a particular animal stood in the way of profit. Many commercial fishermen killed every brown bear they encountered because they competed for the valuable salmon stocks. They even fostered a bounty on all brown bears, which fortunately was never passed.

As big-game sport hunting became more popular, aided by advanced mobile equipment, enforcement agents had to be trained as investigators. This was necessary if we were to cope with the new breed of hunter and guide. The guiding industry began to flourish, and for substantial fees, many guides were willing to conduct quickie illegal kills. These were usually accomplished with the aid of Super Cubs, commonly called "harvesters," on big wheels capable of landing almost anywhere. Game could easily be herded to the wealthy killers, many of whom were unable to walk even a short distance to where they could hide in wait. It was illegal killing at its worst, but it was also big money.

The federal Lacey Act prohibits shipping any wildlife taken illegally from a state or territory. Our agents stayed busy conducting investigations of hunters who had taken game illegally in Alaska and then transported the trophies to other states and countries. As more pressure was applied to commercial violators, the value of trophies increased, and guides became more efficient and nefarious in their activities.

The FWS hired additional agents, and Congress finally updated the game laws and put more teeth into the penalty section. But this became moot with statehood. After 1959, the newly created Alaska Department of Fish and Game installed a Fish and Wildlife Protection Division to protect state laws and regulations governing all indigenous wildlife within its boundaries. This reduced the federal agent force in

During a career spanning three decades, my mission was to stop poor hunting practices and urge protection of the resource. Even with more complicated game laws, it's just as tough for today's wildlife agents to enforce them.

Alaska and the emphasis changed from one of patrol warden to patrol investigator, involving intensive investigations of wildlife taken in violation and shipped out of the state.

Change came again in 1974, when the FWS Enforcement Division was reorganized and our titles changed to that of "Special Agents." Wildlife was becoming a bigger business, and guides, taxidermists, outfitters, and importers organized themselves into a multimillion dollar industry. It was necessary to infiltrate the illegal dealers with undercover agents. Congress finally realized this and made funds available.

As the "Special Agent in Charge," I set up the first of these operations in Alaska. We were able to get an agent and his hunter friend to pose as hunter-clients on an illegal polar bear hunt. The results were rewarding since the guides were linked with a big taxidermy firm in Seattle known to be dealing in unlawful hides and furs. The case reached out to illegal hunts in Montana and California and opened everyone's eyes as to how big a business this kind of hunting really was. Unfortunately, the results in court were less than rewarding because we were dealing with misdemeanor crimes. Most district court judges weren't happy having their courts cluttered with complicated misdemeanor trials lasting days and weeks, and this one involving several hunters, guides, a booking agency, and taxidermy firm would definitely be lengthy. After all, rape and murder trials gathered more attention and had to be given priority.

Today agents are faced with a whole new generation of complicated conservation laws to enforce. The Marine Mammal Act, the Endangered Species Act, the Alaska Native Claims Settlement Act, and the Alaska National Interest Lands Conservation Act, to name a few, are making the job even more complex. There are now inspectors checking all incoming wildlife shipments entering the United States. It is illegal to allow entry to the United States any animal classified as endangered in another country. Many unsuspecting tourists who have bought wildlife souvenirs have been irate to have them seized as they returned home. On the other hand, drug smugglers have tried to ship illegal drugs into the country inside wildlife products that have been made up into trinkets and trophies.

Our efforts weren't in vain, however. Our success encouraged the state legislature to fund the Alaska Department of Fish and Game Protection Division with undercover funds to conduct operations against the growing illegal-hunting trade. The results were excellent, planes were confiscated, and substantial fines levied. This work is ongoing because the illegitimate trade will continue as long as there are those prepared to pay the fee. Greed knows no bounds, and as long as there is a person willing to pay for an illegal hunt, there will be a guide willing to risk all to accommodate him. The big question to most legal hunters and nonconsumptive users is, "Why?" Why spend thousands of dollars to get an illegal animal and risk heavy fines, jail, and the loss of the trophy, and the possibility of being ostracized by his peers? The answer has to be ego. These are not hunters; they are killers after a quick-and-easy entry into a record book.

A good example of how far a person with the means will go to get into a record book occurred in Alaska several years back. A nationally known "sportsman" with many recorded kills to his credit was also a board member of a museum of natural history in one of the southwestern states. The directors of this museum requested and were granted a permit from the Fish and Wildlife Service to obtain a musk-ox bull from the Nunivak Island Refuge. This bull was to be made into a full mount for a habitat group that would include a cow and calf, which would be collected at a later date when funds became available. A permit was issued with the stipulation that the refuge manager would collect the animal, much to the consternation of the sportsman-board member. He requested and was granted permission to accompany the biologist to oversee the preparation and shipment of the hide, skull, and leg bones. Prolonged bad weather and a tight schedule required him to leave before a bull could be taken. The animal was prepared in accordance to the instructions and shipped to New Mexico.

Imagine everyone's surprise when the next edition of the Boone and Crockett record book listed this musk ox as taken by the famous hunter. If that were not enough, the hide had been reduced to a cape and made into head mount that adorned his trophy room. We advised the Boone and Crockett authorities, and they retracted the record. The head was seized and confiscated by our agents. An isolated case, you say? Not so, and Fish and Wildlife Service records have many examples of the extremes people will go to be listed in the "record book."

When Theodore Roosevelt and his colleagues formed the "Boone and Crockett Club" in 1887, they envisioned a society that would foster sportsmanlike methods of hunting. They encouraged the hunting of big game as a sport for vigorous and masterful people pursuing wildlife by foot, horseback, canoe, or dogsled. The "Credo of Fair Chase" was developed to stop the wanton killing of helpless animals and those caught in traps or deep snow. In 1963 the club added to the fair chase code rule "no spotting or herding game from the air." Other rules precluded pursuing game from a motor-powered vehicle.

Since most authorities, including the board members of organizations like the Boone and Crocket and the Safari Club International, agree that sportsmanship cannot be legislated, maybe it's time to close the book. Certainly by now there are enough records by which hunters can gauge their trophies. There is no need to continue recognizing "hero hunters."

Unfortunately, too many organizations foster the kill image, and they too should rewrite their bylaws to end "head hunting." Surely, we can all improve the image of hunting and bring back the nuts and bolts of fair chase. The bandit guide and his combustion engine would fade out of the picture without these people. He would be forced to conduct a "hunt" instead of a "thrill kill." Poor hunting practices must stop some time, either voluntarily or by mandate, or all our hunting will be legislated out of existence. The choice is ours and we better make it soon.

Our rural neighbors and Bush relatives are not so clean either. While hunting was once a necessary way of life, it has now become a lifestyle. The subsistence issue in Alaska has divided residents into hostile groups, each claiming certain "rights" to the wildlife resources. This battle is being fought in courts, both federal and state, by fish and game boards, Alaska Department of Fish and Game, and U.S. Fish and Wildlife Service in the papers, radio, television, bars, and everywhere else people congregate. Although many claim it is not an issue of Native versus non-Native, it certainly has divided many from each culture. It appears this issue will be in the courts with appeals and counter-appeals for many years.

Nowadays it seems everyone is an expert on wildlife, and many are taking his or her preconceived viewpoints to the ballot box. This has resulted in changes in the laws and regulations that have nothing to do with good game management. One of the Kingston Trio's ballads, *Where Have All the Flowers Gone?* says "When will they ever learn, when will they ever learn?"

Where will it end? Maybe we should just say, "Let it run its course, and as each species is eliminated, we can record it for posterity as we did the passenger pigeon and the great auk, to name a few." This is facetious of course, but after years of losing ground, more than one game protector has hung up his badge wondering what, if anything, he really accomplished during his career for the wildlife resource. Quoting one old-timer in Maryland who had spent most of his life chasing illegal duck hunters, especially the market hunters, "We should just forget about protecting the game. Once it's gone, it's gone, and we won't have to worry about it anymore."

We all knew Alaska would change some day, but those of us who loved the country for itself were not prepared for the onslaught that began with the discovery of oil. I know now how the mountain man felt when the homesteaders invaded "his" country or how the Indians felt as they watched the white man destroy "his" buffalo. I wonder at times how well we learned our lesson. A new manifest destiny has taken over this country called the Great Land. One has to only look at the Anchorage skyline to be convinced. Much of the land is now going into private ownership, and the "No Trespassing" signs are appearing. A great fight is looming over ownership of navigable rivers.

When we flew around the country in the early 1950s, it was a thrill to land a floatplane on a newly discovered lake and wonder if we were the first to throw a fishing lure into the water. My good friend Jay Hammond, former governor of Alaska, once said over a cup of coffee, "We really had it the best back in the '50s. The old-timers at the turn of the century knew the old Alaska, but they were only able to see a limited part of the country. We were able to see it all while flying over the territory before all the big changes were made that so drastically changed the old Alaska into what it is today."

You don't have to ask the question anymore because soon after landing, a beer can lying along the lakeshore tells it all. I landed at Old John Lake where Jim King and I had fished several years ago. With me was a group of law enforcement officials. We were on our way back from a meeting with Canadian officials at the town of Inuvik. The once-pristine lakeshore was now littered with garbage, oil cans (some airplane driver had changed his oil and failed to take the empty cans back with him), empty dog food bags and, of course, the inevitable beer cans.

The Alaska game warden today is a mixture of the old and the new. He is unionized and is plagued by rules that dictate his effectiveness. Unless overtime funds are available, he can only work 37½ hours a week. Some have businesses on the side, while others are dedicated and spend longer hours on the job in spite of union rules. In 1972 the Fish and Wildlife Protection Division was moved from the Department of Fish and Game to the Department of Public Safety. The officers are now administered under the same procedures as the State Troopers. This was a highly controversial, political move that resulted in better law enforcement procedures. However, while the men are better police officers, they understand less about conservation theories because they no longer work with wildlife managers. There now exists a large breach between biologists and law enforcement officers. So we now have many officers enforcing wildlife laws without understanding the reason for their existence, and we have managers requesting regulations that are often unenforceable.

Fortunately I see some bright young people with fresh ideas and common sense trying to balance wildlife management principles and law enforcement. They will have to walk a delicate tightrope if hunting and fishing are to remain a part of our heritage. It's time for me to move on and let someone else take over, but remember, I'm not ready to hang up my rifle and fishing rod yet.

READY FOR MORE ALASKAN ADVENTURE?

Pick up these true-life spellbinders from Alaska Northwest Books®!

Alaska Bear Tales
By Larry Kaniut

More Alaska Bear Tales
By Larry Kaniut

Alone across the Arctic
By Pam Flowers with Ann Dixon

Two in the Far North
By Margaret E. Murie

Frank Barr: Bush Pilot in Alaska and the Yukon
By Dermot Cole

In the Shadow of Eagles
From Barnstormer to Bush Pilot, A Flyer's Story
By Rudy Billberg as told to Jim Rearden

One Man's Wilderness
An Alaskan Odyssey
By Sam Keith
from the journals and photographs of Richard Proenneke

Alaska Northwest Books®
An imprint of Graphic Arts Center Publishing Co.
P.O. Box 10306, Portland, OR 97296-0306
www.gacpc.com / (503) 226-2402